Thank yous

Thank you to my daugthers who have coauthored, my parents and my pup for being my rocks in life.

Thank you to the friends that have cheered me on for years on this project.

Thank you to the crowdfunding supporters for your patience.

Thank you to planet Earth for tolerating us Humans this long, may we all work to restore you.

Published in the United States
by Angelo D' Amore Publishing

Copyright 2024 | All Rights Reserved | First Edition

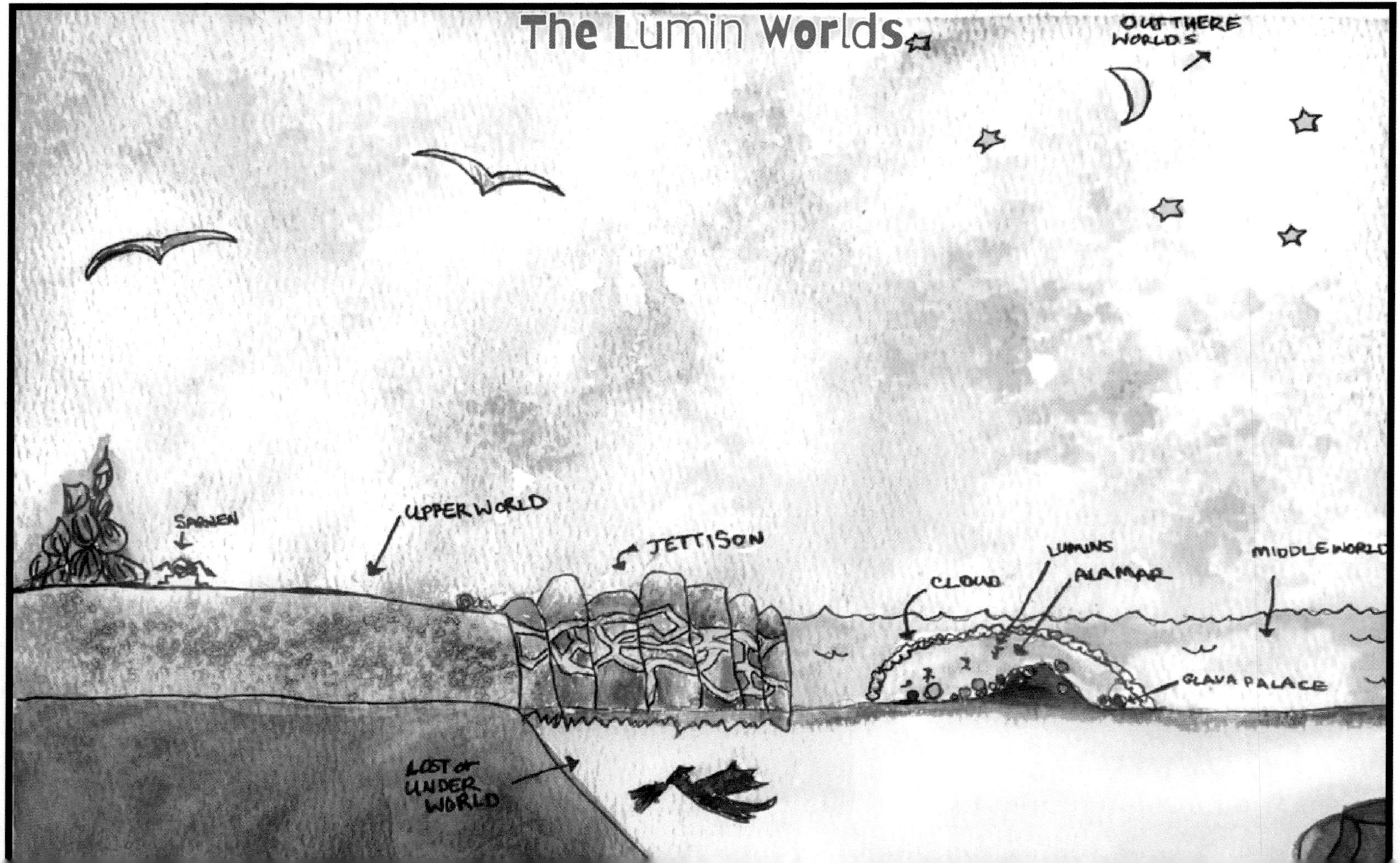
The Lumin Worlds
OUTTHERE WORLDS
SARNEN
UPPER WORLD
JETTISON
LUMINS
CLOUD
ALAMAR
MIDDLE WORLD
GLAVA PALACE
LOST or UNDER WORLD

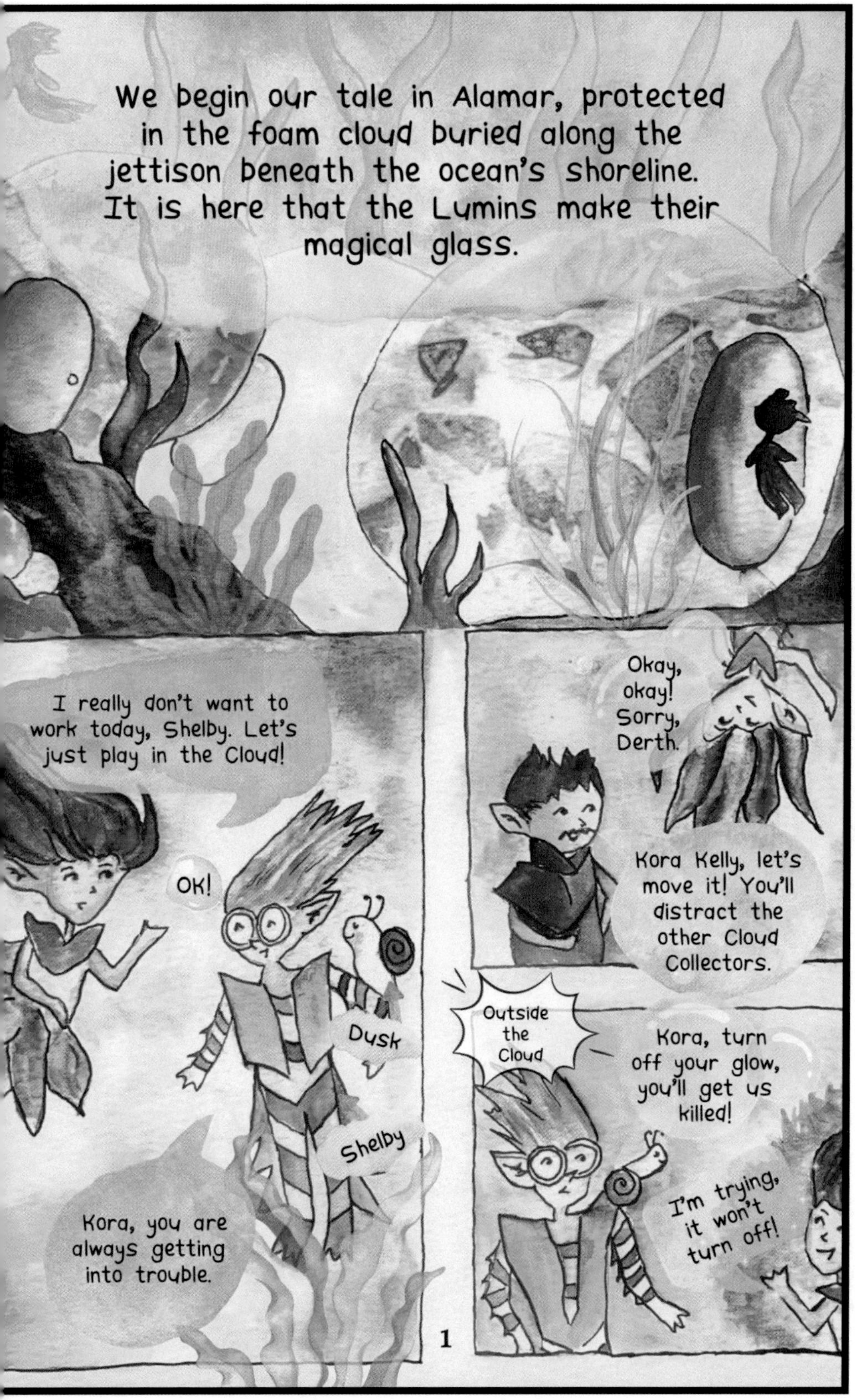
We begin our tale in Alamar, protected in the foam cloud buried along the jettison beneath the ocean's shoreline. It is here that the Lumins make their magical glass.
I really don't want to work today, Shelby. Let's just play in the Cloud!
OK!
Dusk
Shelby
Kora, you are always getting into trouble.
Okay, okay! Sorry, Derth.
Kora Kelly, let's move it! You'll distract the other Cloud Collectors.
Outside the Cloud
Kora, turn off your glow, you'll get us killed!
I'm trying, it won't turn off!

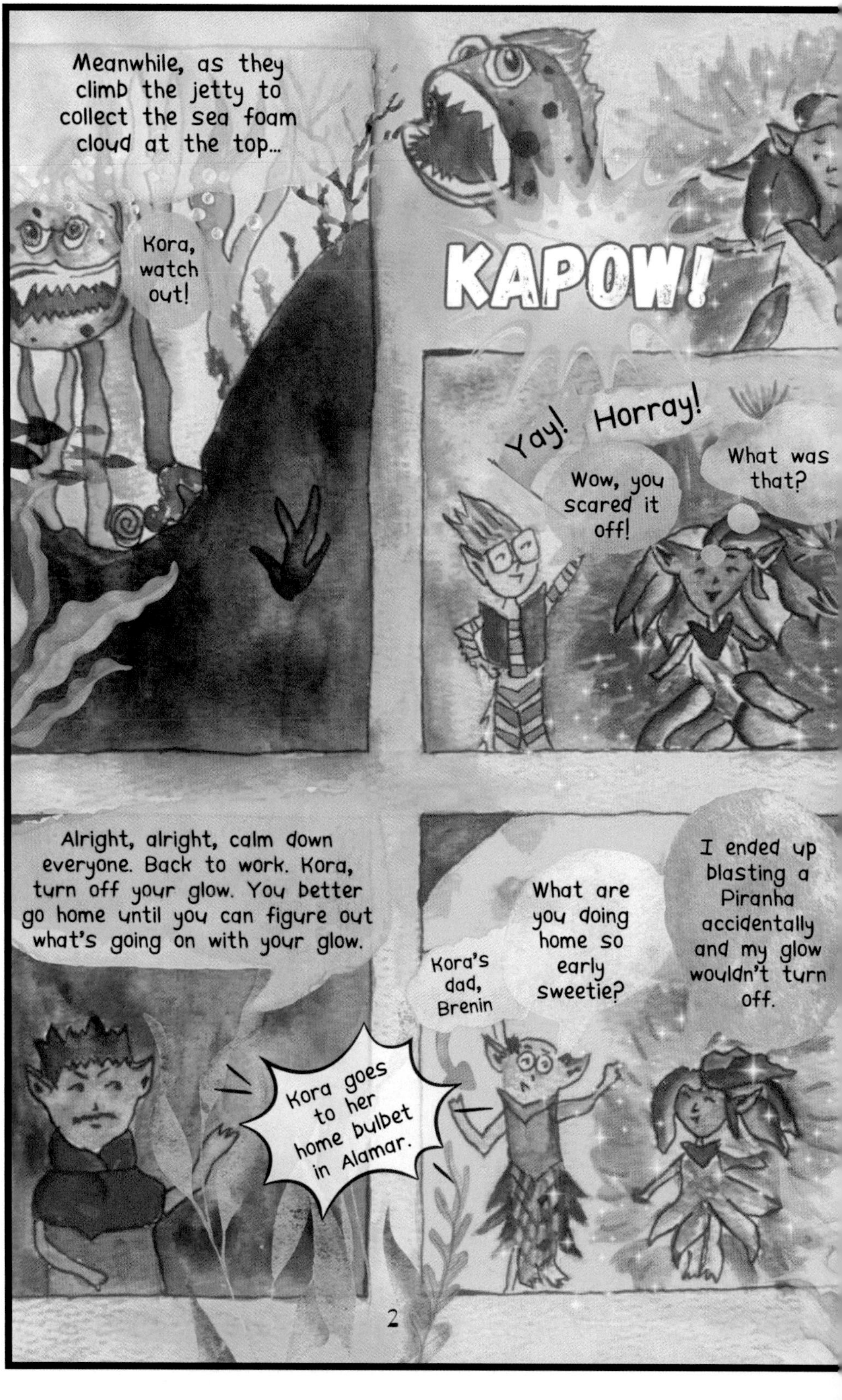
Meanwhile, as they climb the jetty to collect the sea foam cloud at the top...
Kora, watch out!
KAPOW!
Yay!
Horray!
Wow, you scared it off!
What was that?
Alright, alright, calm down everyone. Back to work. Kora, turn off your glow. You better go home until you can figure out what's going on with your glow.
Kora goes to her home bulbet in Alamar.
Kora's dad, Brenin
What are you doing home so early sweetie?
I ended up blasting a Piranha accidentally and my glow wouldn't turn off.

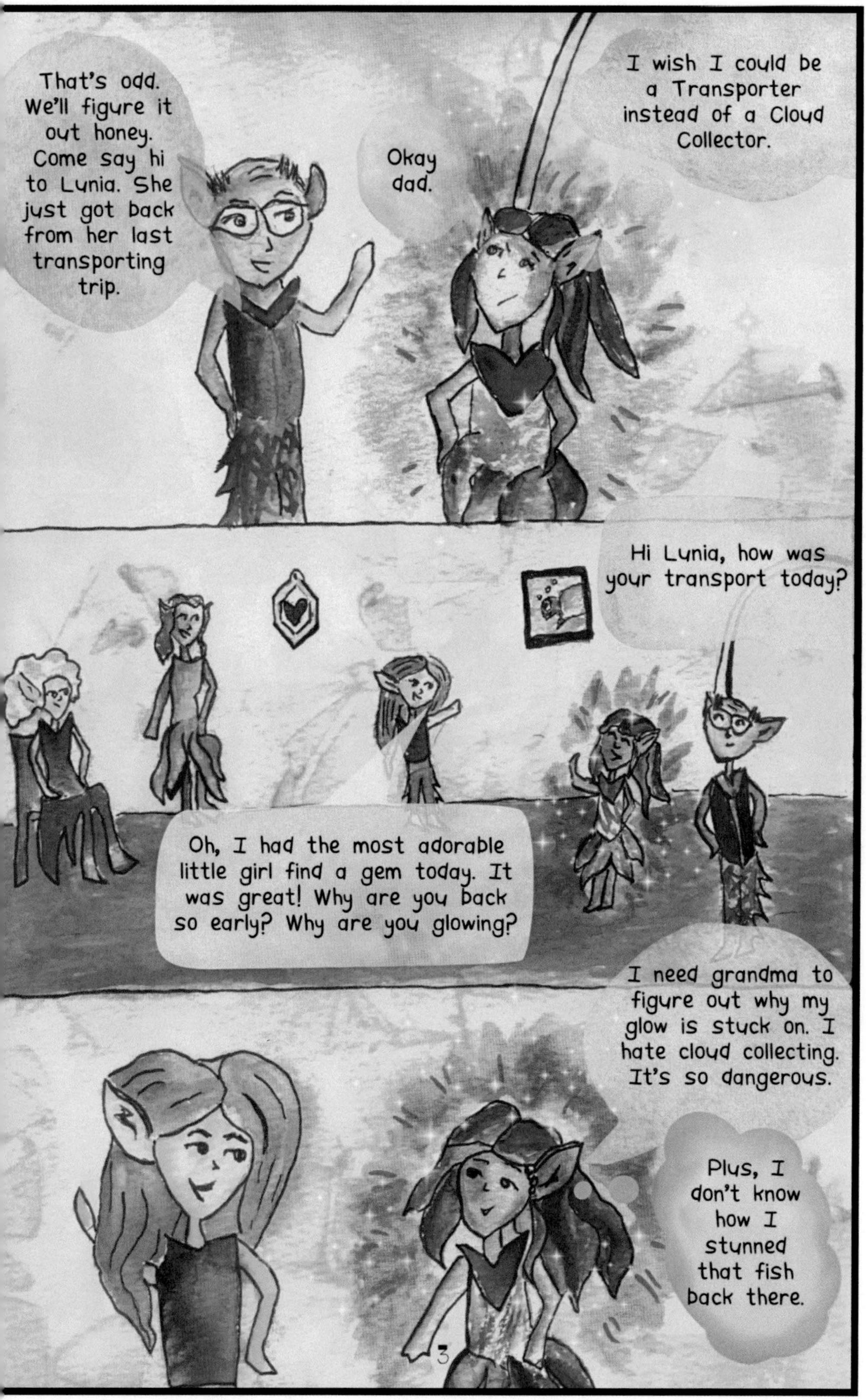
That's odd. We'll figure it out honey. Come say hi to Lunia. She just got back from her last transporting trip.
Okay dad.
I wish I could be a Transporter instead of a Cloud Collector.
Hi Lunia, how was your transport today?
Oh, I had the most adorable little girl find a gem today. It was great! Why are you back so early? Why are you glowing?
I need grandma to figure out why my glow is stuck on. I hate cloud collecting. It's so dangerous.
Plus, I don't know how I stunned that fish back there.

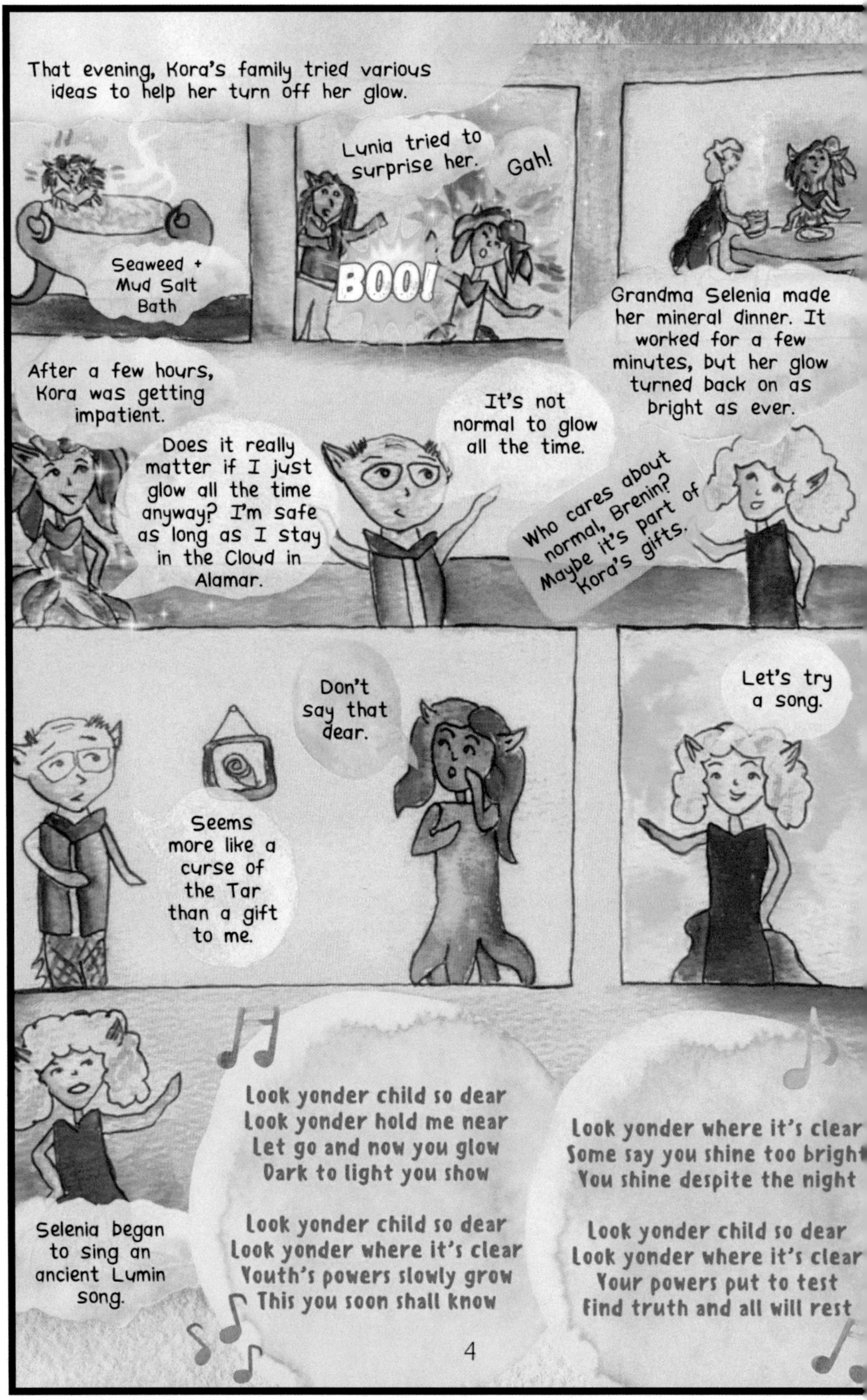
That evening, Kora's family tried various ideas to help her turn off her glow.
Seaweed + Mud Salt Bath
Lunia tried to surprise her.
Gah!
BOO!
Grandma Selenia made her mineral dinner. It worked for a few minutes, but her glow turned back on as bright as ever.
After a few hours, Kora was getting impatient.
Does it really matter if I just glow all the time anyway? I'm safe as long as I stay in the Cloud in Alamar.
It's not normal to glow all the time.
Who cares about normal, Brenin? Maybe it's part of Kora's gifts.
Seems more like a curse of the Tar than a gift to me.
Don't say that dear.
Let's try a song.
Selenia began to sing an ancient Lumin song.
Look yonder child so dear
Look yonder hold me near
Let go and now you glow
Dark to light you show
Look yonder child so dear
Look yonder where it's clear
Youth's powers slowly grow
This you soon shall know
Look yonder where it's clear
Some say you shine too bright
You shine despite the night
Look yonder child so dear
Look yonder where it's clear
Your powers put to test
Find truth and all will rest

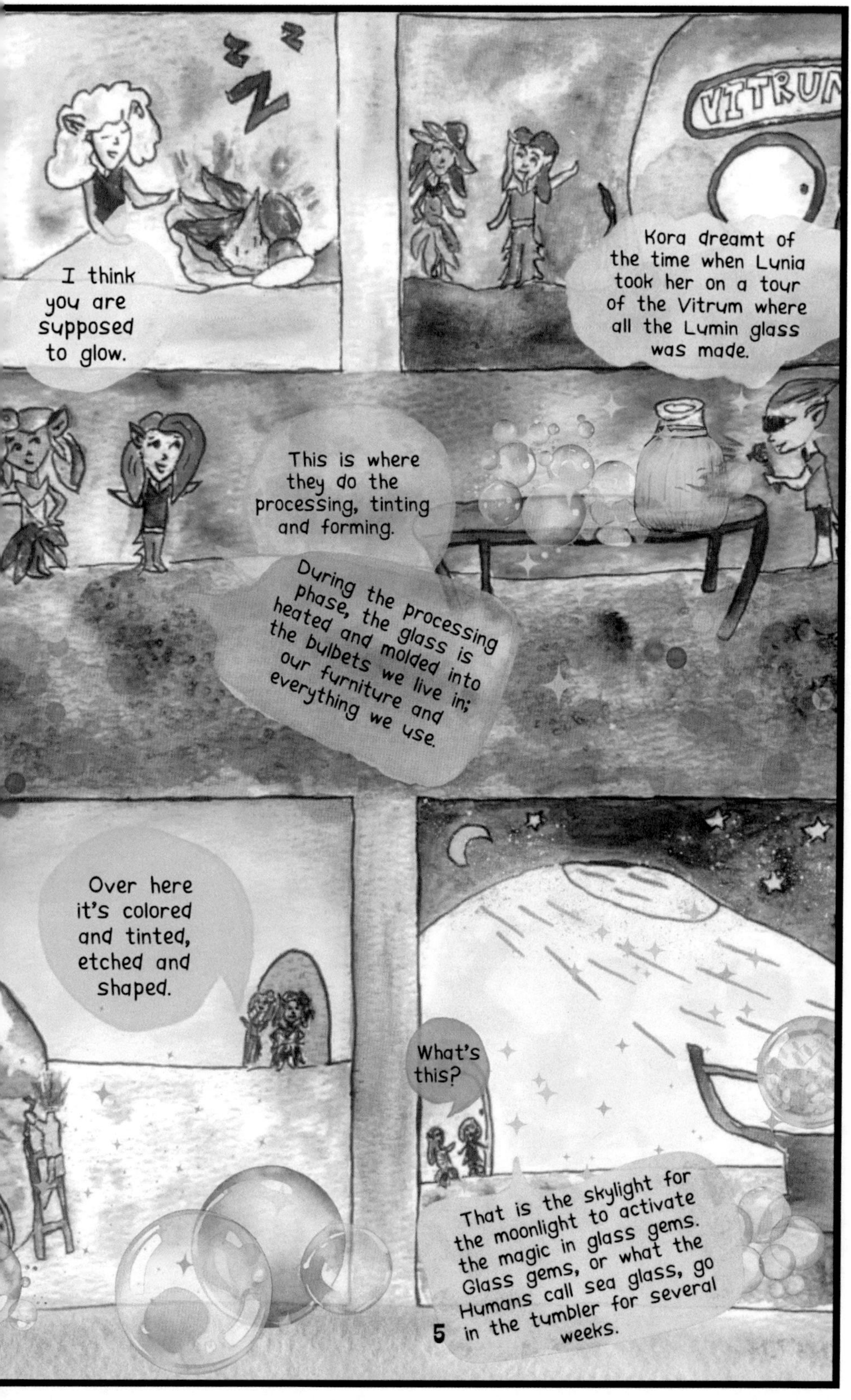
I think you are supposed to glow.
Kora dreamt of the time when Lunia took her on a tour of the Vitrum where all the Lumin glass was made.
This is where they do the processing, tinting and forming.
During the processing phase, the glass is heated and molded into the bulbets we live in; our furniture and everything we use.
Over here it's colored and tinted, etched and shaped.
What's this?
That is the skylight for the moonlight to activate the magic in glass gems. Glass gems, or what the Humans call sea glass, go in the tumbler for several weeks.

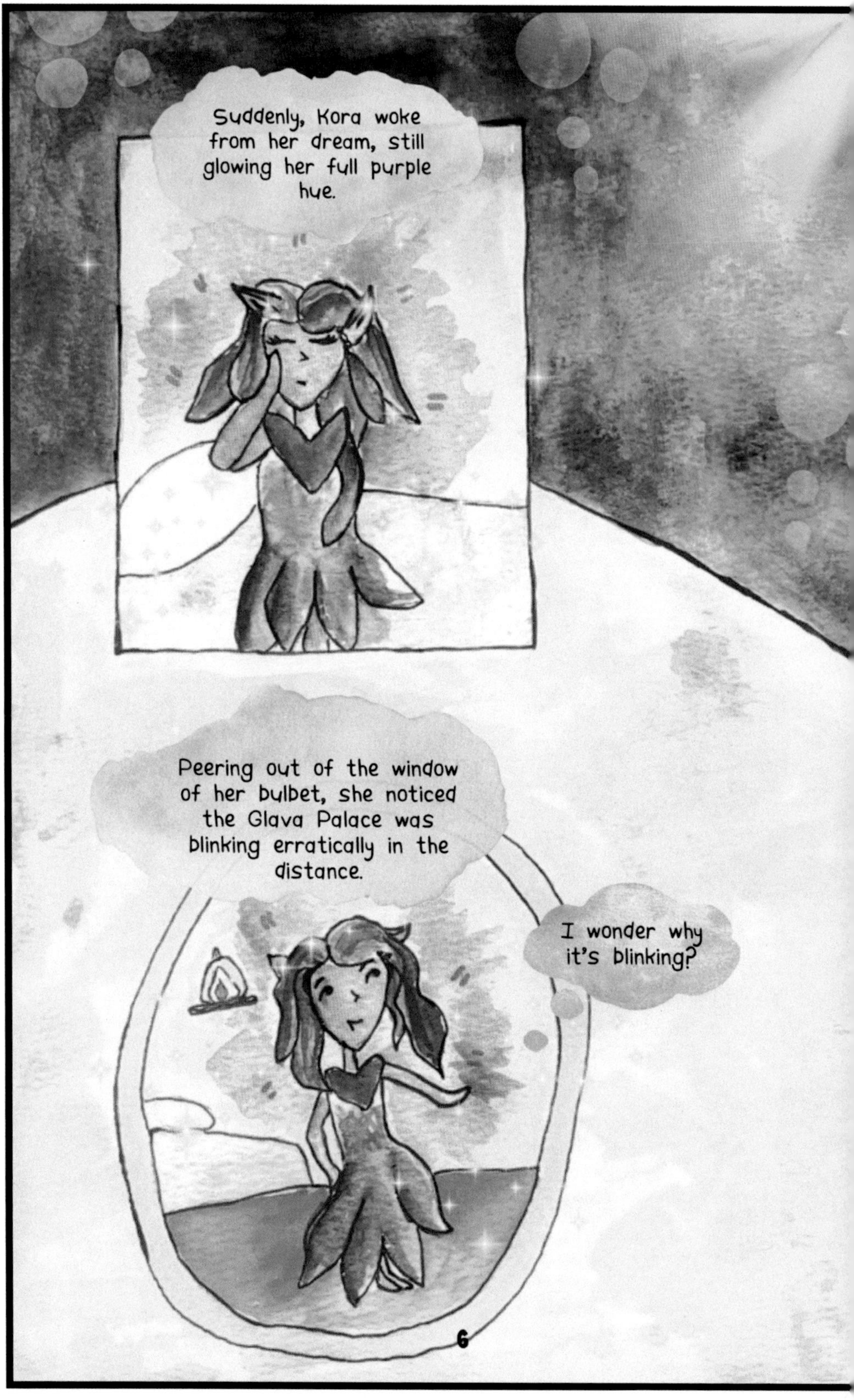
Suddenly, Kora woke from her dream, still glowing her full purple hue.
Peering out of the window of her bulbet, she noticed the Glava Palace was blinking erratically in the distance.
I wonder why it's blinking?

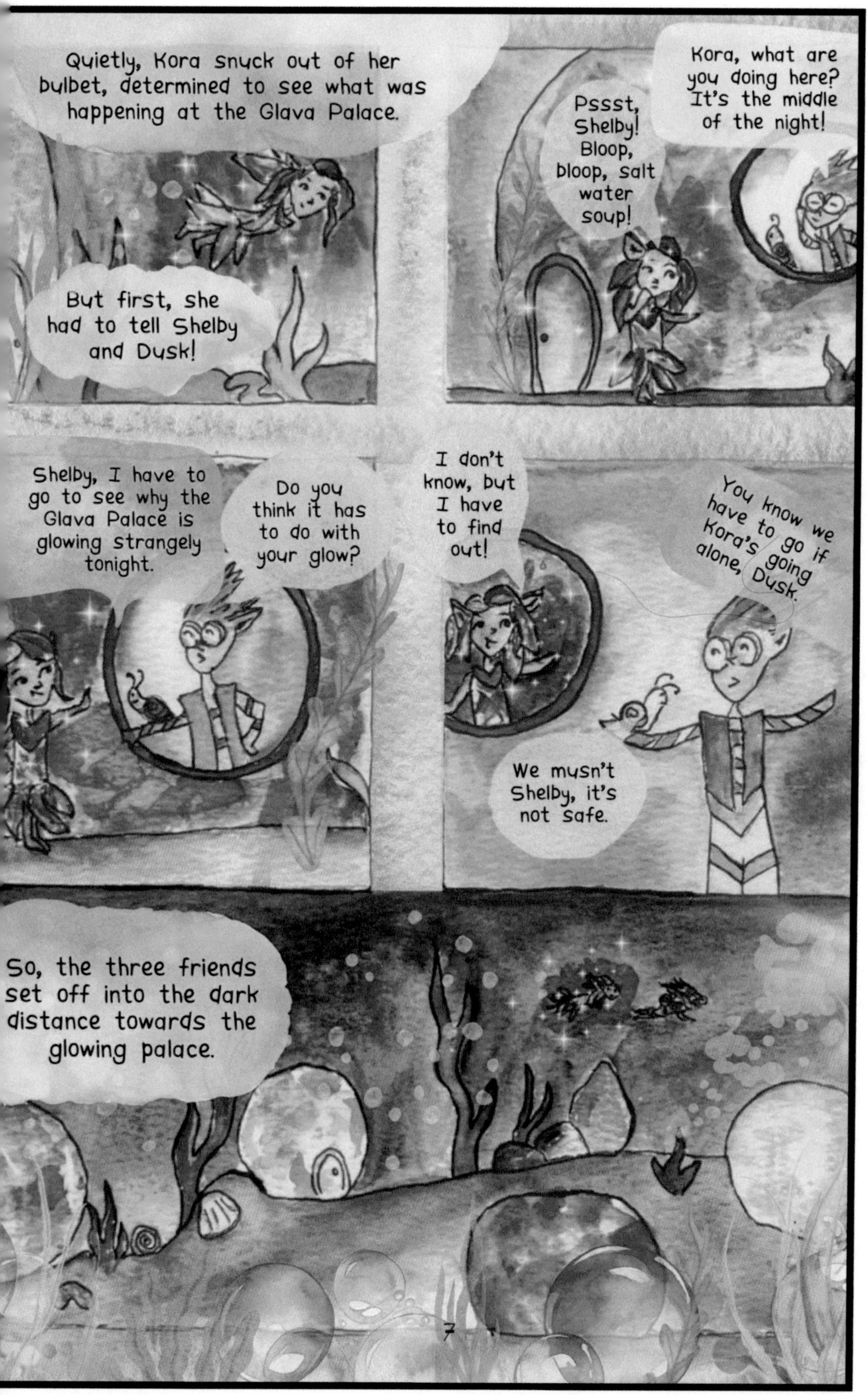

Quietly, Kora snuck out of her bulbet, determined to see what was happening at the Glava Palace.
But first, she had to tell Shelby and Dusk!
Pssst, Shelby! Bloop, bloop, salt water soup!
Kora, what are you doing here? It's the middle of the night!
Shelby, I have to go to see why the Glava Palace is glowing strangely tonight.
Do you think it has to do with your glow?
I don't know, but I have to find out!
You know we have to go if Kora's going alone, Dusk.
We musn't Shelby, it's not safe.
So, the three friends set off into the dark distance towards the glowing palace.

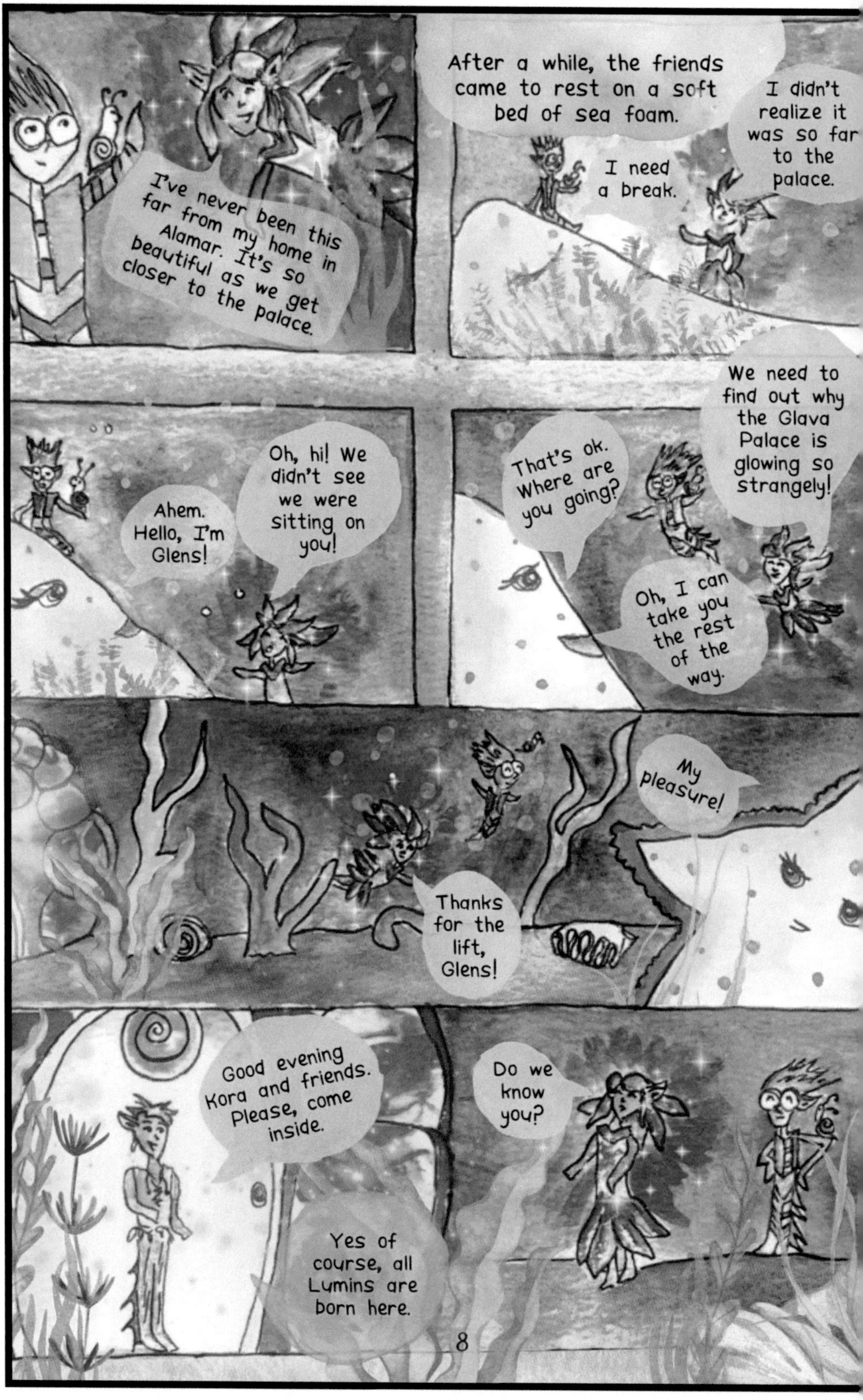
I've never been this far from my home in Alamar. It's so beautiful as we get closer to the palace.
After a while, the friends came to rest on a soft bed of sea foam.
I need a break.
I didn't realize it was so far to the palace.
Ahem. Hello, I'm Glens!
Oh, hi! We didn't see we were sitting on you!
That's ok. Where are you going?
We need to find out why the Glava Palace is glowing so strangely!
Oh, I can take you the rest of the way.
My pleasure!
Thanks for the lift, Glens!
Good evening Kora and friends. Please, come inside.
Do we know you?
Yes of course, all Lumins are born here.

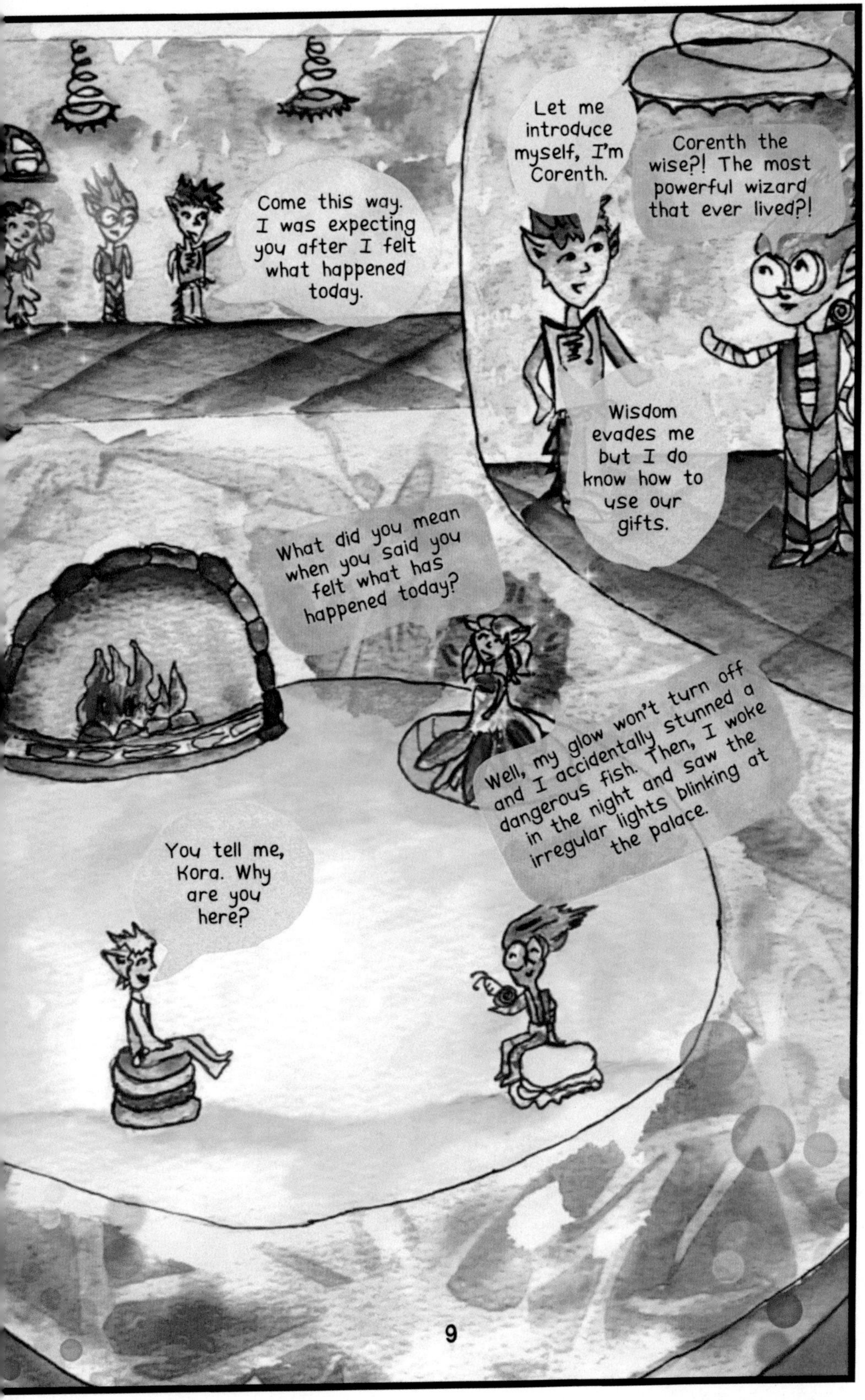
Come this way. I was expecting you after I felt what happened today.
Let me introduce myself, I'm Corenth.
Corenth the wise?! The most powerful wizard that ever lived?!
Wisdom evades me but I do know how to use our gifts.
What did you mean when you said you felt what has happened today?
Well, my glow won't turn off and I accidentally stunned a dangerous fish. Then, I woke in the night and saw the irregular lights blinking at the palace.
You tell me, Kora. Why are you here?

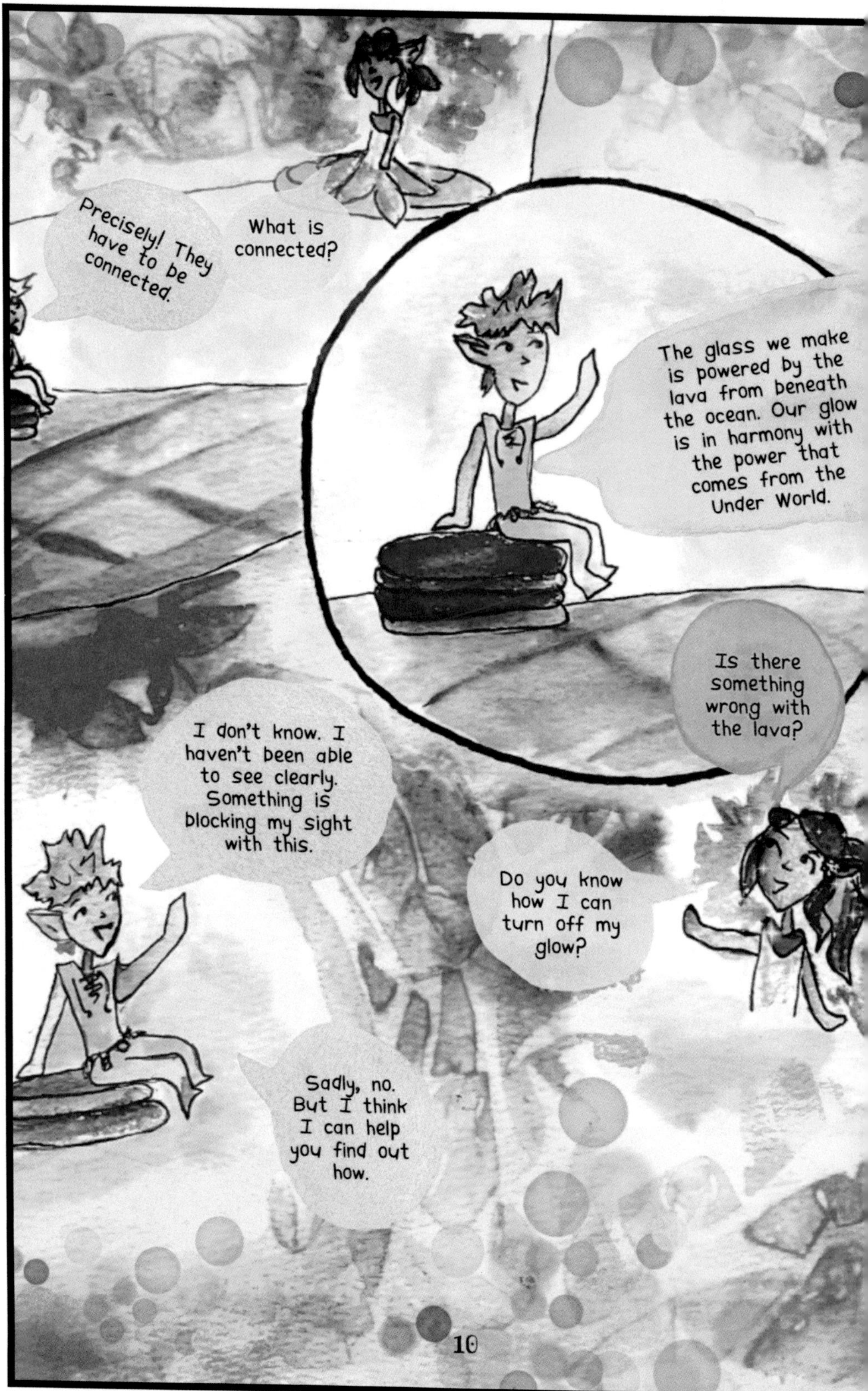
What is connected?
Precisely! They have to be connected.
The glass we make is powered by the lava from beneath the ocean. Our glow is in harmony with the power that comes from the Under World.
Is there something wrong with the lava?
I don't know. I haven't been able to see clearly. Something is blocking my sight with this.
Do you know how I can turn off my glow?
Sadly, no. But I think I can help you find out how.

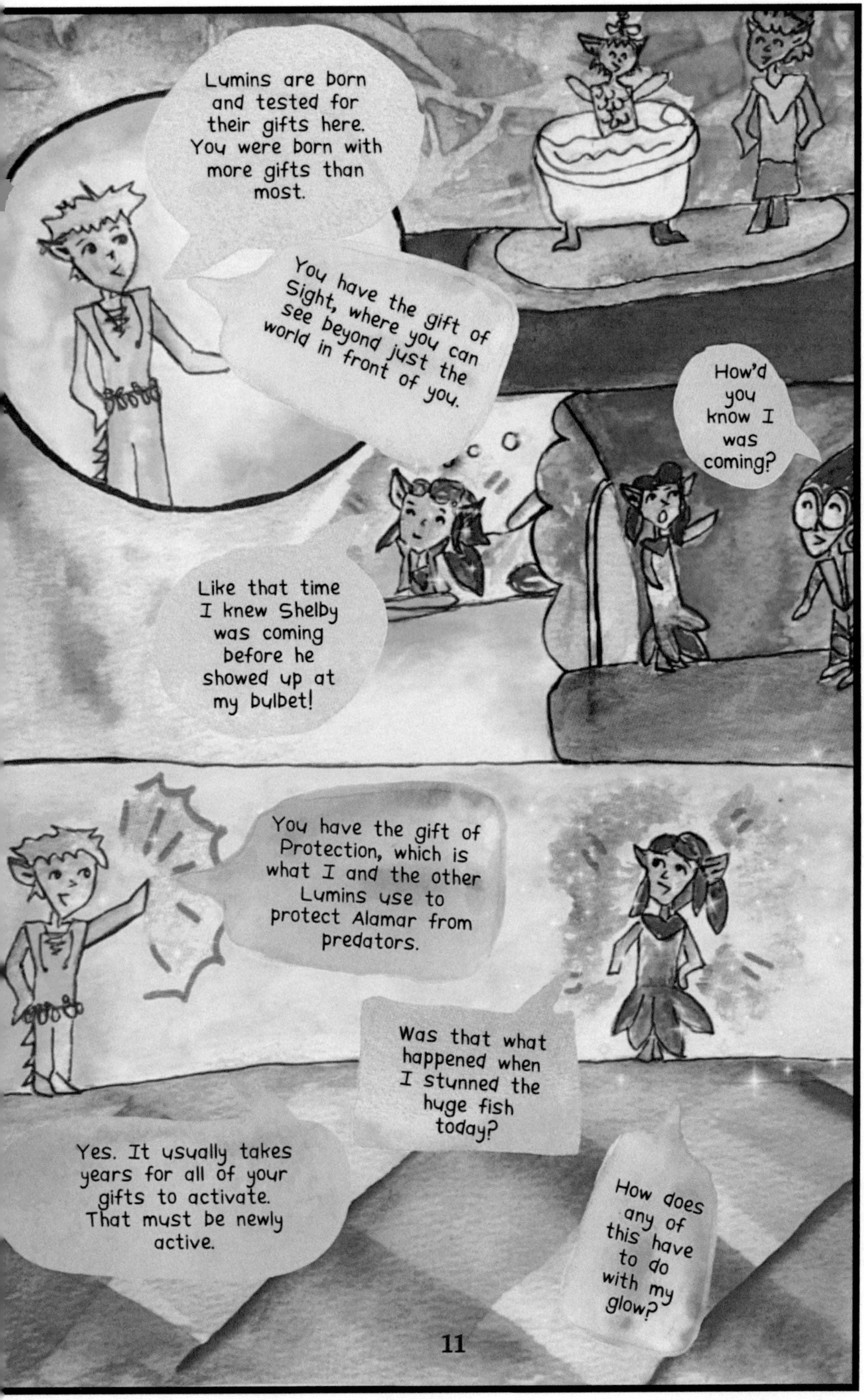

Lumins are born and tested for their gifts here. You were born with more gifts than most.
You have the gift of Sight, where you can see beyond just the world in front of you.
How'd you know I was coming?
Like that time I knew Shelby was coming before he showed up at my bulbet!
You have the gift of Protection, which is what I and the other Lumins use to protect Alamar from predators.
Was that what happened when I stunned the huge fish today?
Yes. It usually takes years for all of your gifts to activate. That must be newly active.
How does any of this have to do with my glow?

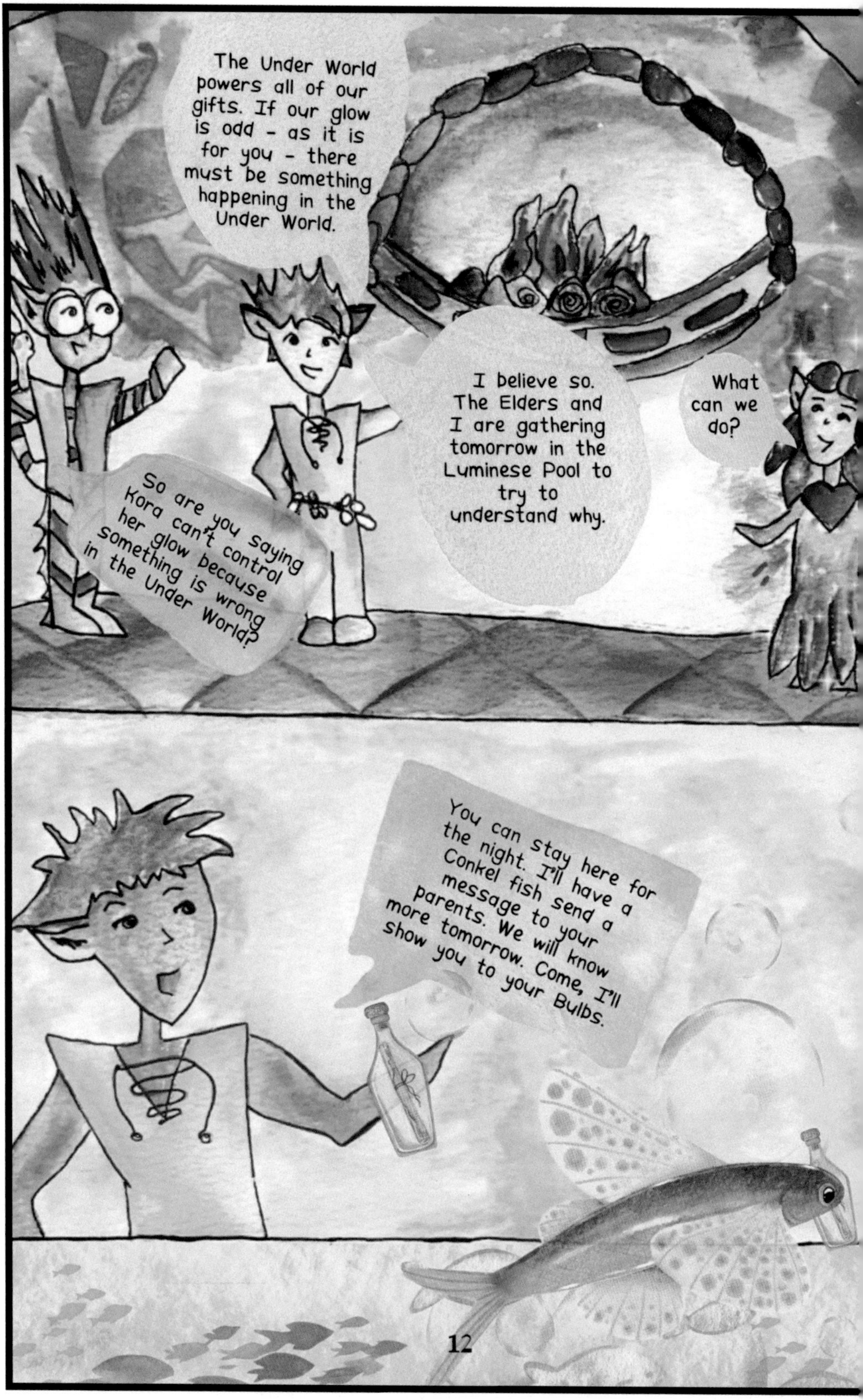
The Under World powers all of our gifts. If our glow is odd - as it is for you - there must be something happening in the Under World.
So are you saying Kora can't control her glow because something is wrong in the Under World?
I believe so. The Elders and I are gathering tomorrow in the Luminese Pool to try to understand why.
What can we do?
You can stay here for the night. I'll have a Conkel fish send a message to your parents. We will know more tomorrow. Come, I'll show you to your Bulbs.

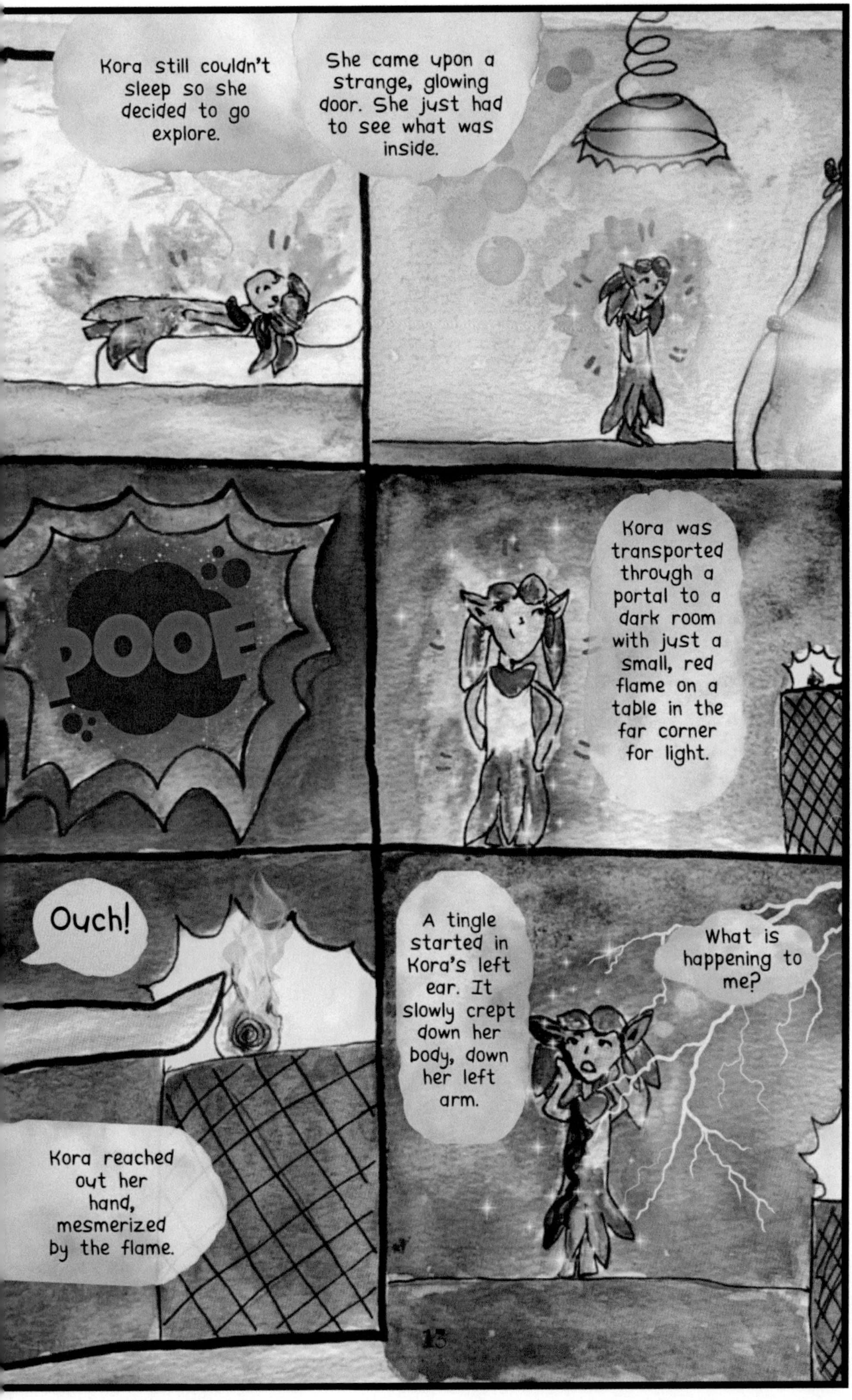
Kora still couldn't sleep so she decided to go explore.
She came upon a strange, glowing door. She just had to see what was inside.
POOF
Kora was transported through a portal to a dark room with just a small, red flame on a table in the far corner for light.
Ouch!
Kora reached out her hand, mesmerized by the flame.
A tingle started in Kora's left ear. It slowly crept down her body, down her left arm.
What is happening to me?

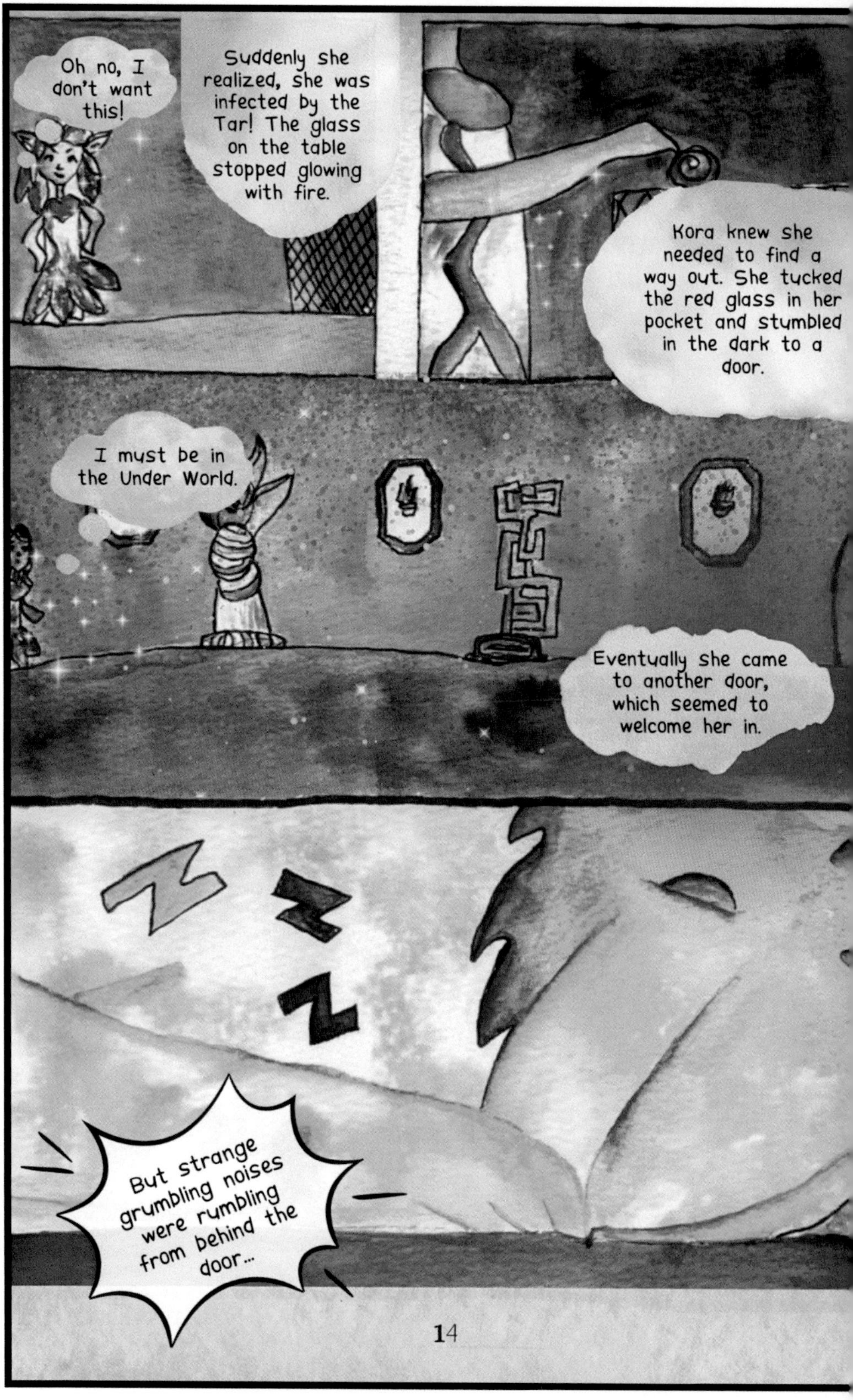
Oh no, I don't want this!
Suddenly she realized, she was infected by the Tar! The glass on the table stopped glowing with fire.
Kora knew she needed to find a way out. She tucked the red glass in her pocket and stumbled in the dark to a door.
I must be in the Under World.
Eventually she came to another door, which seemed to welcome her in.
But strange grumbling noises were rumbling from behind the door...

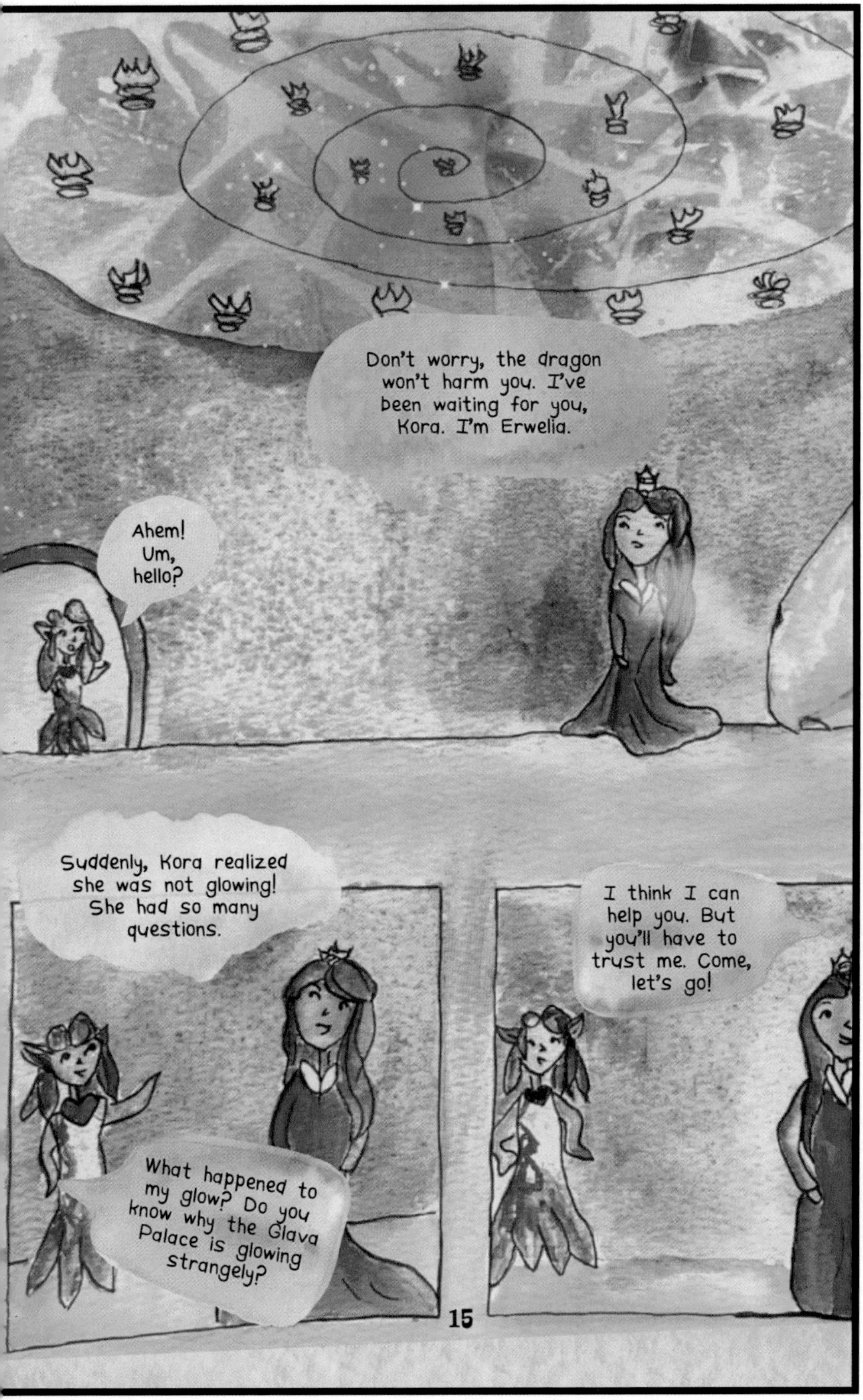
Don't worry, the dragon won't harm you. I've been waiting for you, Kora. I'm Erwelia.
Ahem! Um, hello?
Suddenly, Kora realized she was not glowing! She had so many questions.
What happened to my glow? Do you know why the Glava Palace is glowing strangely?
I think I can help you. But you'll have to trust me. Come, let's go!

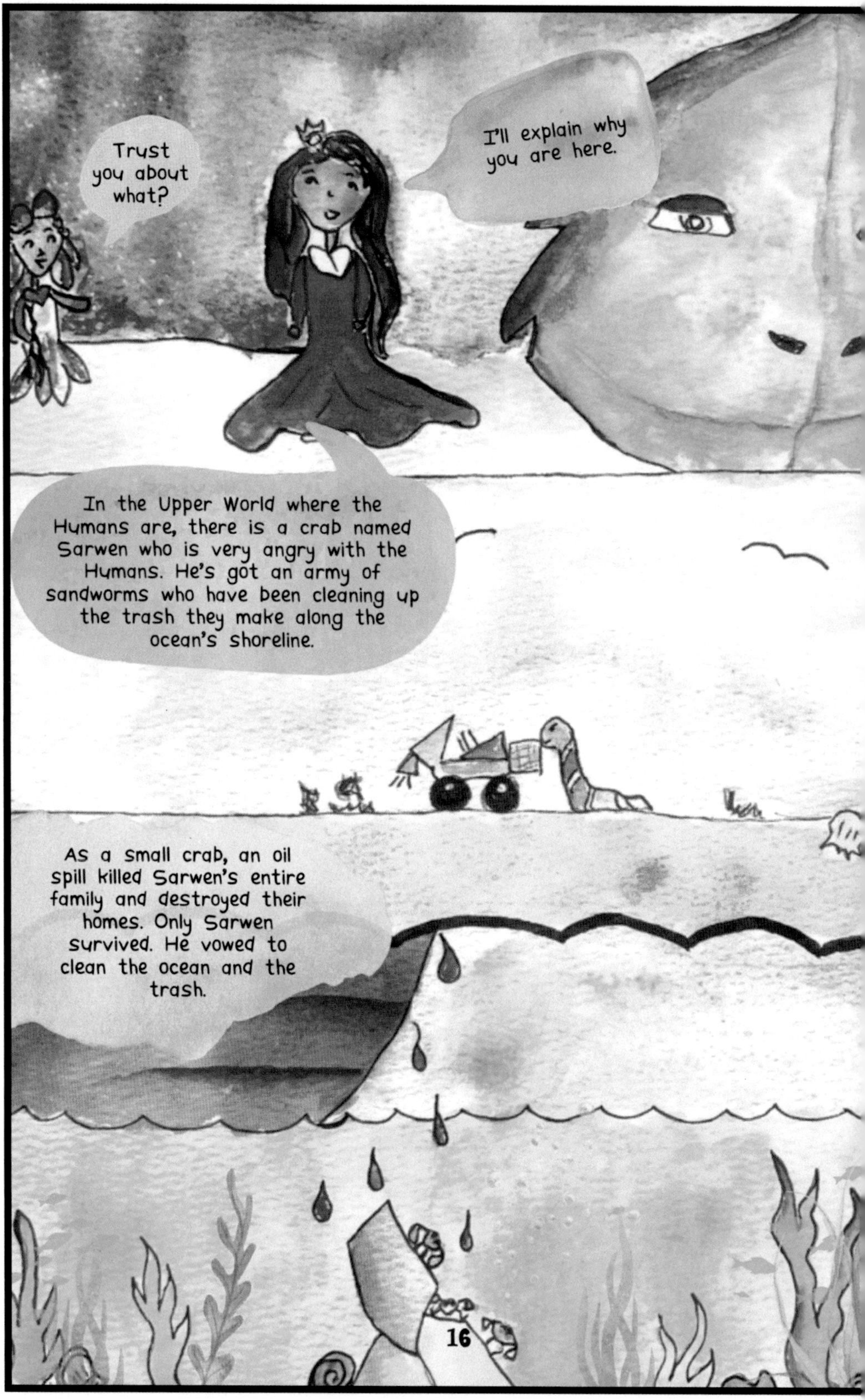
Trust you about what?
I'll explain why you are here.
In the Upper World where the Humans are, there is a crab named Sarwen who is very angry with the Humans. He's got an army of sandworms who have been cleaning up the trash they make along the ocean's shoreline.
As a small crab, an oil spill killed Sarwen's entire family and destroyed their homes. Only Sarwen survived. He vowed to clean the ocean and the trash.

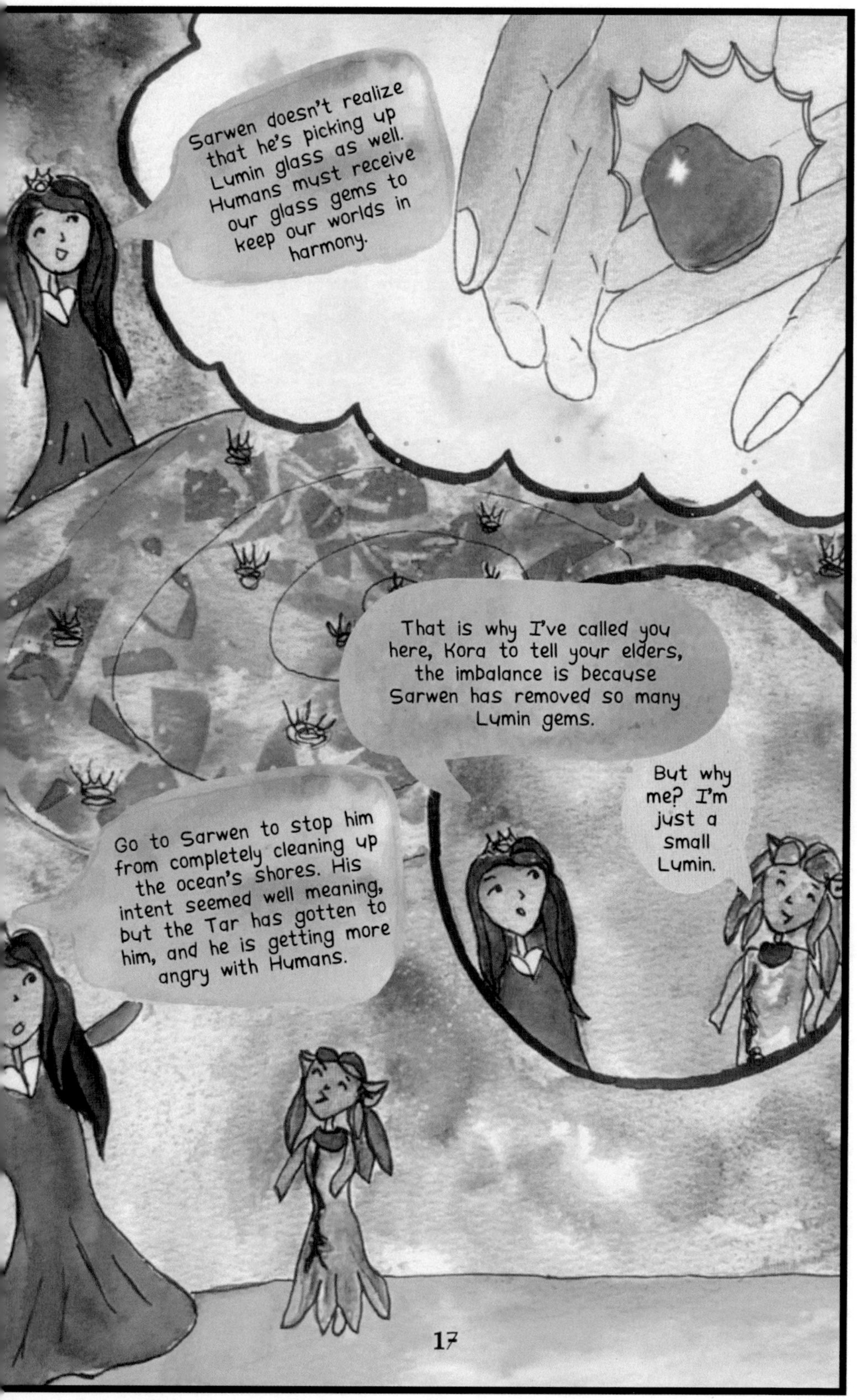
Sarwen doesn't realize that he's picking up Lumin glass as well. Lumin glass. Humans must receive our glass gems to keep our worlds in harmony.
That is why I've called you here, Kora to tell your elders, the imbalance is because Sarwen has removed so many Lumin gems.
But why me? I'm just a small Lumin.
Go to Sarwen to stop him from completely cleaning up the ocean's shores. His intent seemed well meaning, but the Tar has gotten to him, and he is getting more angry with Humans.

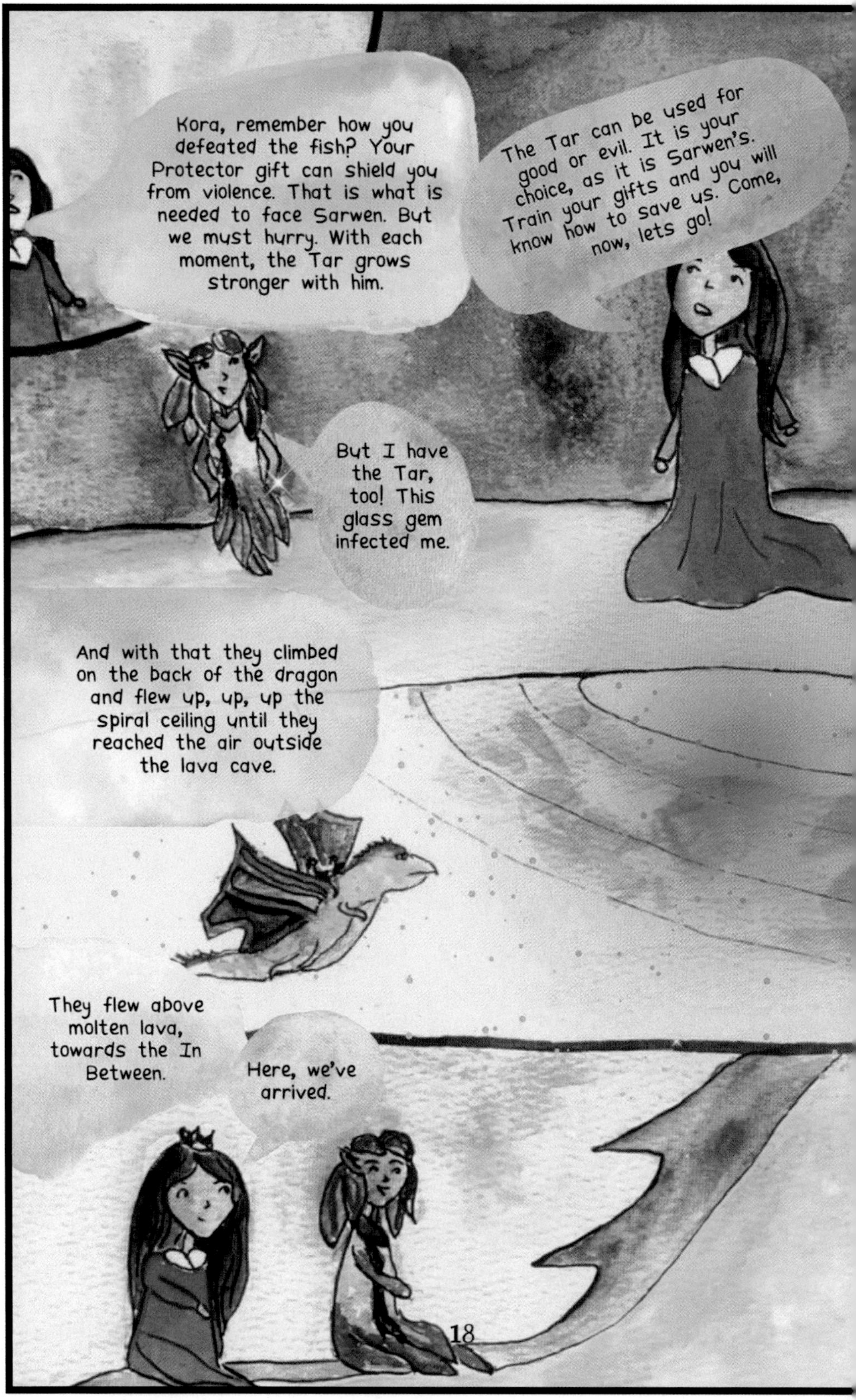

Kora, remember how you defeated the fish? Your Protector gift can shield you from violence. That is what is needed to face Sarwen. But we must hurry. With each moment, the Tar grows stronger with him.
The Tar can be used for good or evil. It is your choice, as it is Sarwen's. Train your gifts and you will know how to save us. Come, now, lets go!
But I have the Tar, too! This glass gem infected me.
And with that they climbed on the back of the dragon and flew up, up, up the spiral ceiling until they reached the air outside the lava cave.
They flew above molten lava, towards the In Between.
Here, we've arrived.

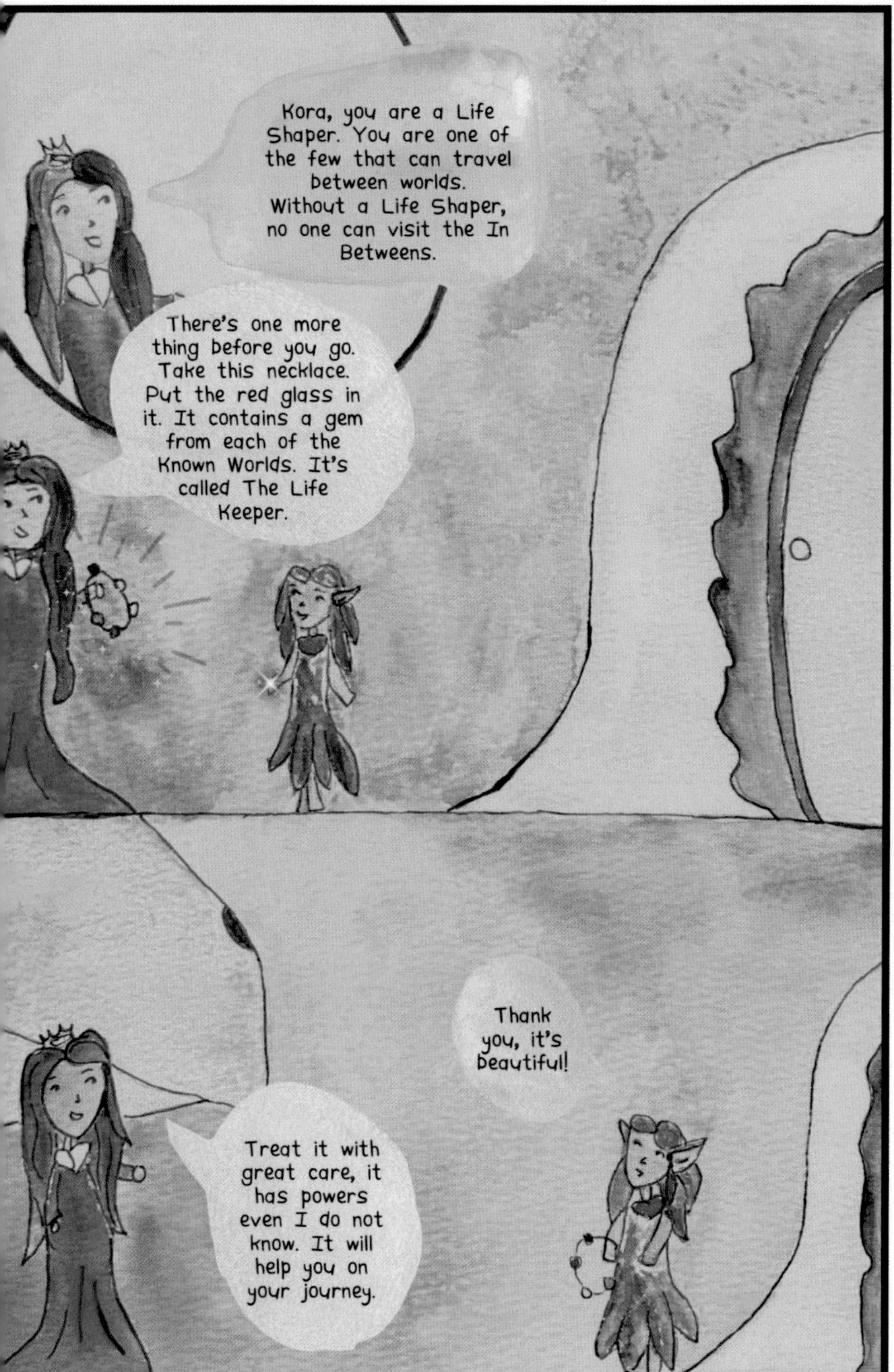
Kora, you are a Life Shaper. You are one of the few that can travel between worlds. Without a Life Shaper, no one can visit the In Betweens.
There's one more thing before you go. Take this necklace. Put the red glass in it. It contains a gem from each of the Known Worlds. It's called The Life Keeper.
Thank you, it's beautiful!
Treat it with great care, it has powers even I do not know. It will help you on your journey.

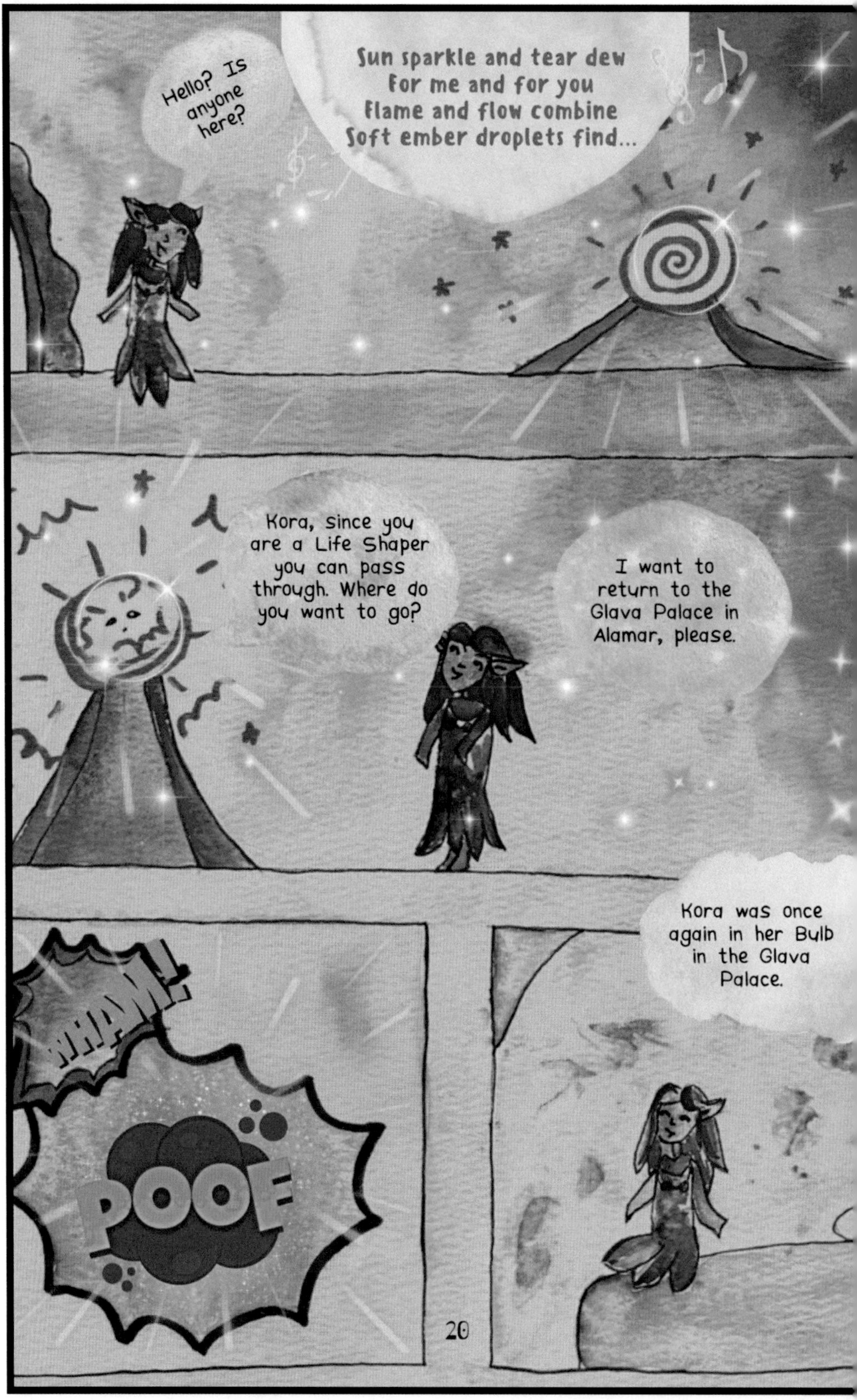
Hello? Is anyone here?
Sun sparkle and tear dew
For me and for you
Flame and flow combine
Soft ember droplets find...
Kora, since you are a Life Shaper you can pass through. Where do you want to go?
I want to return to the Glava Palace in Alamar, please.
WHAM!
POOF
Kora was once again in her Bulb in the Glava Palace.

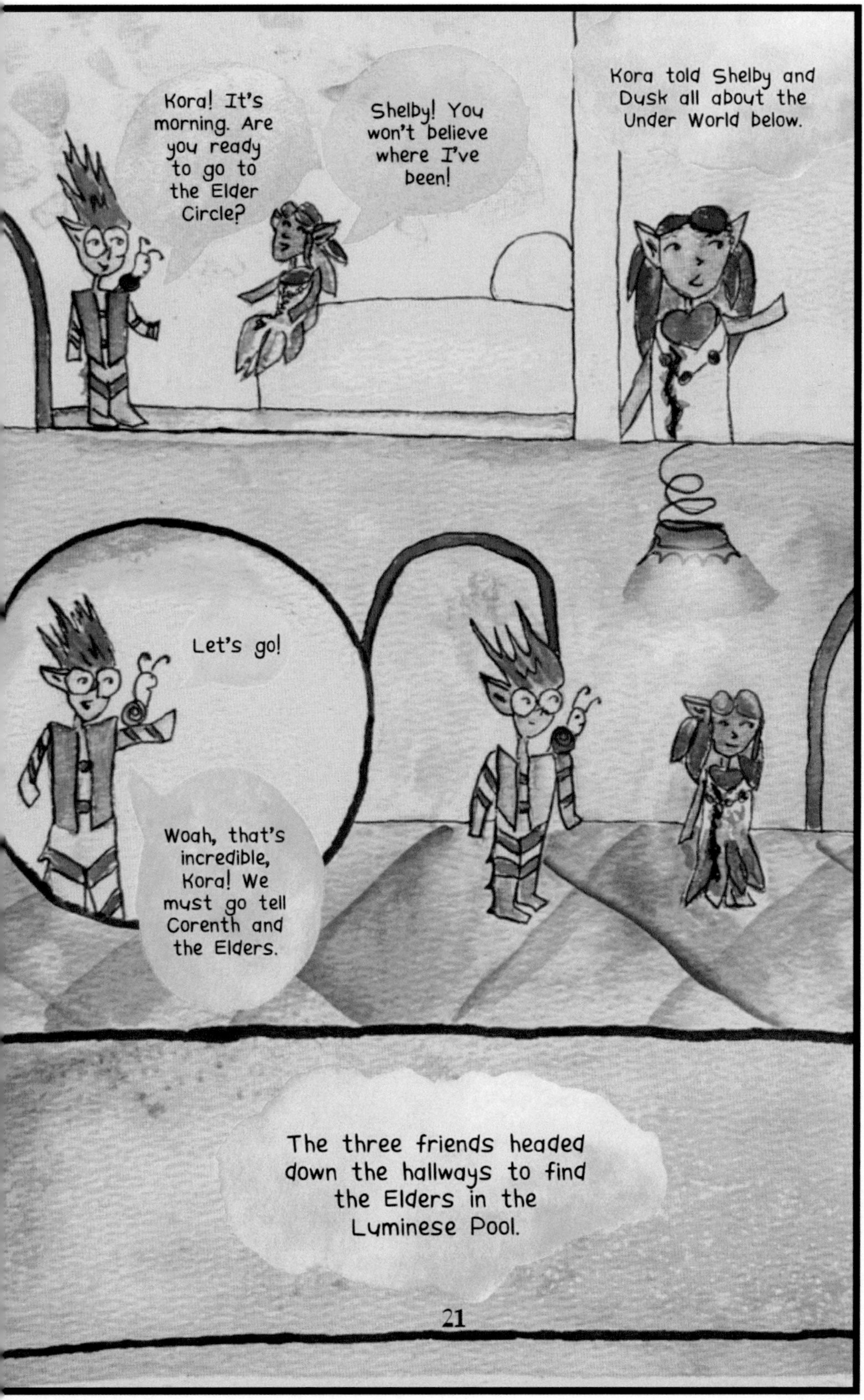
Kora! It's morning. Are you ready to go to the Elder Circle?
Shelby! You won't believe where I've been!
Kora told Shelby and Dusk all about the Under World below.
Let's go!
Woah, that's incredible, Kora! We must go tell Corenth and the Elders.
The three friends headed down the hallways to find the Elders in the Luminese Pool.

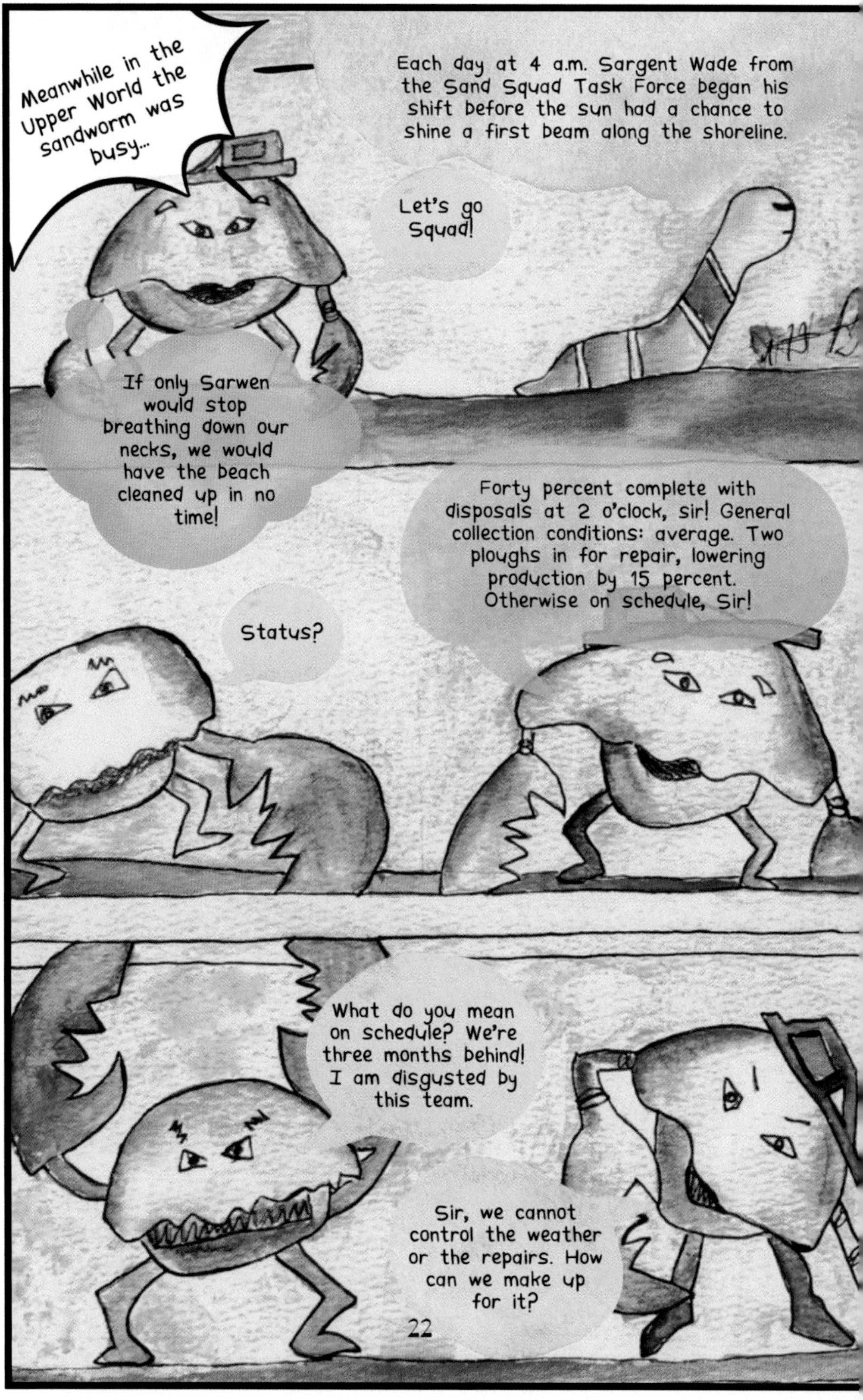
Meanwhile in the Upper World the sandworm was busy...
Each day at 4 a.m. Sargent Wade from the Sand Squad Task Force began his shift before the sun had a chance to shine a first beam along the shoreline.
Let's go Squad!
If only Sarwen would stop breathing down our necks, we would have the beach cleaned up in no time!
Status?
Forty percent complete with disposals at 2 o'clock, sir! General collection conditions: average. Two ploughs in for repair, lowering production by 15 percent. Otherwise on schedule, Sir!
What do you mean on schedule? We're three months behind! I am disgusted by this team.
Sir, we cannot control the weather or the repairs. How can we make up for it?

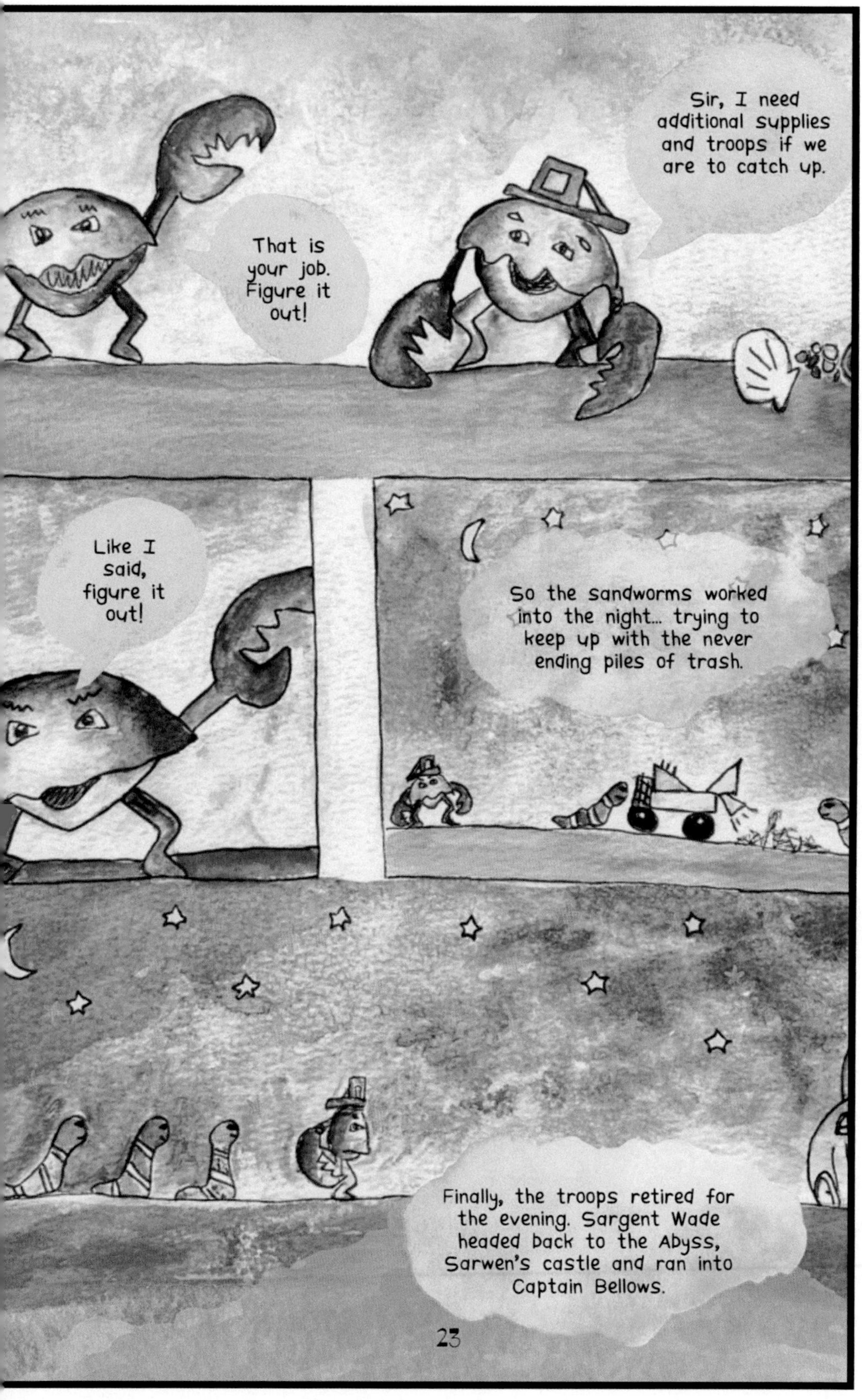
Sir, I need additional supplies and troops if we are to catch up.
That is your job. Figure it out!
Like I said, figure it out!
So the sandworms worked into the night... trying to keep up with the never ending piles of trash.
Finally, the troops retired for the evening. Sargent Wade headed back to the Abyss, Sarwen's castle and ran into Captain Bellows.

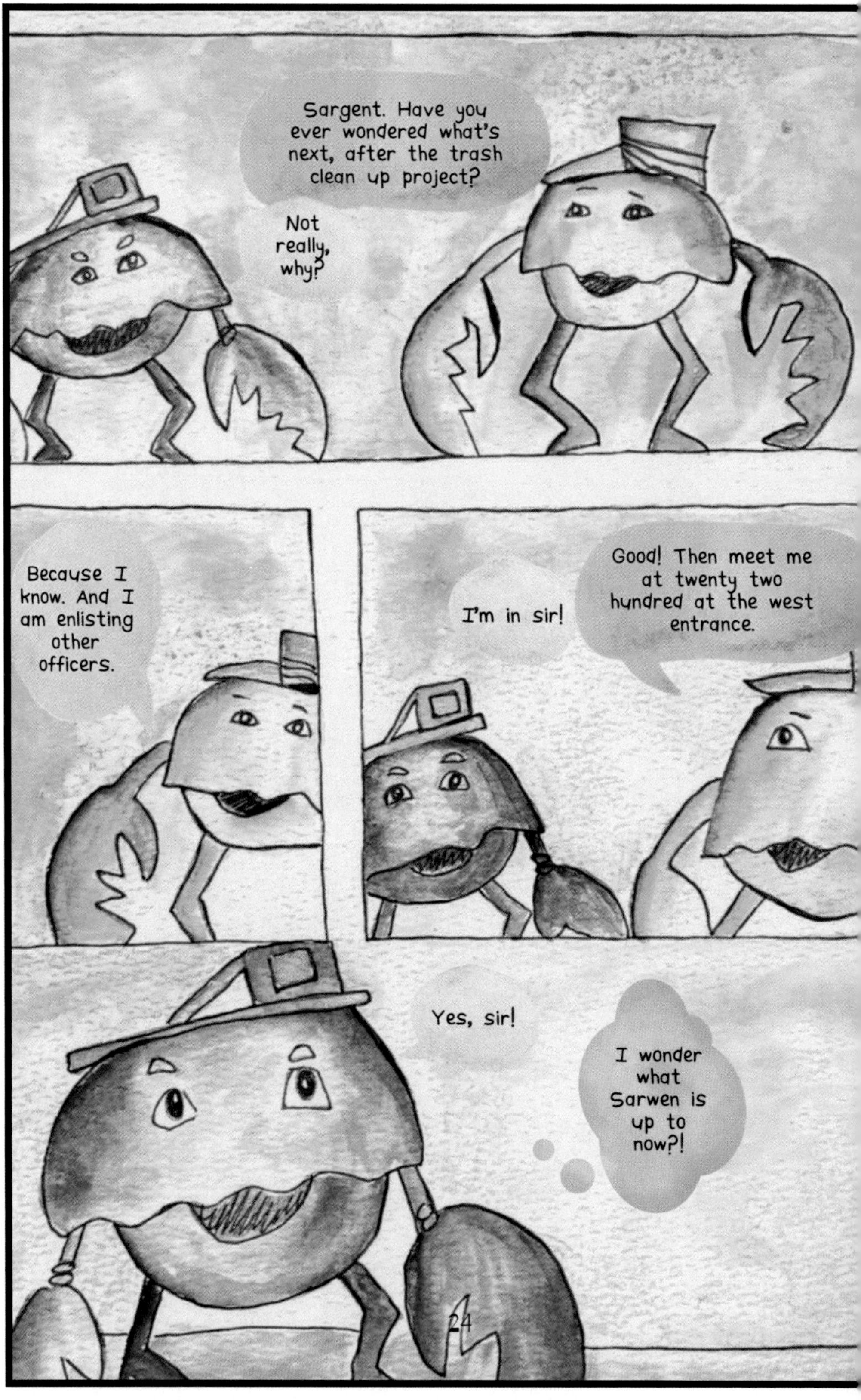
Sargent. Have you ever wondered what's next, after the trash clean up project?
Not really, why?
Because I know. And I am enlisting other officers.
I'm in sir!
Good! Then meet me at twenty two hundred at the west entrance.
Yes, sir!
I wonder what Sarwen is up to now?!

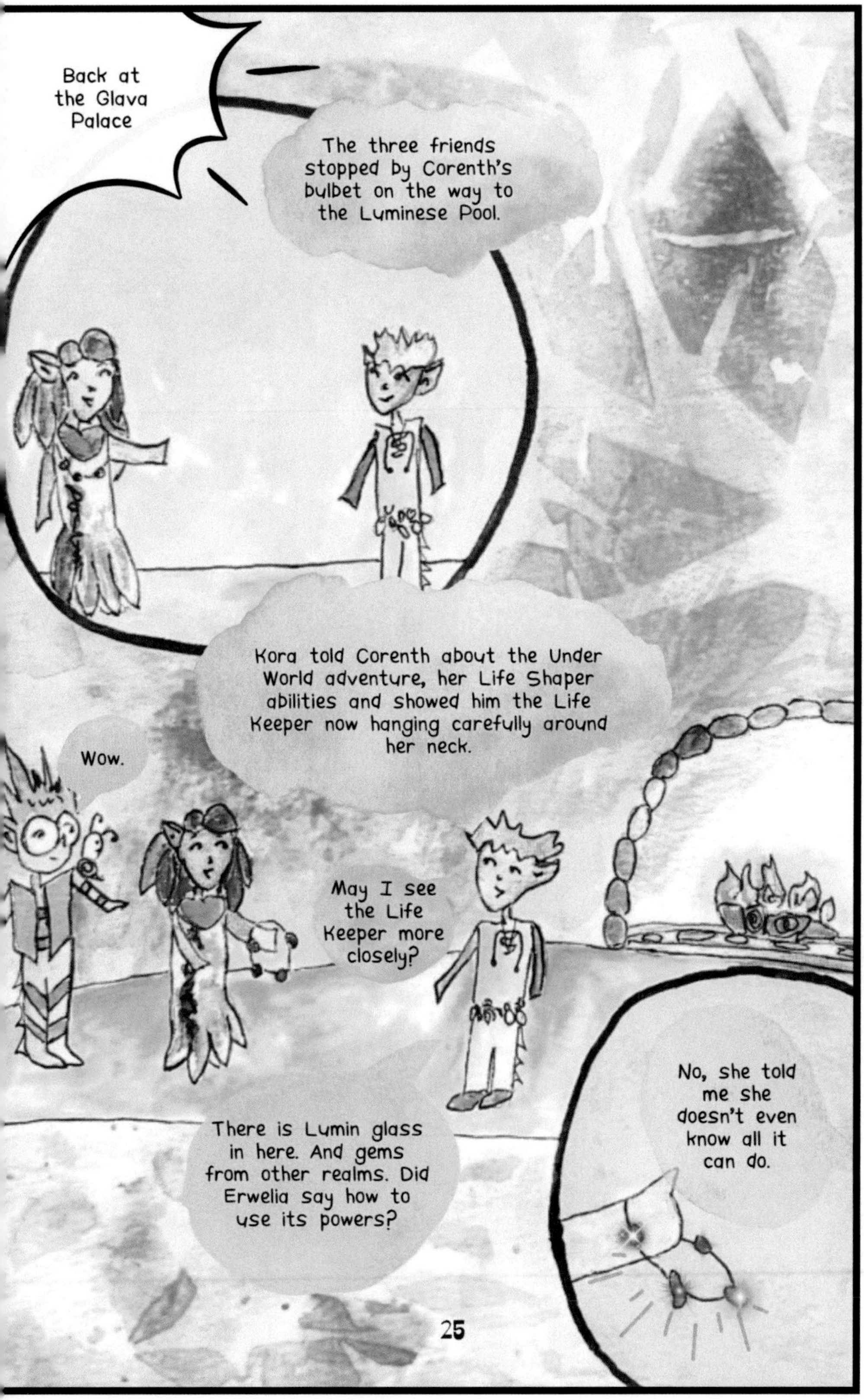
Back at the Glava Palace
The three friends stopped by Corenth's bulbet on the way to the Luminese Pool.
Kora told Corenth about the Under World adventure, her Life Shaper abilities and showed him the Life Keeper now hanging carefully around her neck.
Wow.
May I see the Life Keeper more closely?
There is Lumin glass in here. And gems from other realms. Did Erwelia say how to use its powers?
No, she told me she doesn't even know all it can do.

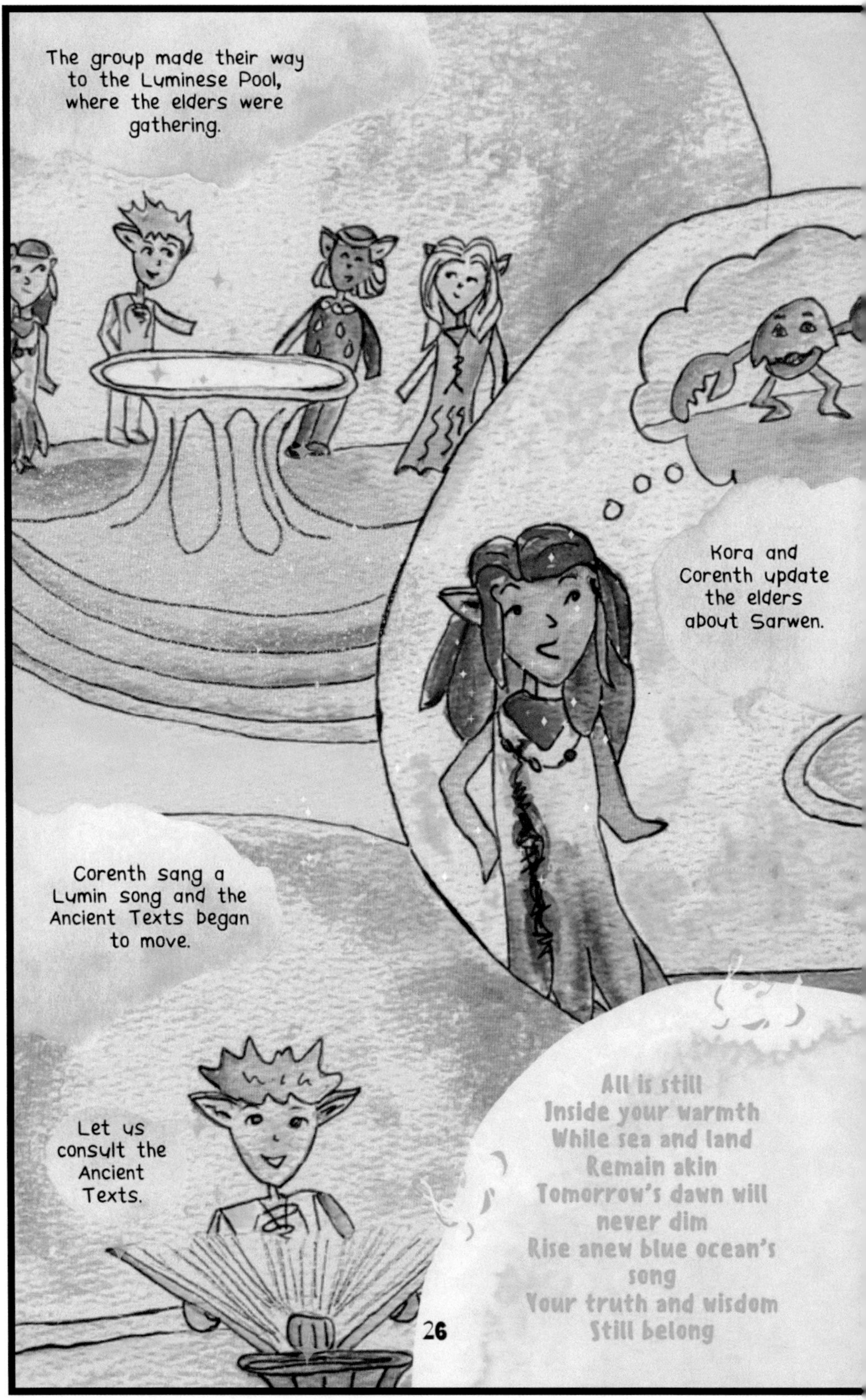

The group made their way to the Luminese Pool, where the elders were gathering.
Kora and Corenth update the elders about Sarwen.
Corenth sang a Lumin song and the Ancient Texts began to move.
Let us consult the Ancient Texts.
All is still
Inside your warmth
While sea and land
Remain akin
Tomorrow's dawn will
never dim
Rise anew blue ocean's
song
Your truth and wisdom
Still belong

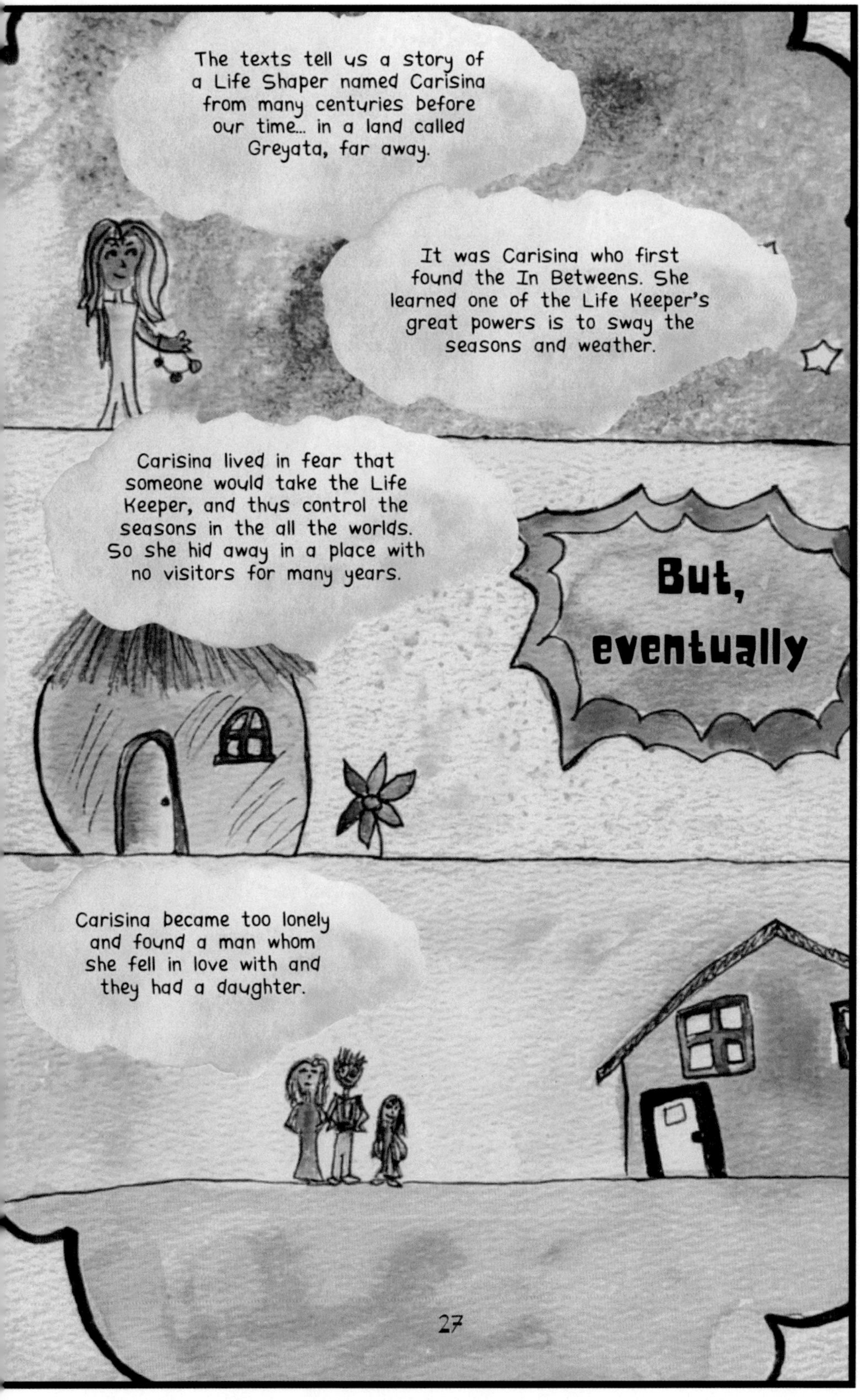
The texts tell us a story of a Life Shaper named Carisina from many centuries before our time... in a land called Greyata, far away.
It was Carisina who first found the In Betweens. She learned one of the Life Keeper's great powers is to sway the seasons and weather.
Carisina lived in fear that someone would take the Life Keeper, and thus control the seasons in the all the worlds. So she hid away in a place with no visitors for many years.
But, eventually
Carisina became too lonely and found a man whom she fell in love with and they had a daughter.

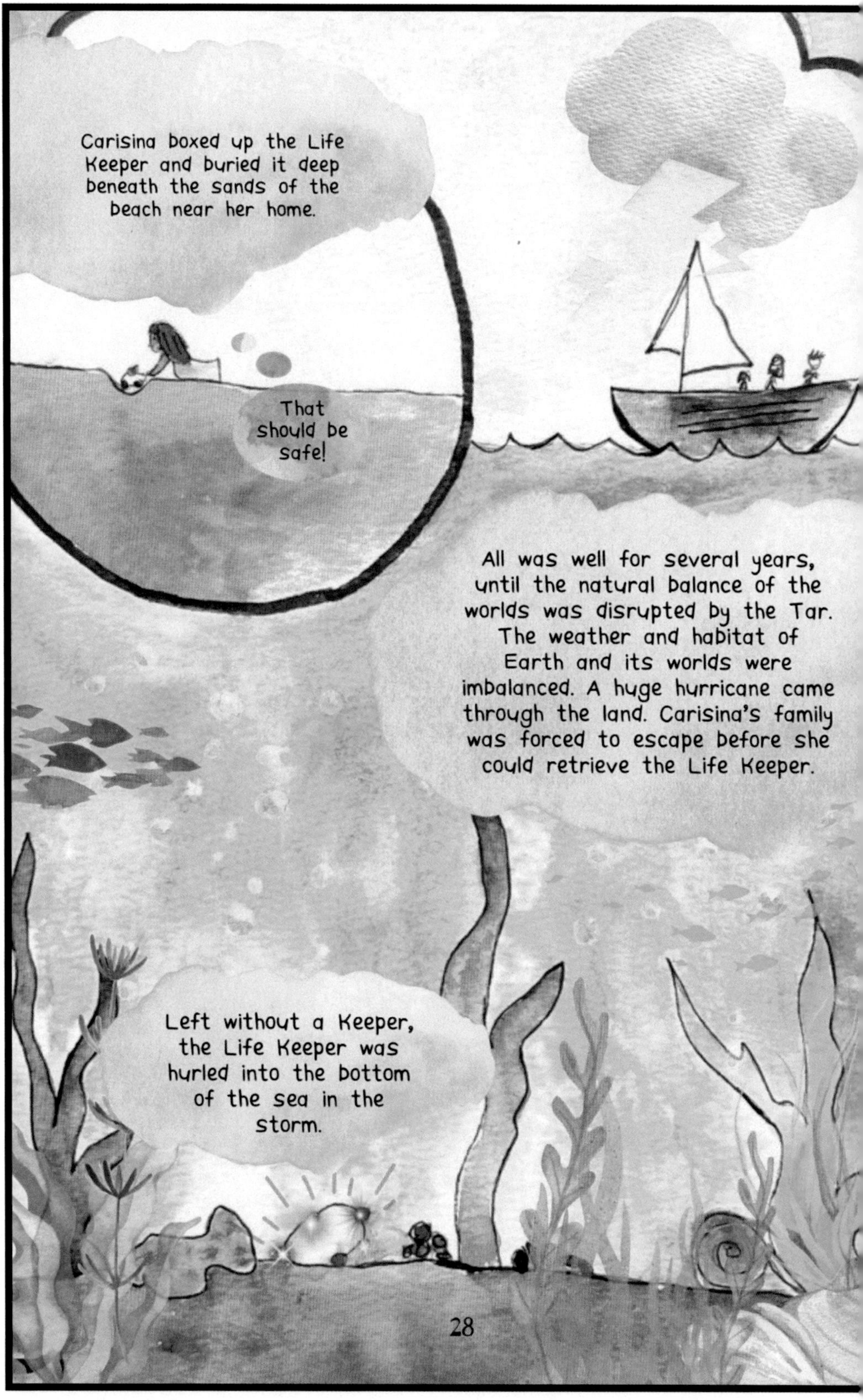

Carisina boxed up the Life Keeper and buried it deep beneath the sands of the beach near her home.
That should be safe!
All was well for several years, until the natural balance of the worlds was disrupted by the Tar. The weather and habitat of Earth and its worlds were imbalanced. A huge hurricane came through the land. Carisina's family was forced to escape before she could retrieve the Life Keeper.
Left without a Keeper, the Life Keeper was hurled into the bottom of the sea in the storm.

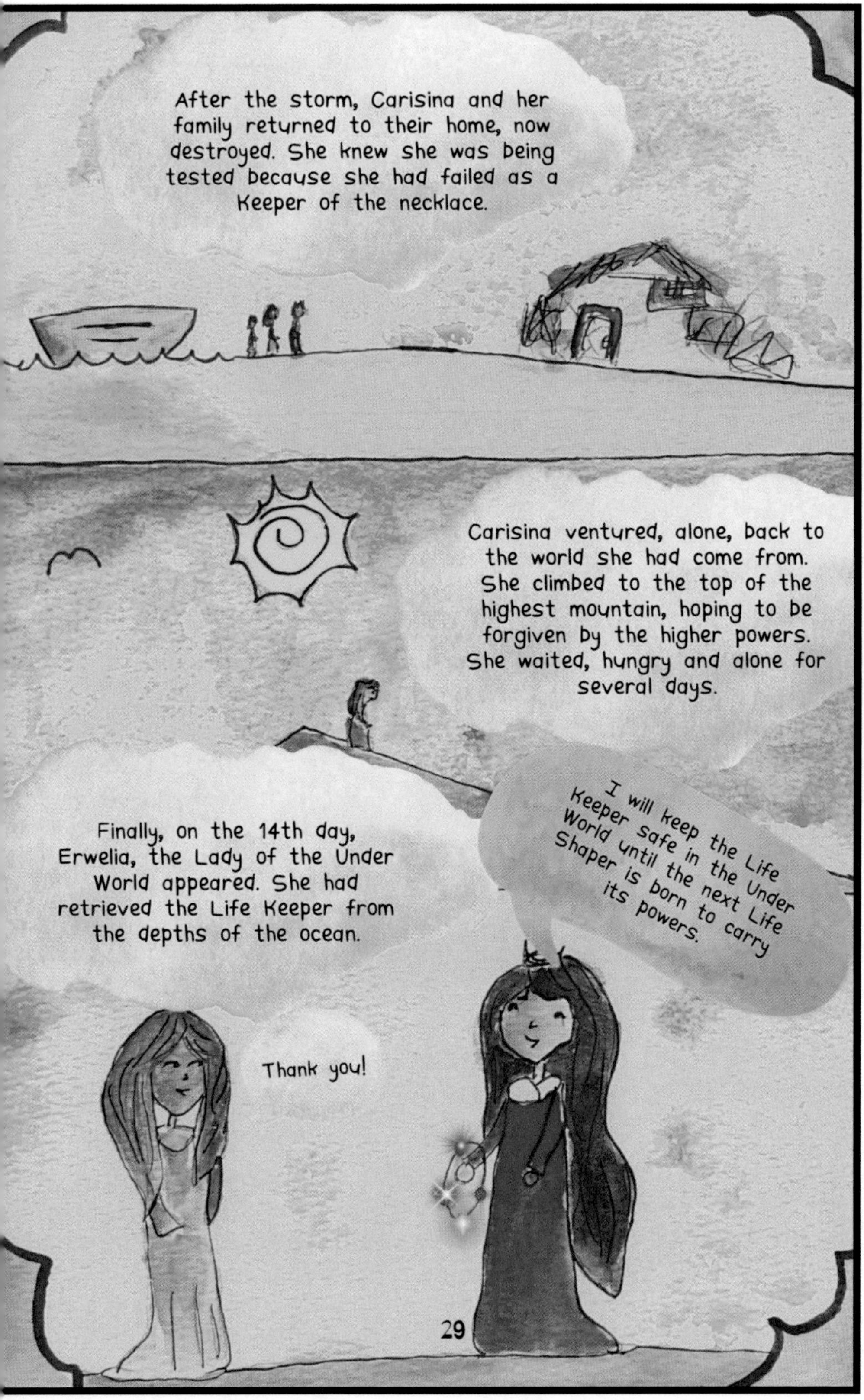
After the storm, Carisina and her family returned to their home, now destroyed. She knew she was being tested because she had failed as a Keeper of the necklace.
Carisina ventured, alone, back to the world she had come from. She climbed to the top of the highest mountain, hoping to be forgiven by the higher powers. She waited, hungry and alone for several days.
Finally, on the 14th day, Erwelia, the Lady of the Under World appeared. She had retrieved the Life Keeper from the depths of the ocean.
I will keep the Life Keeper safe in the Under World until the next Life Shaper is born to carry its powers.
Thank you!

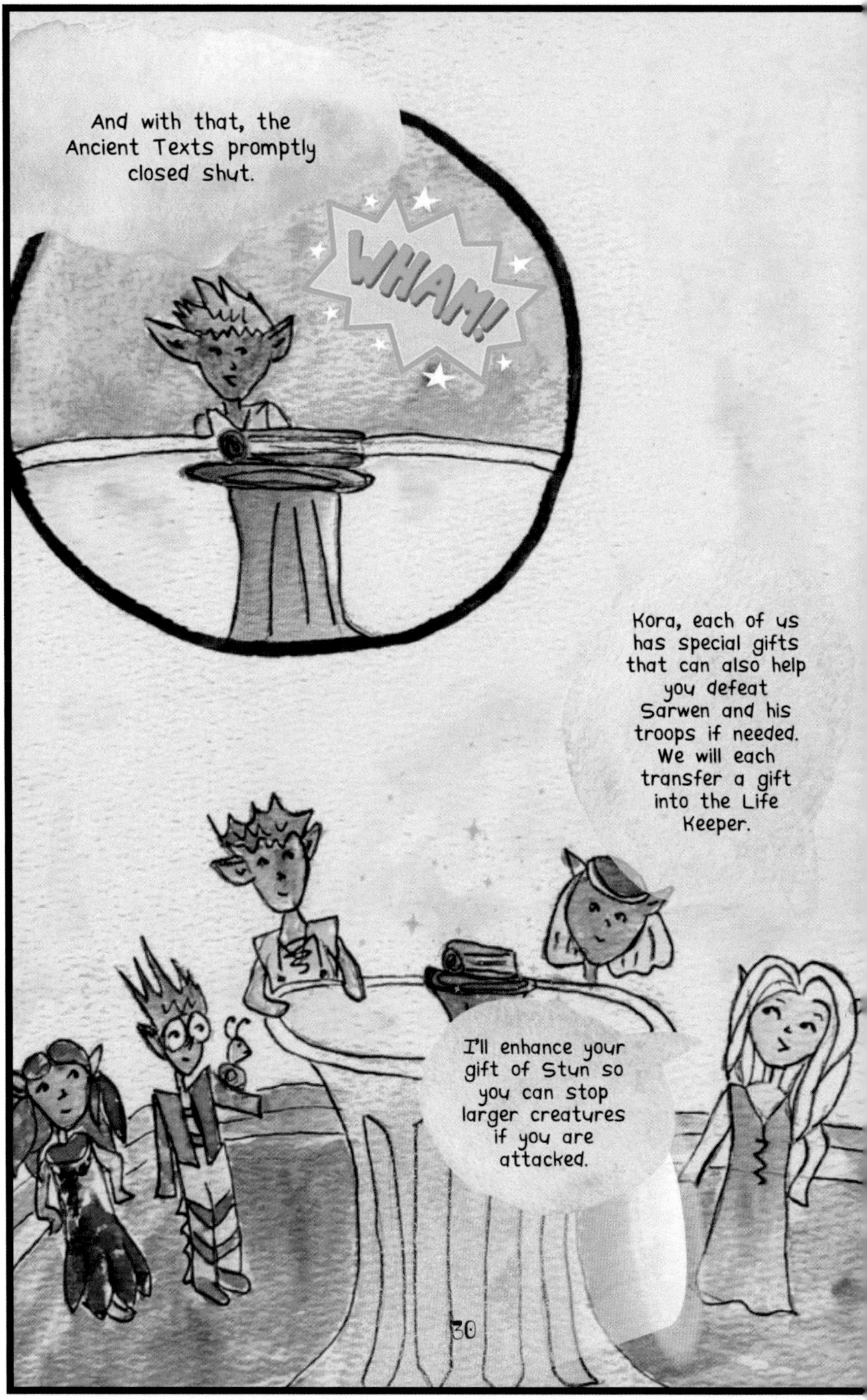
And with that, the Ancient Texts promptly closed shut.
WHAM!
Kora, each of us has special gifts that can also help you defeat Sarwen and his troops if needed. We will each transfer a gift into the Life Keeper.
I'll enhance your gift of Stun so you can stop larger creatures if you are attacked.

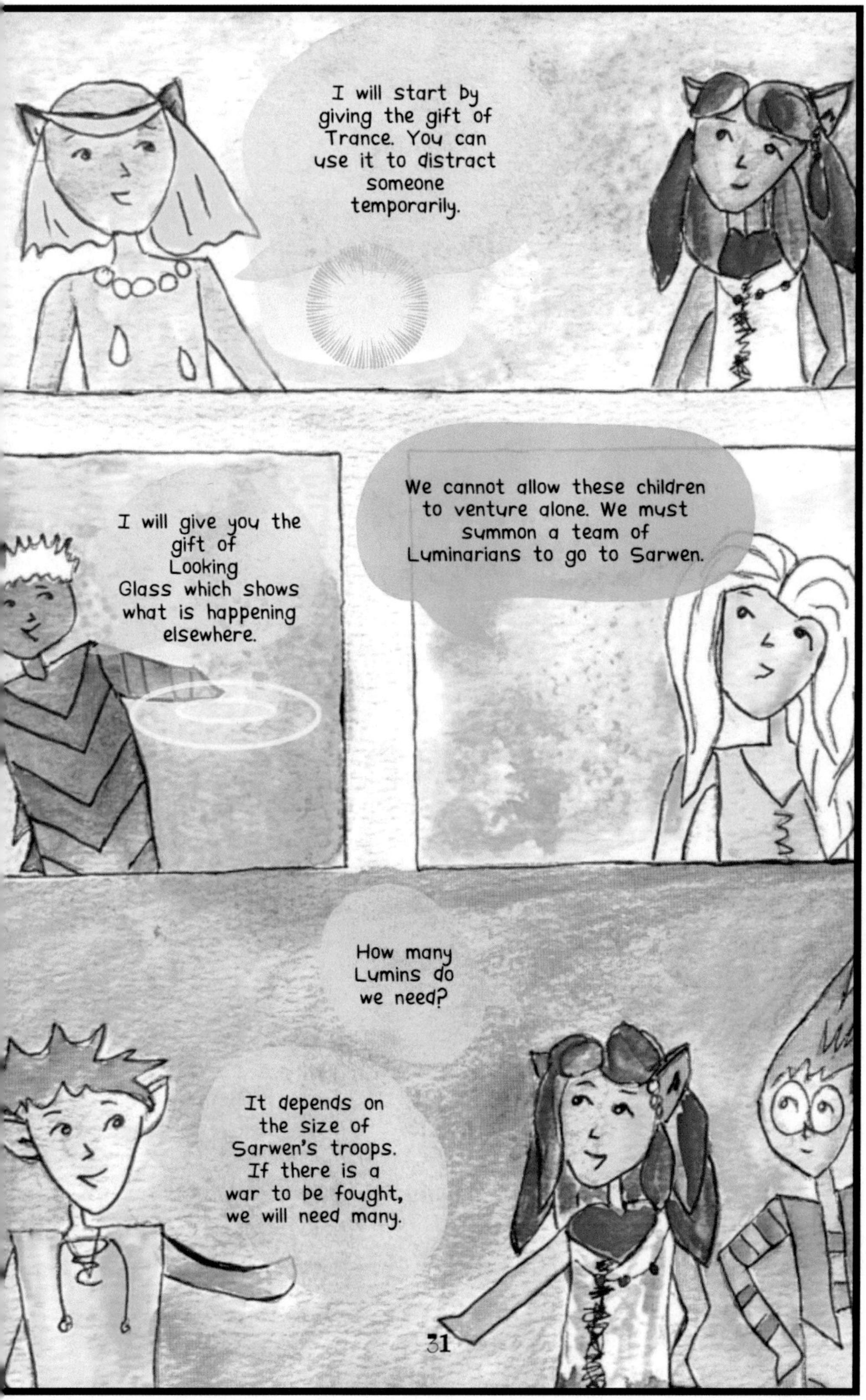
I will start by giving the gift of Trance. You can use it to distract someone temporarily.
I will give you the gift of Looking Glass which shows what is happening elsewhere.
We cannot allow these children to venture alone. We must summon a team of Luminarians to go to Sarwen.
How many Lumins do we need?
It depends on the size of Sarwen's troops. If there is a war to be fought, we will need many.

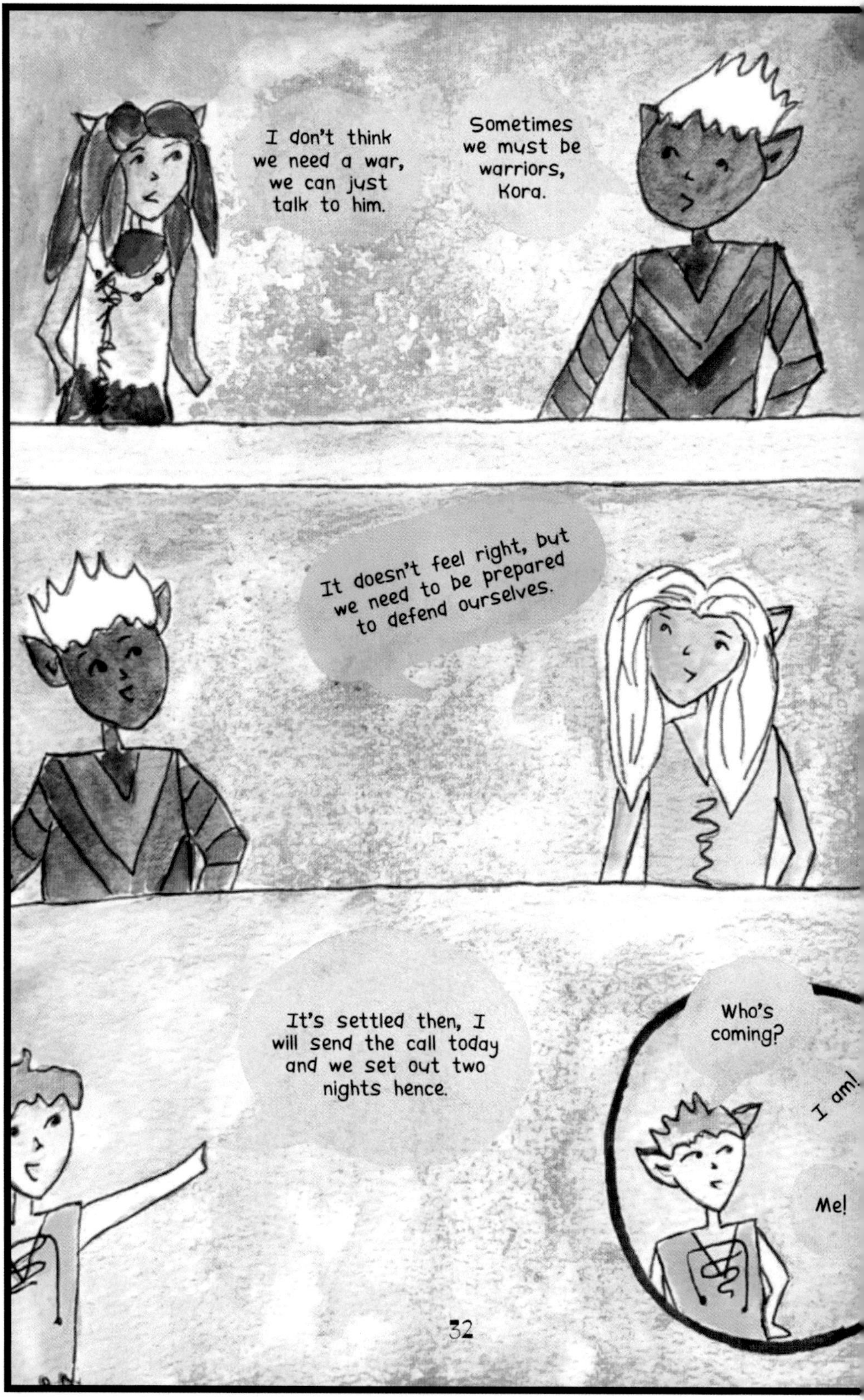
I don't think we need a war, we can just talk to him.
Sometimes we must be warriors, Kora.
It doesn't feel right, but we need to be prepared to defend ourselves.
It's settled then, I will send the call today and we set out two nights hence.
Who's coming?
I am!
Me!

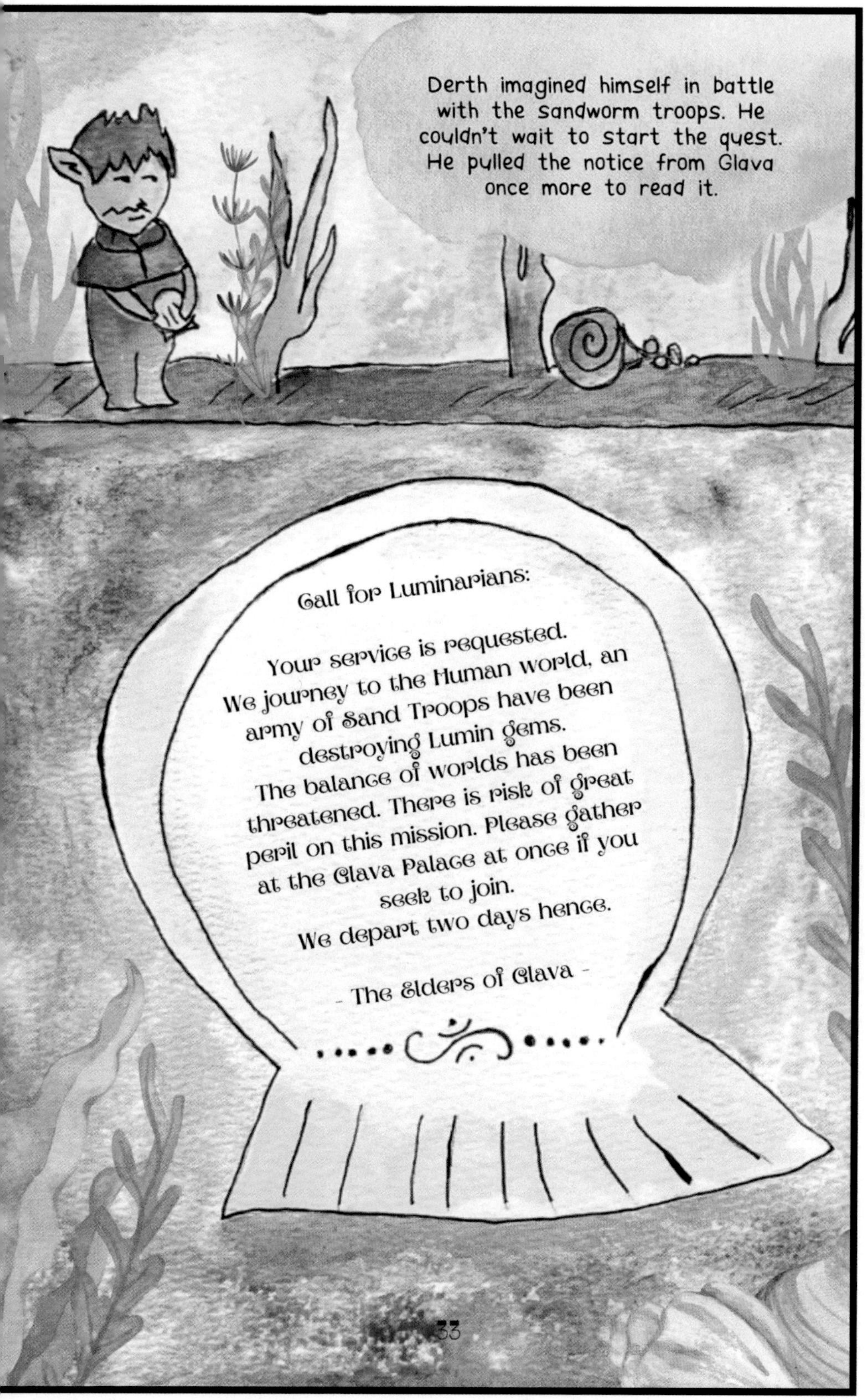

Derth imagined himself in battle with the sandworm troops. He couldn't wait to start the quest. He pulled the notice from Glava once more to read it.
Call for Luminarians:
Your service is requested.
We journey to the Human world, an army of Sand Troops have been destroying Lumin gems.
The balance of worlds has been threatened. There is risk of great peril on this mission. Please gather at the Glava Palace at once if you seek to join.
We depart two days hence.
- The Elders of Glava -

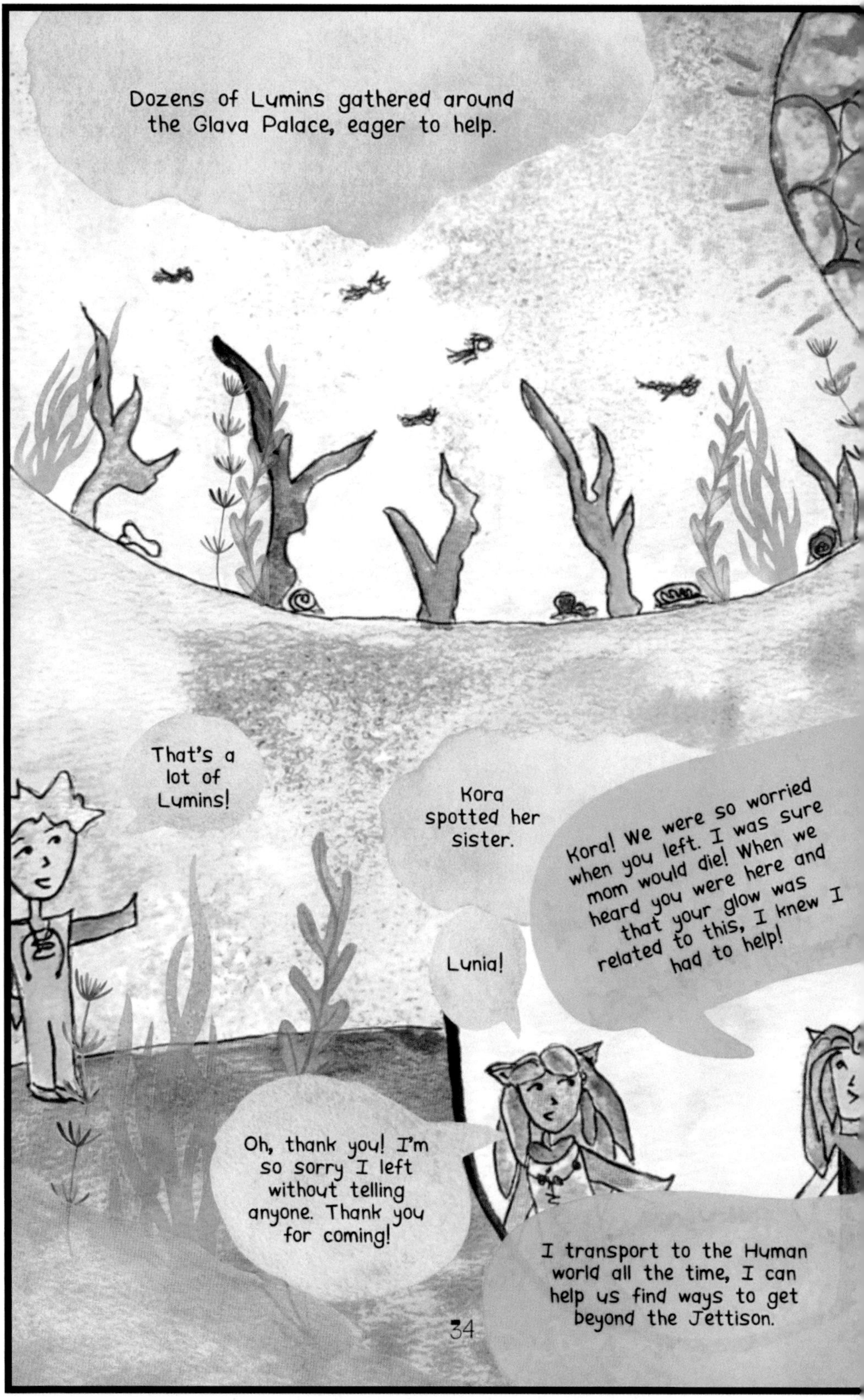
Dozens of Lumins gathered around the Glava Palace, eager to help.
That's a lot of Lumins!
Kora spotted her sister.
Kora! We were so worried when you left. I was sure mom would die! When we heard you were here and that your glow was related to this, I knew I had to help!
Lunia!
Oh, thank you! I'm so sorry I left without telling anyone. Thank you for coming!
I transport to the Human world all the time, I can help us find ways to get beyond the Jettison.

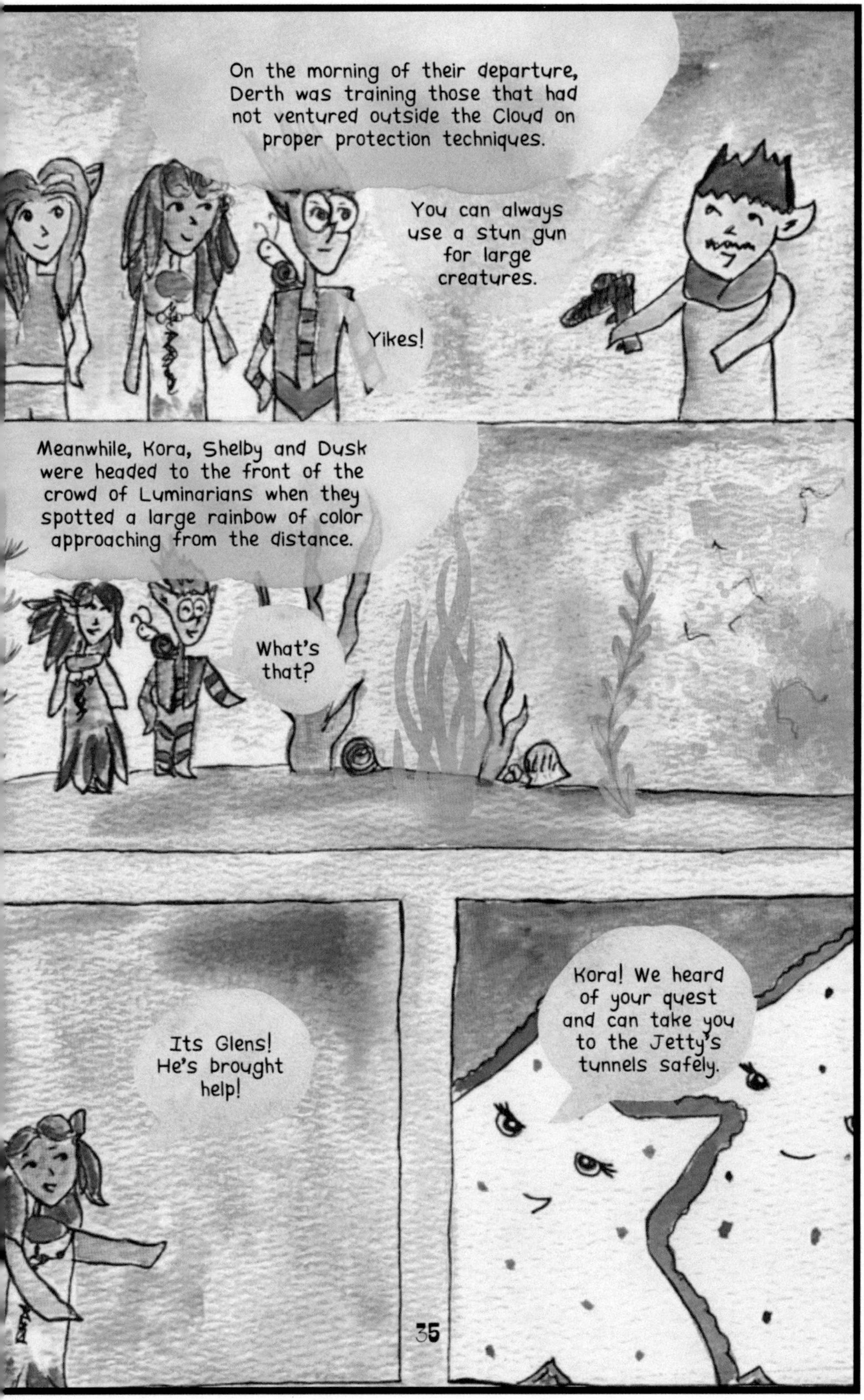
On the morning of their departure, Derth was training those that had not ventured outside the Cloud on proper protection techniques.
You can always use a stun gun for large creatures.
Yikes!
Meanwhile, Kora, Shelby and Dusk were headed to the front of the crowd of Luminarians when they spotted a large rainbow of color approaching from the distance.
What's that?
Its Glens! He's brought help!
Kora! We heard of your quest and can take you to the Jetty's tunnels safely.

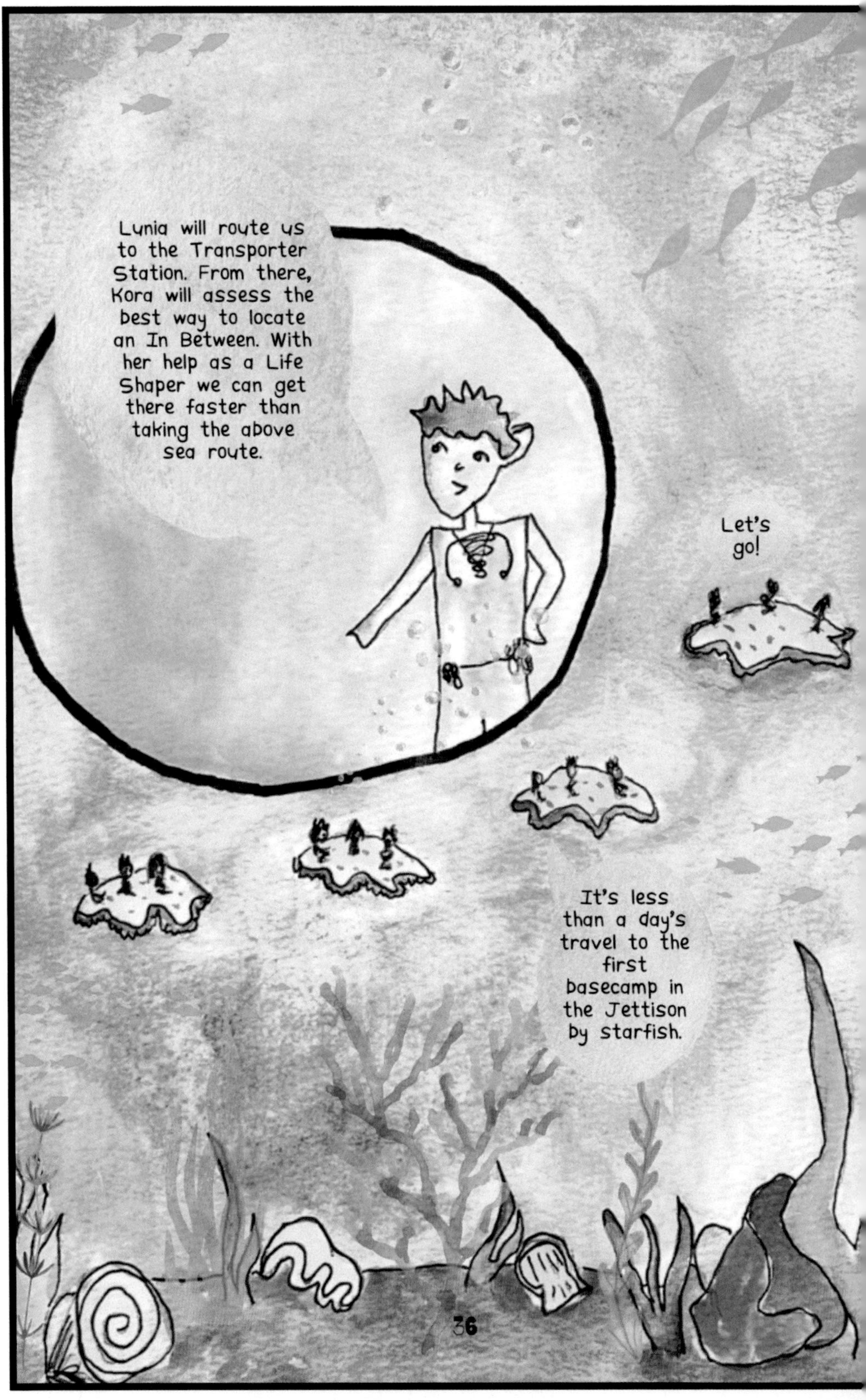
Lunia will route us to the Transporter Station. From there, Kora will assess the best way to locate an In Between. With her help as a Life Shaper we can get there faster than taking the above sea route.
Let's go!
It's less than a day's travel to the first basecamp in the Jettison by starfish.

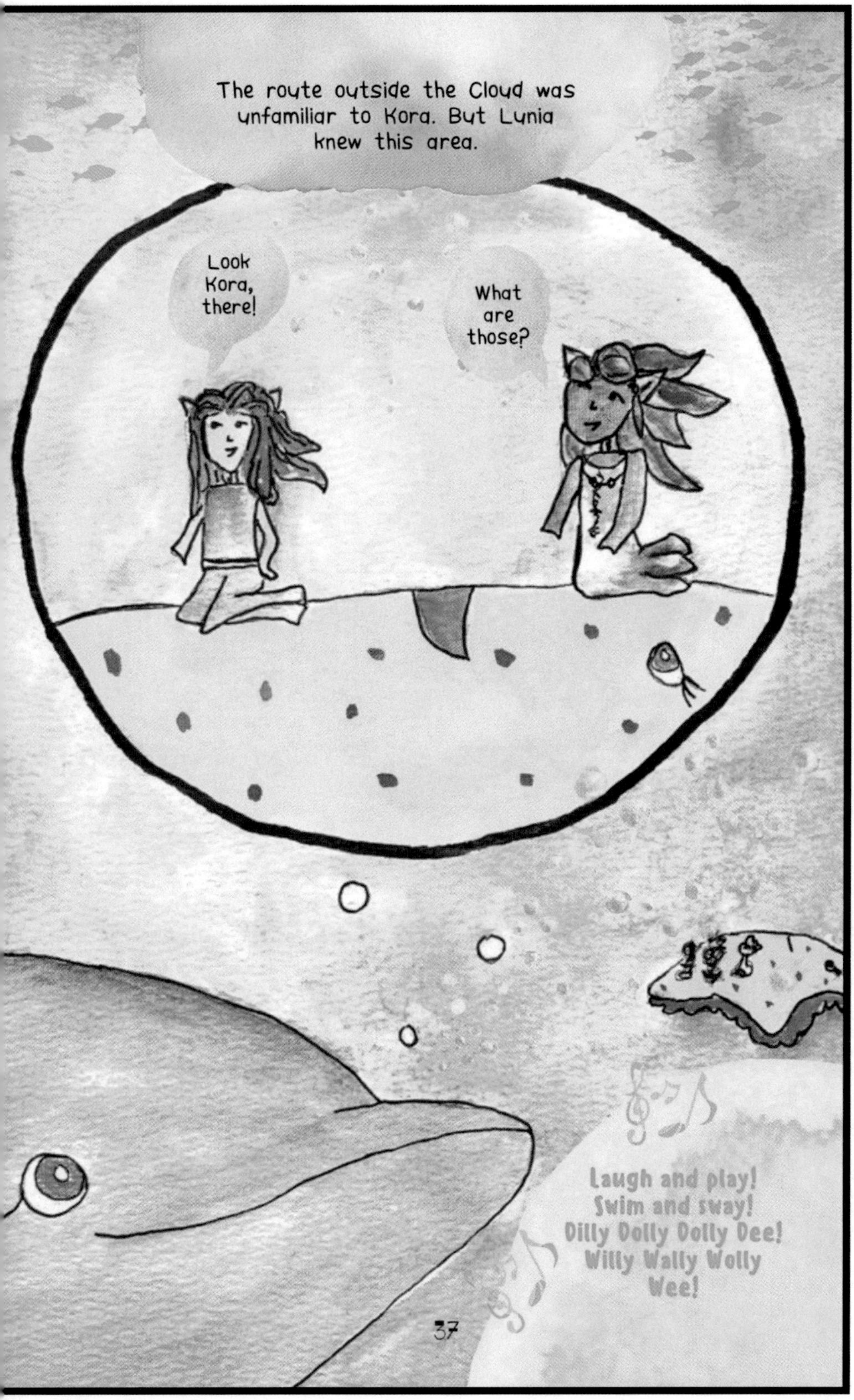
The route outside the Cloud was unfamiliar to Kora. But Lunia knew this area.
Look Kora, there!
What are those?
Laugh and play! Swim and sway! Dilly Dolly Dolly Dee! Willy Wally Wolly Wee!

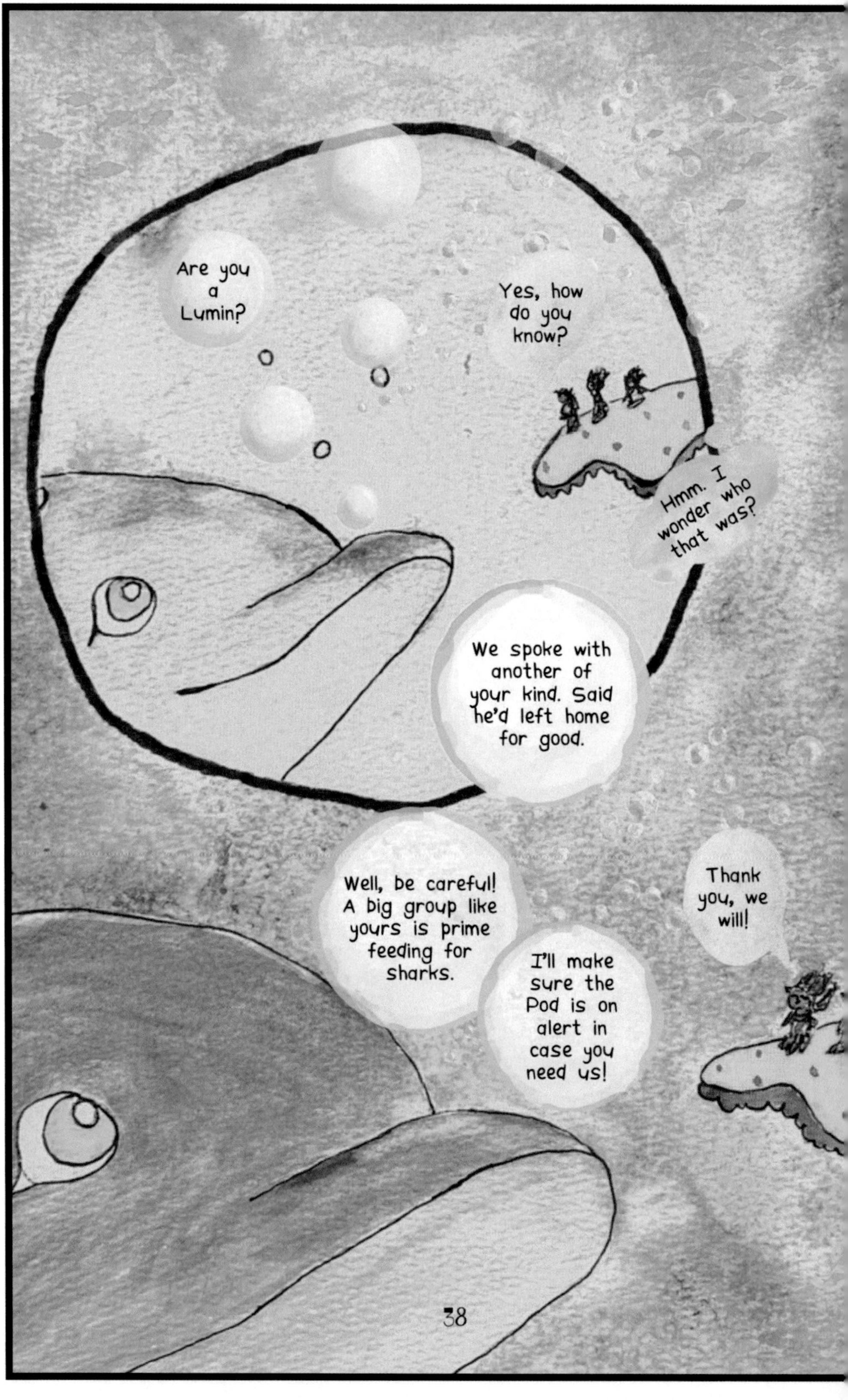
Are you a Lumin?
Yes, how do you know?
Hmm. I wonder who that was?
We spoke with another of your kind. Said he'd left home for good.
Well, be careful! A big group like yours is prime feeding for sharks.
I'll make sure the Pod is on alert in case you need us!
Thank you, we will!

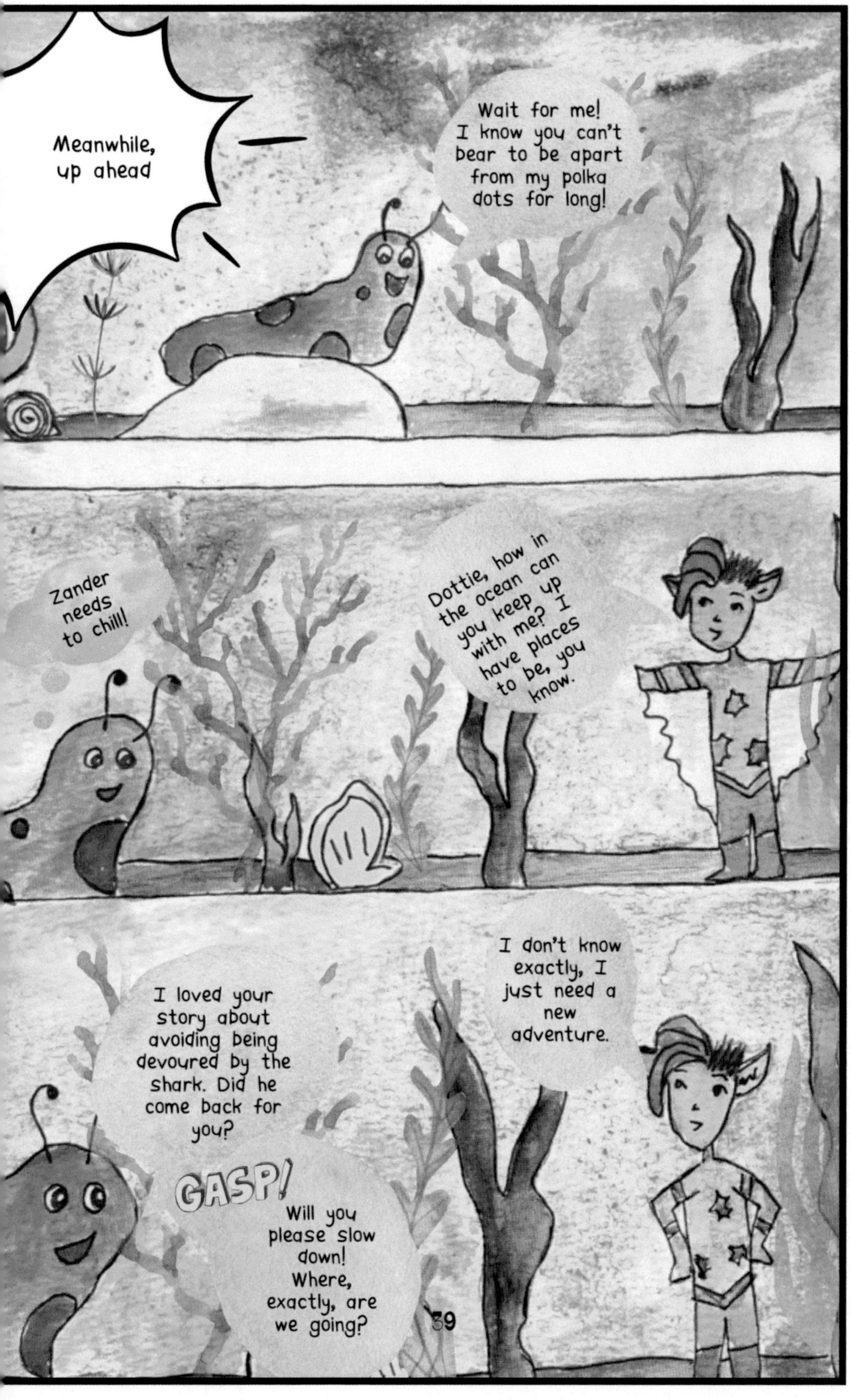
Meanwhile, up ahead
Wait for me! I know you can't bear to be apart from my polka dots for long!
Dottie, how in the ocean can you keep up with me? I have places to be, you know.
Zander needs to chill!
I don't know exactly, I just need a new adventure.
I loved your story about avoiding being devoured by the shark. Did he come back for you?
GASP!
Will you please slow down! Where, exactly, are we going?

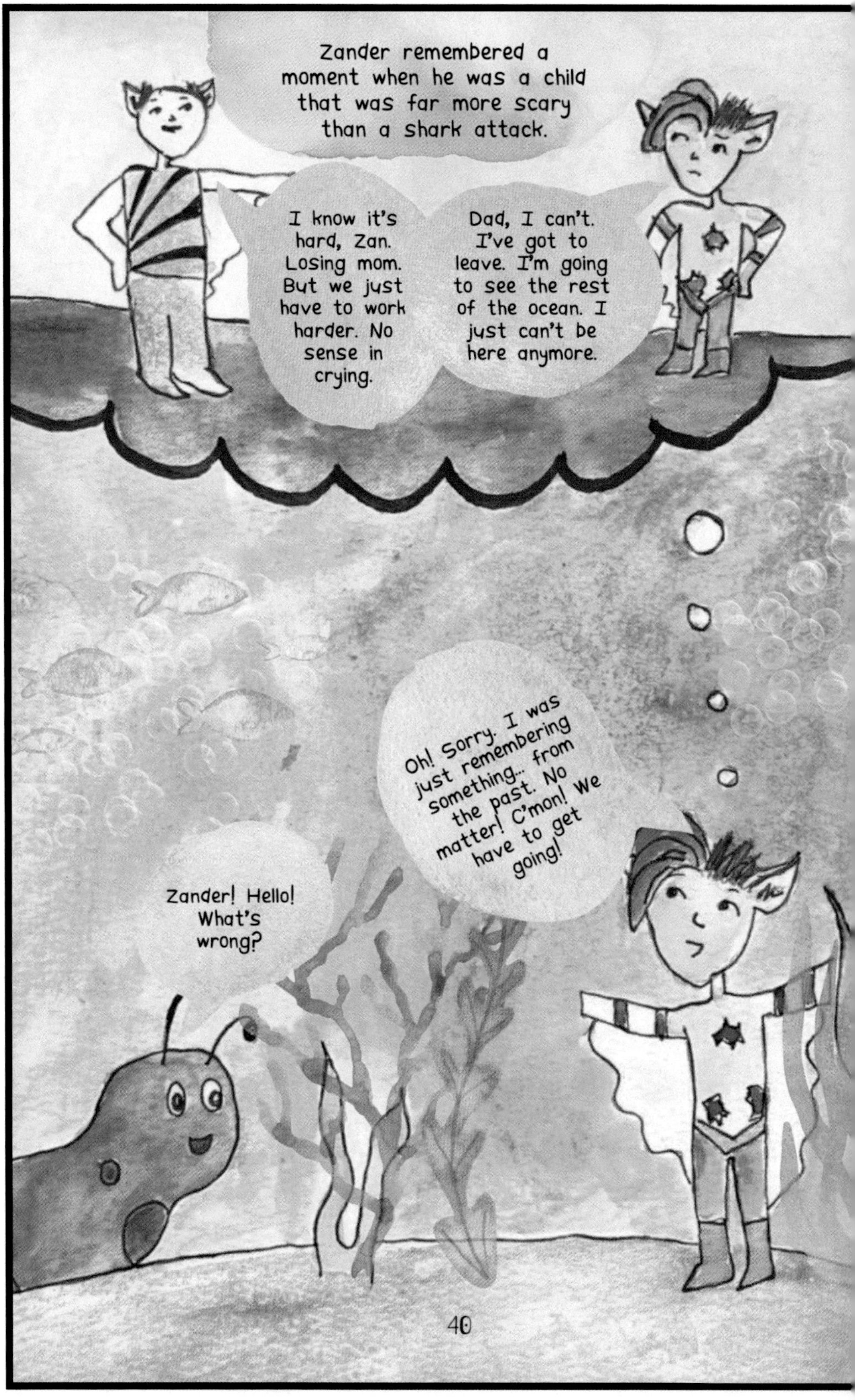
Zander remembered a moment when he was a child that was far more scary than a shark attack.
I know it's hard, Zan. Losing mom. But we just have to work harder. No sense in crying.
Dad, I can't. I've got to leave. I'm going to see the rest of the ocean. I just can't be here anymore.
Zander! Hello! What's wrong?
Oh! Sorry. I was just remembering something... from the past. No matter! C'mon! We have to get going!

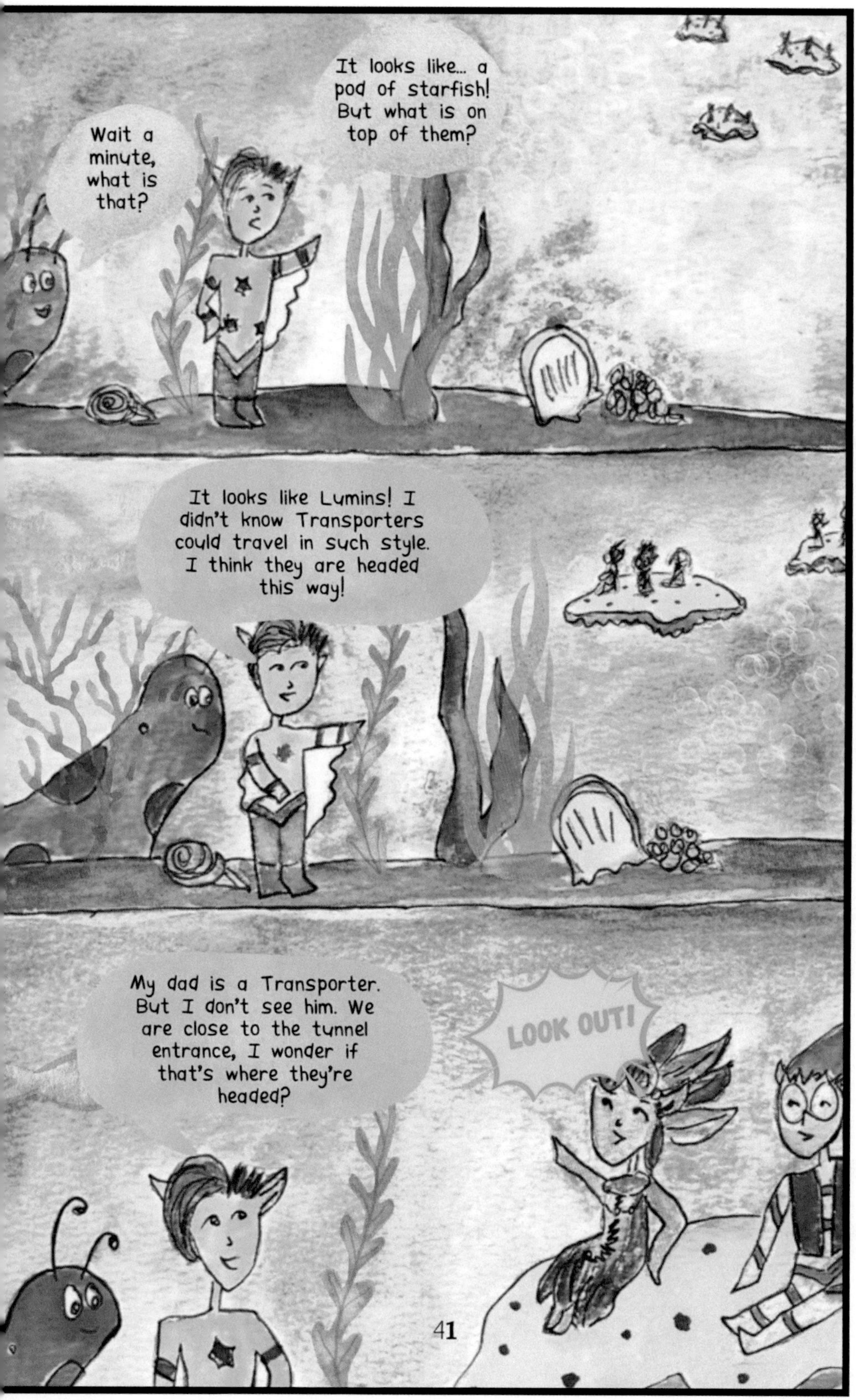
Wait a minute, what is that?
It looks like... a pod of starfish! But what is on top of them?
It looks like Lumins! I didn't know Transporters could travel in such style. I think they are headed this way!
My dad is a Transporter. But I don't see him. We are close to the tunnel entrance, I wonder if that's where they're headed?
LOOK OUT!

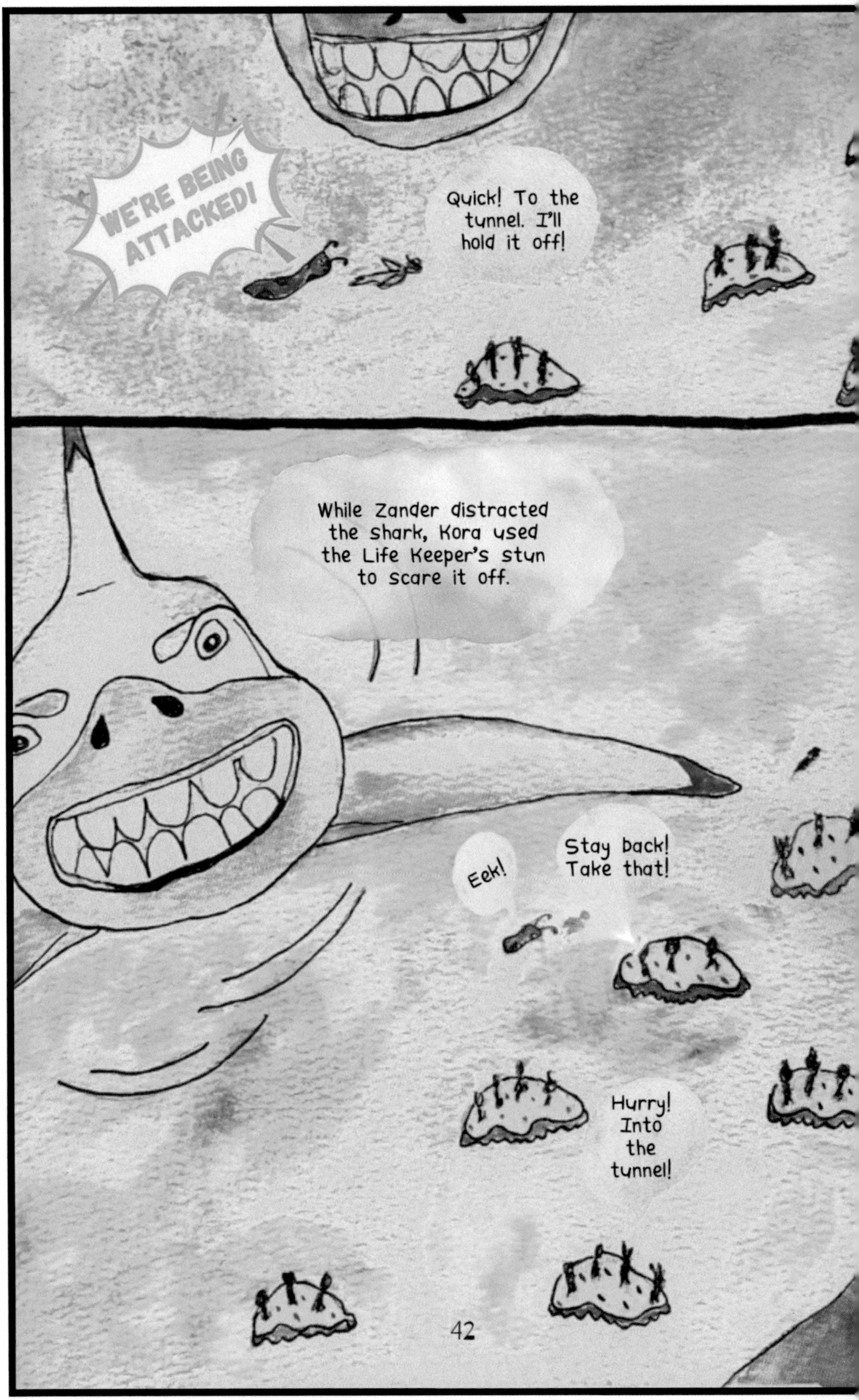
WE'RE BEING ATTACKED!
Quick! To the tunnel. I'll hold it off!
While Zander distracted the shark, Kora used the Life Keeper's stun to scare it off.
Eek!
Stay back! Take that!
Hurry! Into the tunnel!

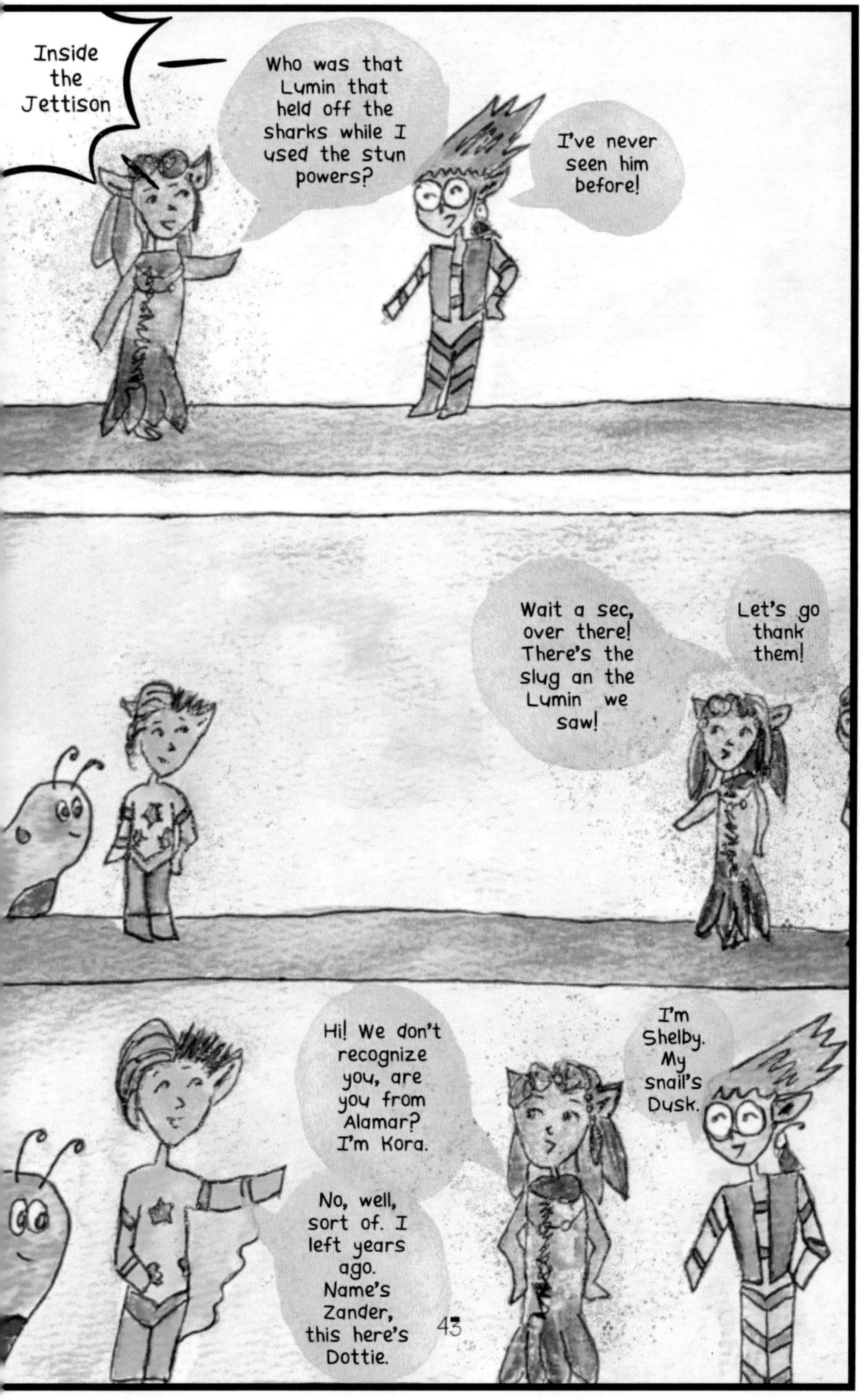
Inside the Jettison
Who was that Lumin that held off the sharks while I used the stun powers?
I've never seen him before!
Wait a sec, over there! There's the slug an the Lumin we saw!
Let's go thank them!
Hi! We don't recognize you, are you from Alamar? I'm Kora.
I'm Shelby. My snail's Dusk.
No, well, sort of. I left years ago. Name's Zander, this here's Dottie.

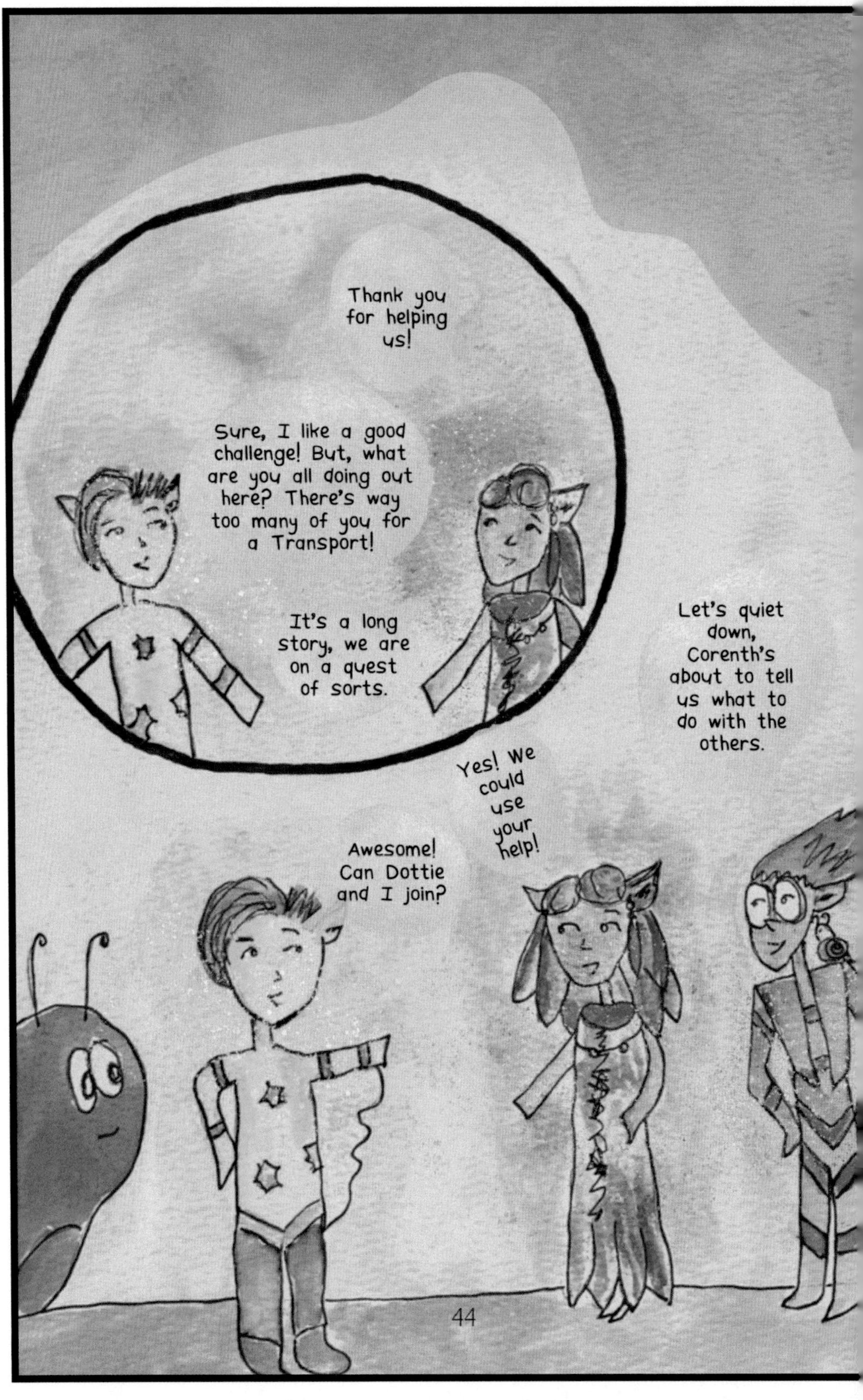
Thank you for helping us!
Sure, I like a good challenge! But, what are you all doing out here? There's way too many of you for a Transport!
It's a long story, we are on a quest of sorts.
Let's quiet down, Corenth's about to tell us what to do with the others.
Yes! We could use your help!
Awesome! Can Dottie and I join?

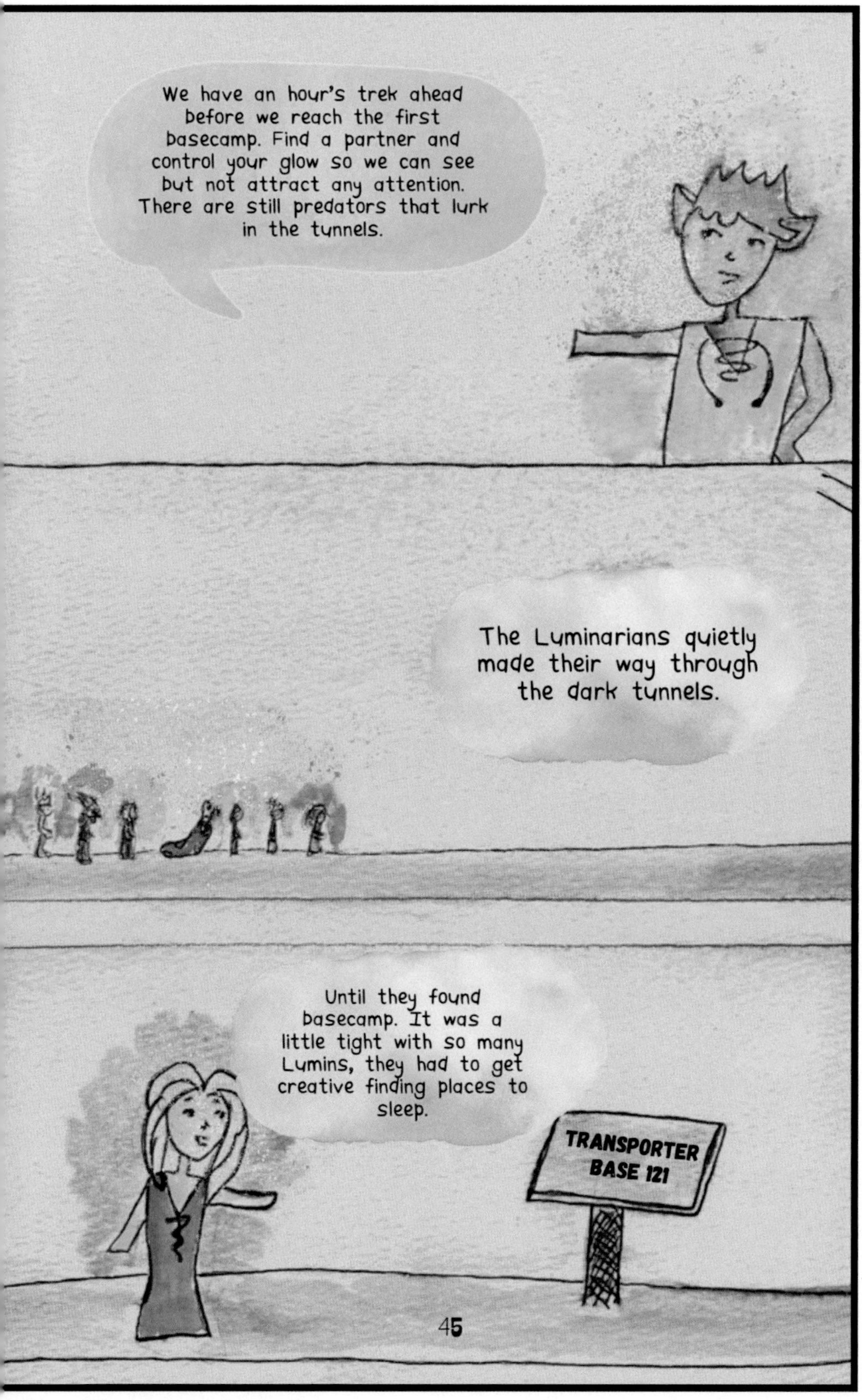
We have an hour's trek ahead before we reach the first basecamp. Find a partner and control your glow so we can see but not attract any attention. There are still predators that lurk in the tunnels.
The Luminarians quietly made their way through the dark tunnels.
Until they found basecamp. It was a little tight with so many Lumins, they had to get creative finding places to sleep.
TRANSPORTER BASE 121

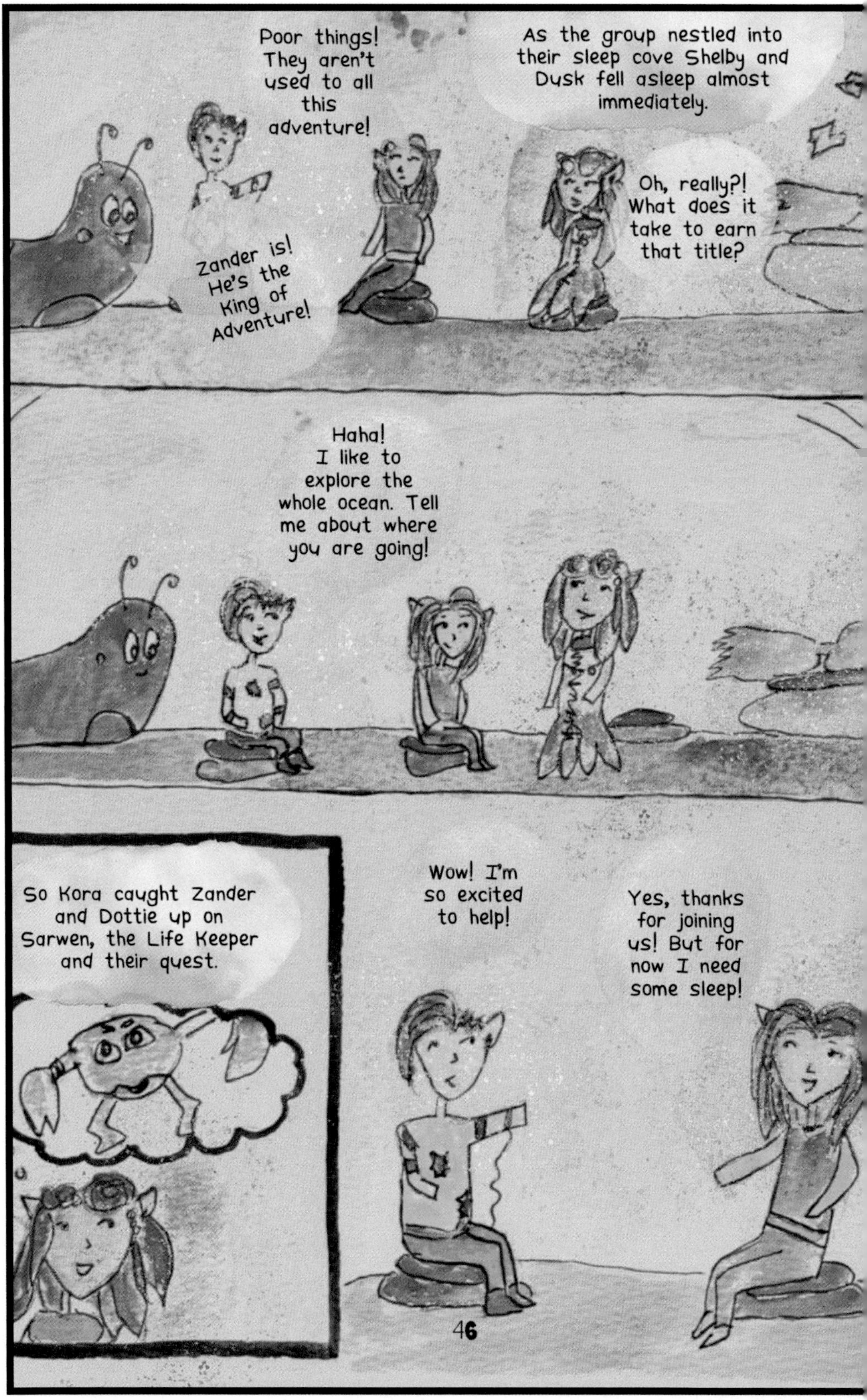

Poor things! They aren't used to all this adventure!
As the group nestled into their sleep cove Shelby and Dusk fell asleep almost immediately.
Zander is! He's the King of Adventure!
Oh, really?! What does it take to earn that title?
Haha! I like to explore the whole ocean. Tell me about where you are going!
So Kora caught Zander and Dottie up on Sarwen, the Life Keeper and their quest.
Wow! I'm so excited to help!
Yes, thanks for joining us! But for now I need some sleep!

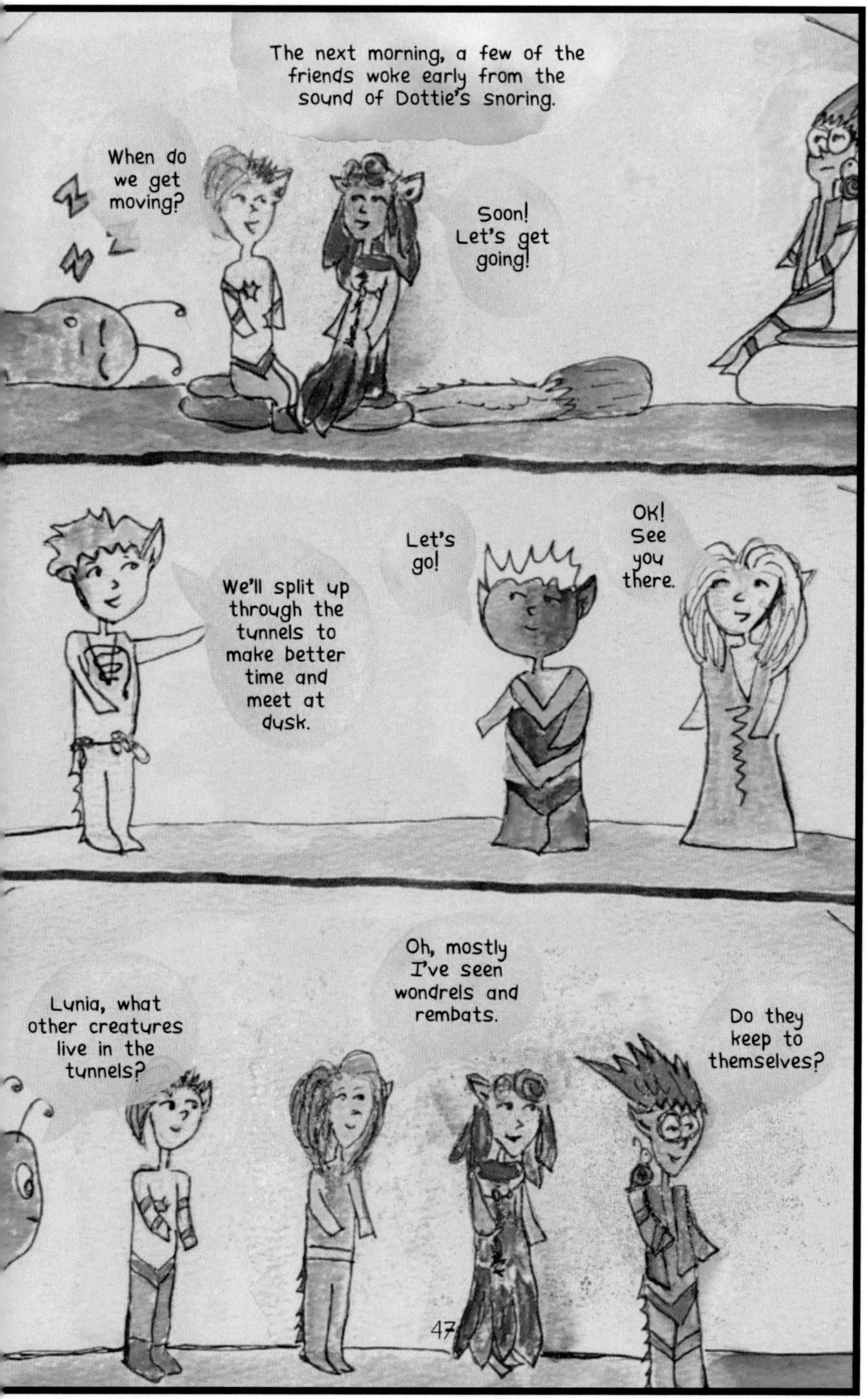
The next morning, a few of the friends woke early from the sound of Dottie's snoring.
When do we get moving?
Soon! Let's get going!
We'll split up through the tunnels to make better time and meet at dusk.
Let's go!
OK! See you there.
Lunia, what other creatures live in the tunnels?
Oh, mostly I've seen wondrels and rembats.
Do they keep to themselves?

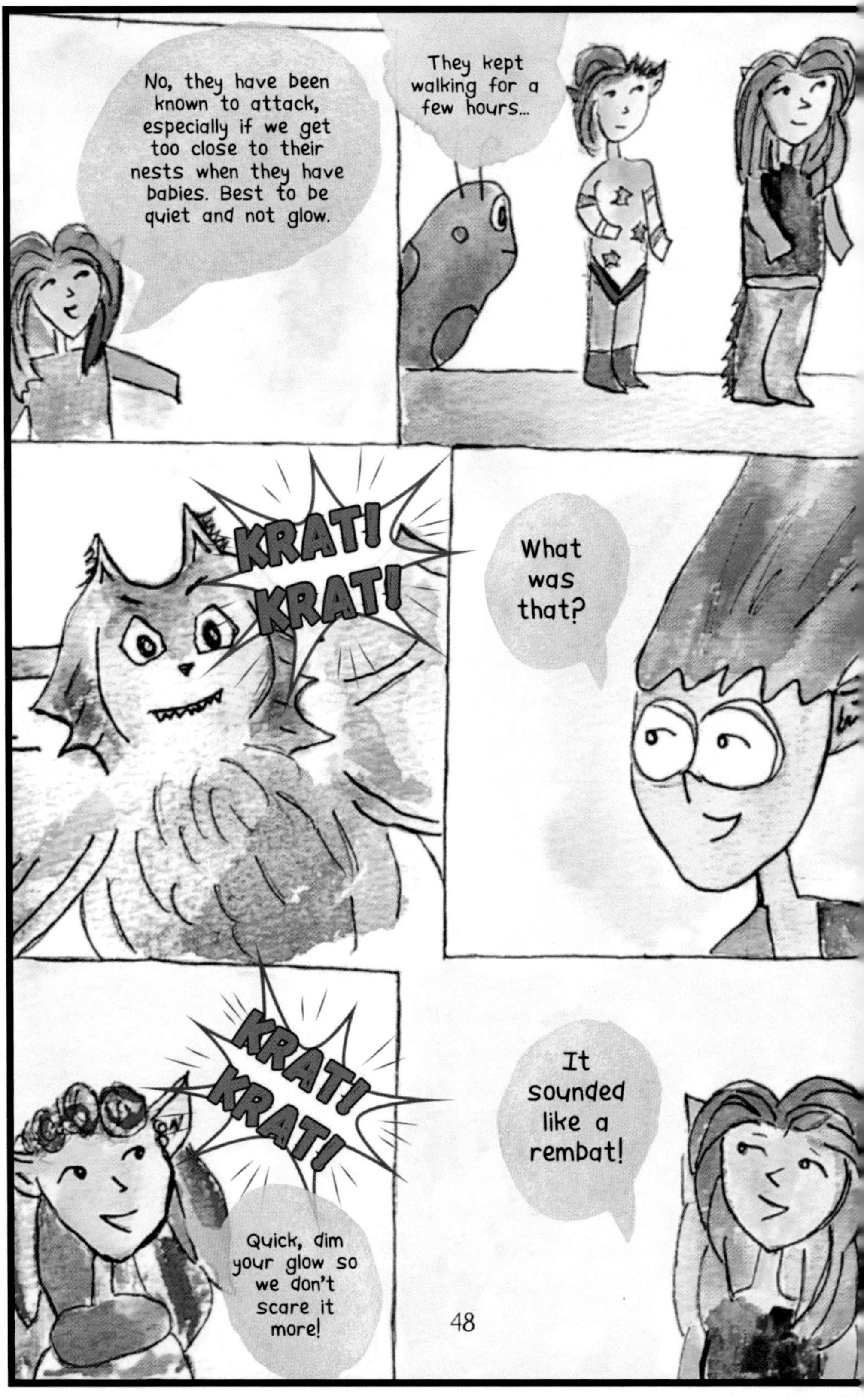
No, they have been known to attack, especially if we get too close to their nests when they have babies. Best to be quiet and not glow.
They kept walking for a few hours...
KRAT! KRAT!
What was that?
KRAT! KRAT!
It sounded like a rembat!
Quick, dim your glow so we don't scare it more!

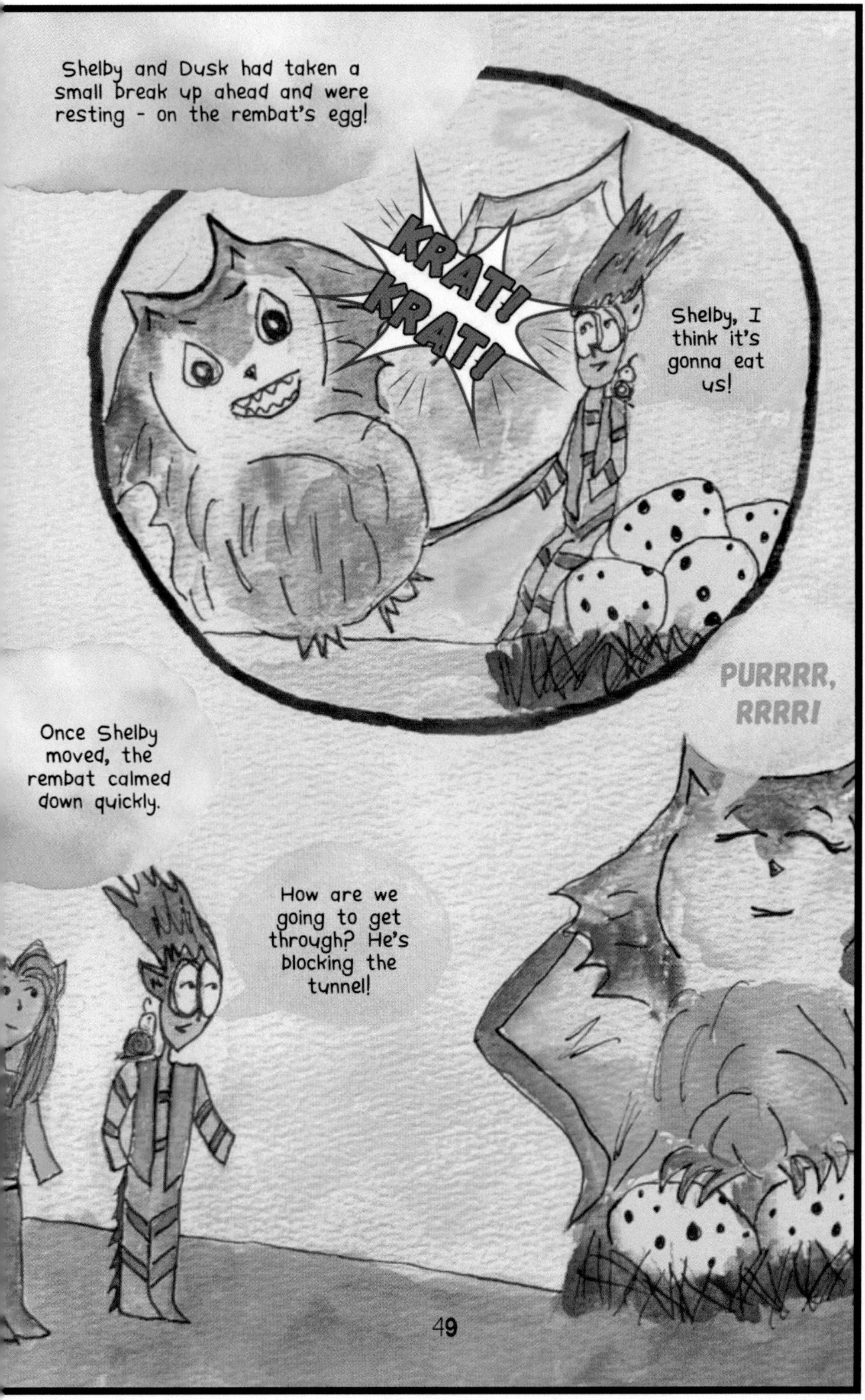

Shelby and Dusk had taken a small break up ahead and were resting - on the rembat's egg!
KRAT! KRAT!
Shelby, I think it's gonna eat us!
PURRRR, RRRR!
Once Shelby moved, the rembat calmed down quickly.
How are we going to get through? He's blocking the tunnel!

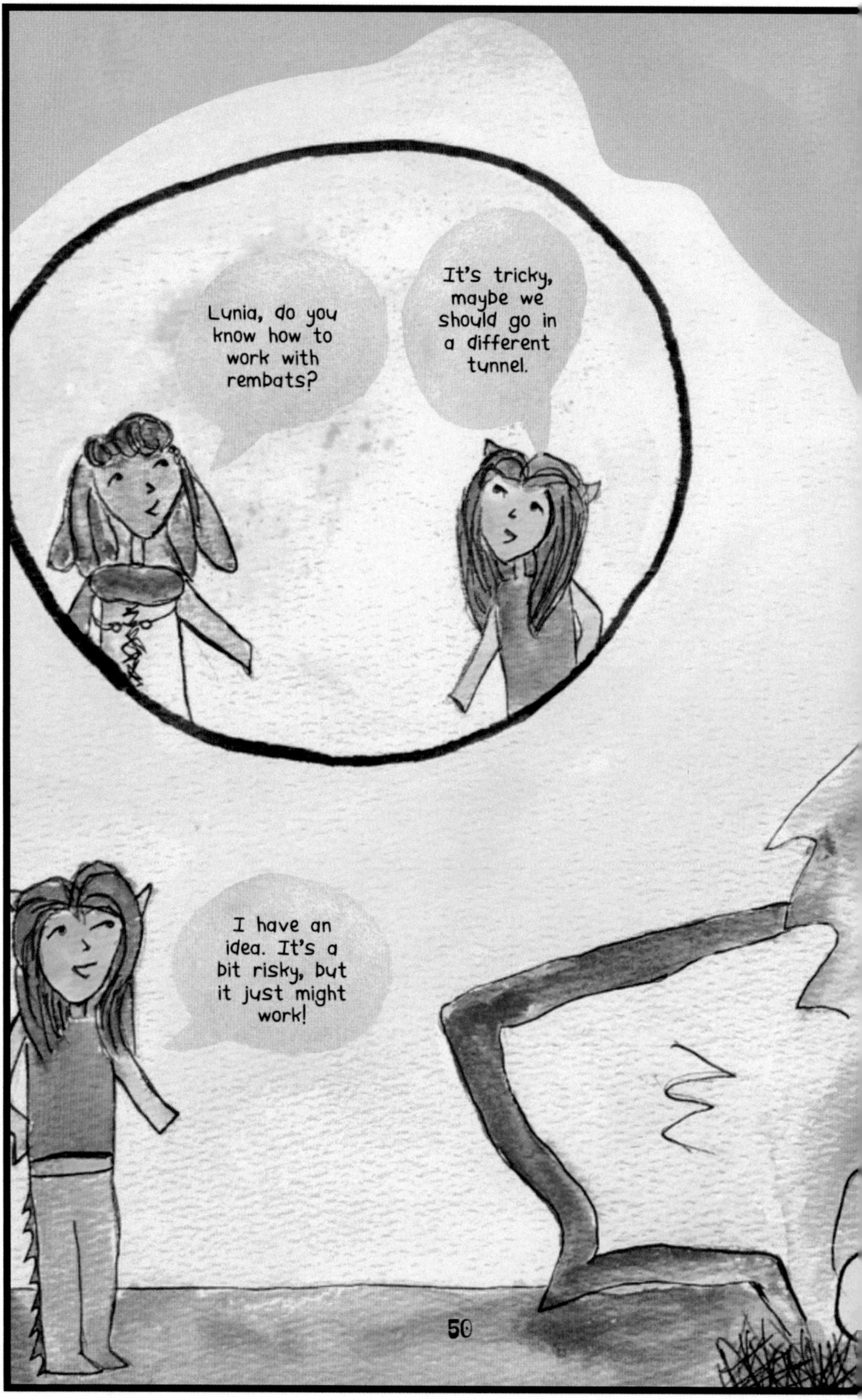
Lunia, do you know how to work with rembats?
It's tricky, maybe we should go in a different tunnel.
I have an idea. It's a bit risky, but it just might work!

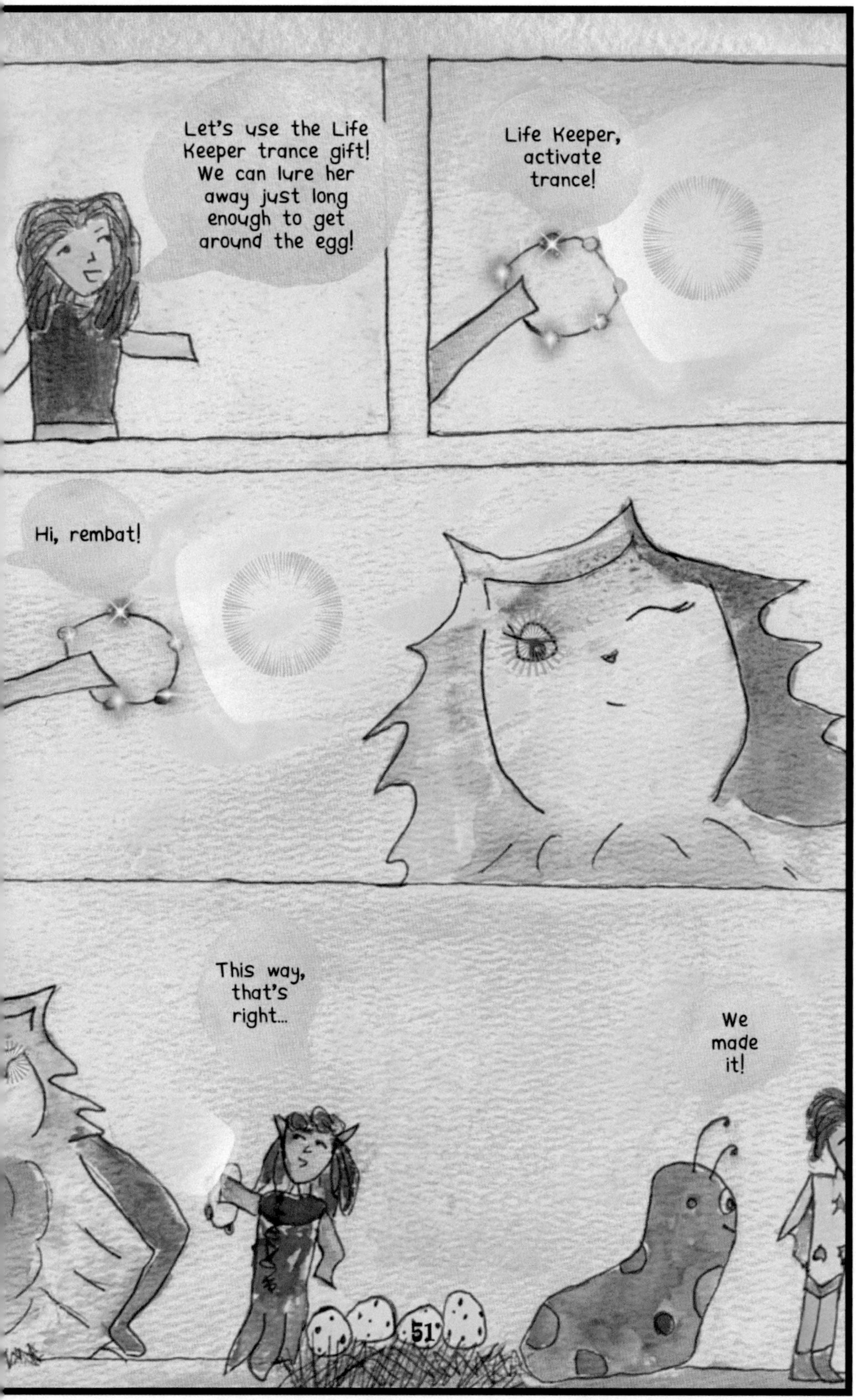
Let's use the Life Keeper trance gift! We can lure her away just long enough to get around the egg!
Life Keeper, activate trance!
Hi, rembat!
This way, that's right...
We made it!

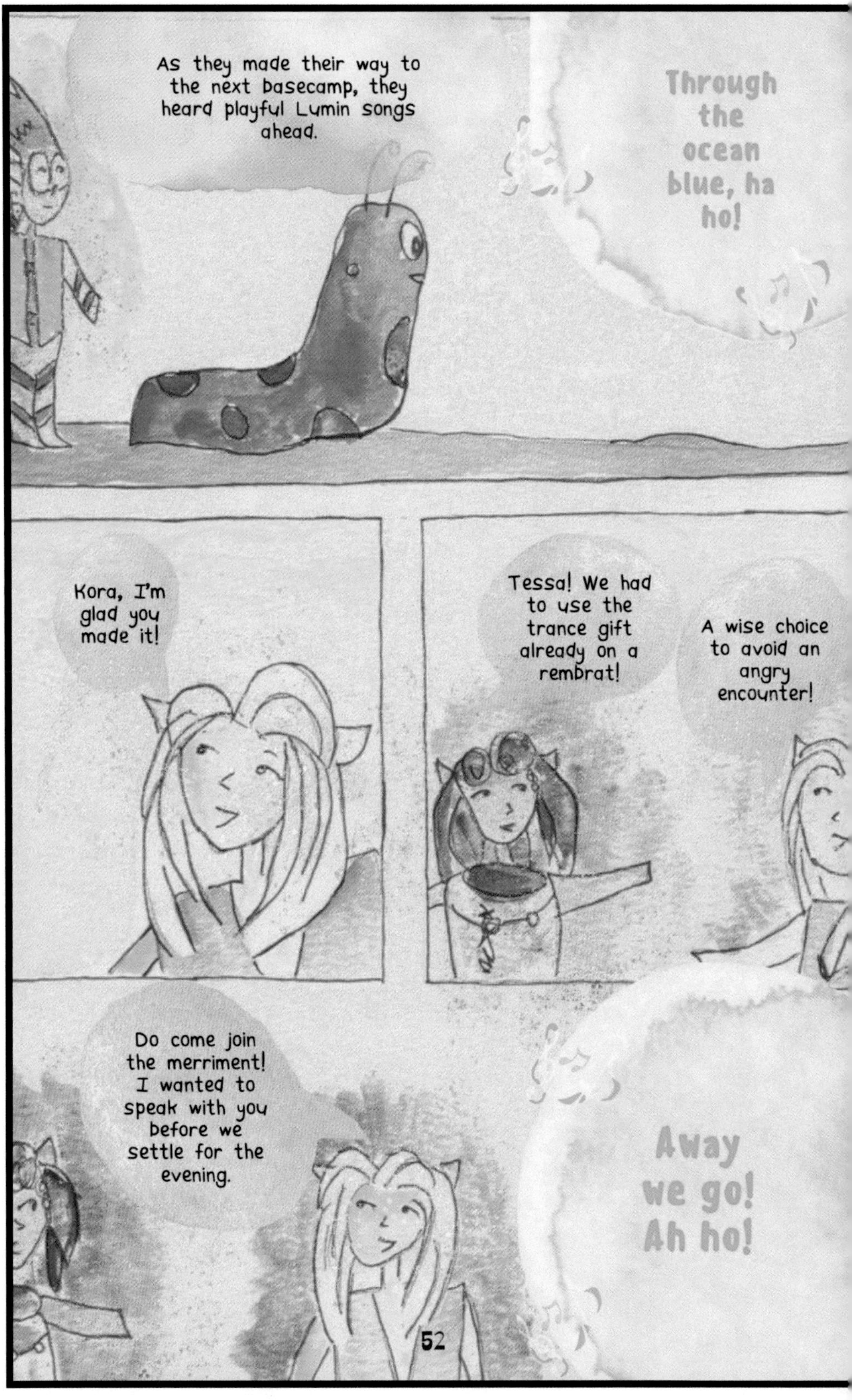
As they made their way to the next basecamp, they heard playful Lumin songs ahead.
Through the ocean blue, ha ho!
Kora, I'm glad you made it!
Tessa! We had to use the trance gift already on a rembrat!
A wise choice to avoid an angry encounter!
Do come join the merriment! I wanted to speak with you before we settle for the evening.
Away we go! Ah ho!

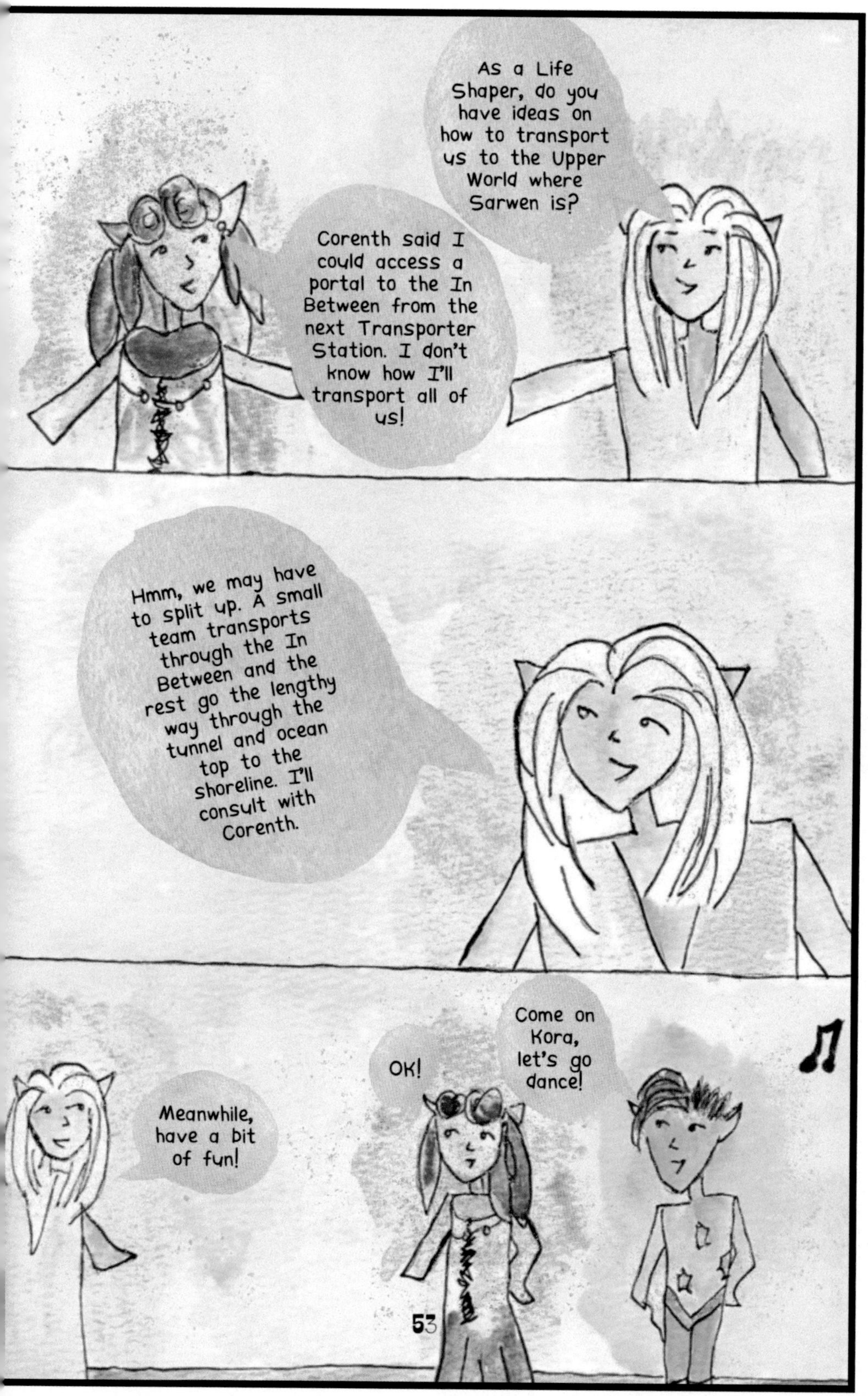
As a Life Shaper, do you have ideas on how to transport us to the Upper World where Sarwen is?
Corenth said I could access a portal to the In Between from the next Transporter Station. I don't know how I'll transport all of us!
Hmm, we may have to split up. A small team transports through the In Between and the rest go the lengthy way through the tunnel and ocean top to the shoreline. I'll consult with Corenth.
Meanwhile, have a bit of fun!
OK!
Come on Kora, let's go dance!

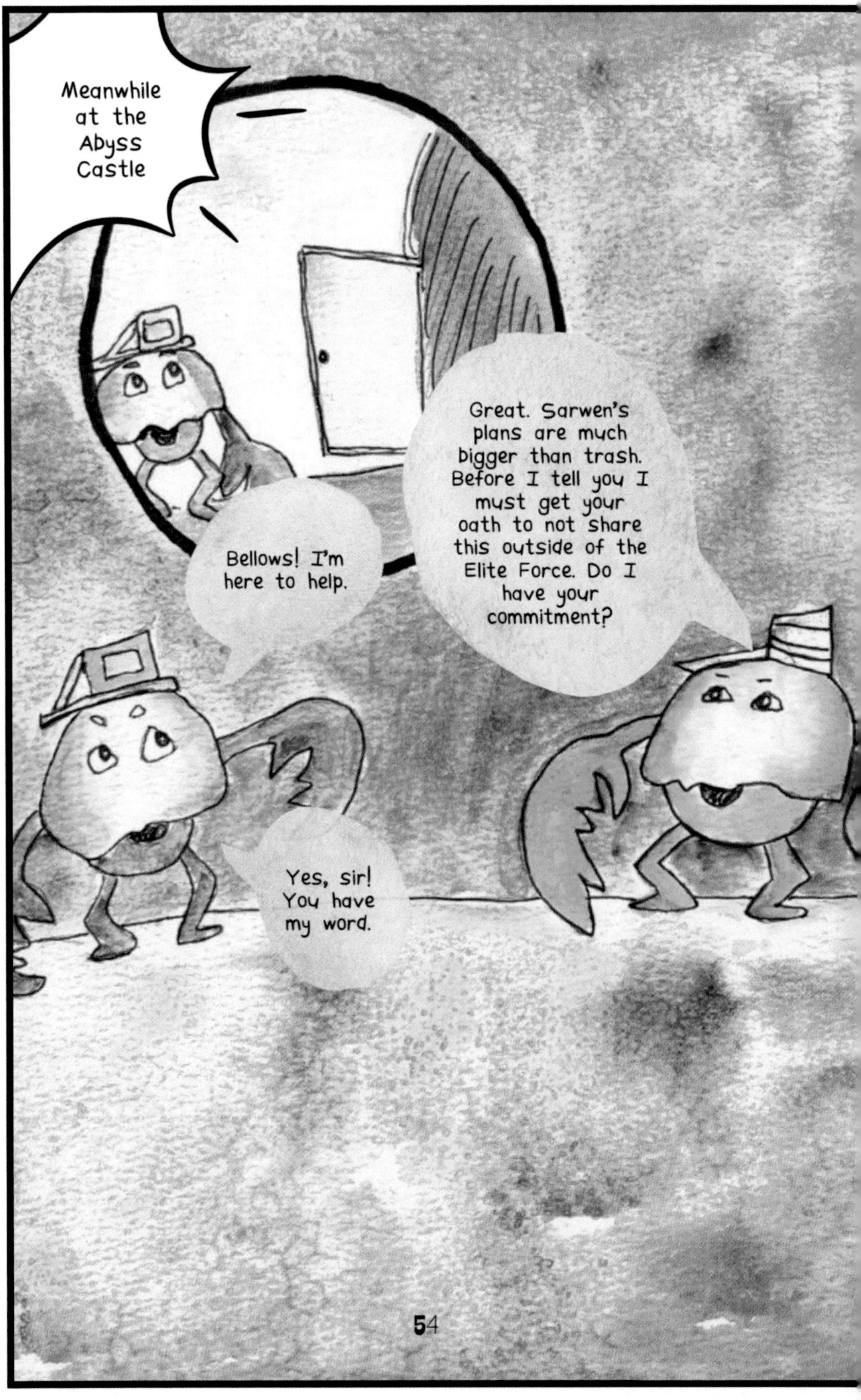
Meanwhile at the Abyss Castle
Bellows! I'm here to help.
Great. Sarwen's plans are much bigger than trash. Before I tell you I must get your oath to not share this outside of the Elite Force. Do I have your commitment?
Yes, sir! You have my word.

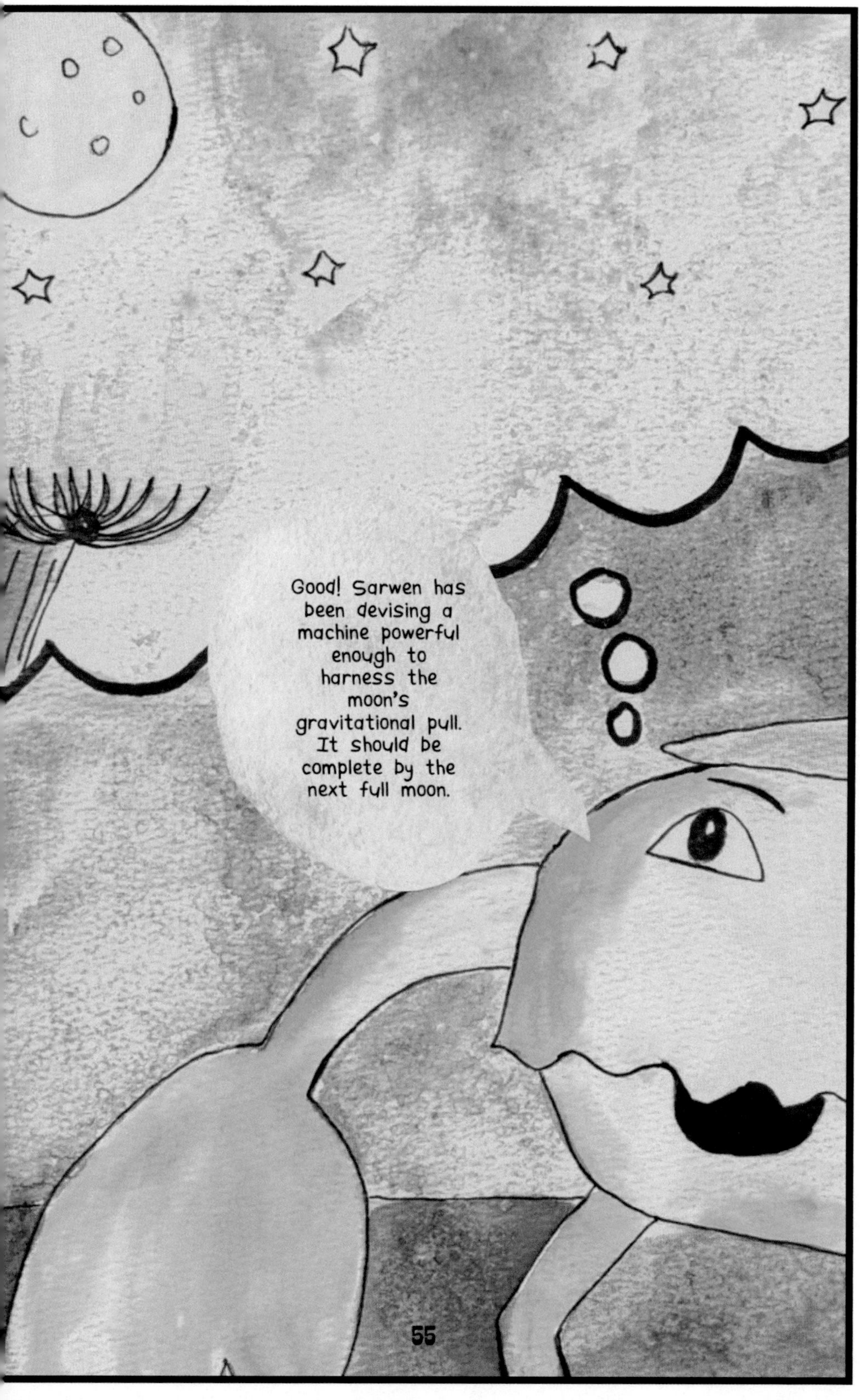
Good! Sarwen has been devising a machine powerful enough to harness the moon's gravitational pull. It should be complete by the next full moon.

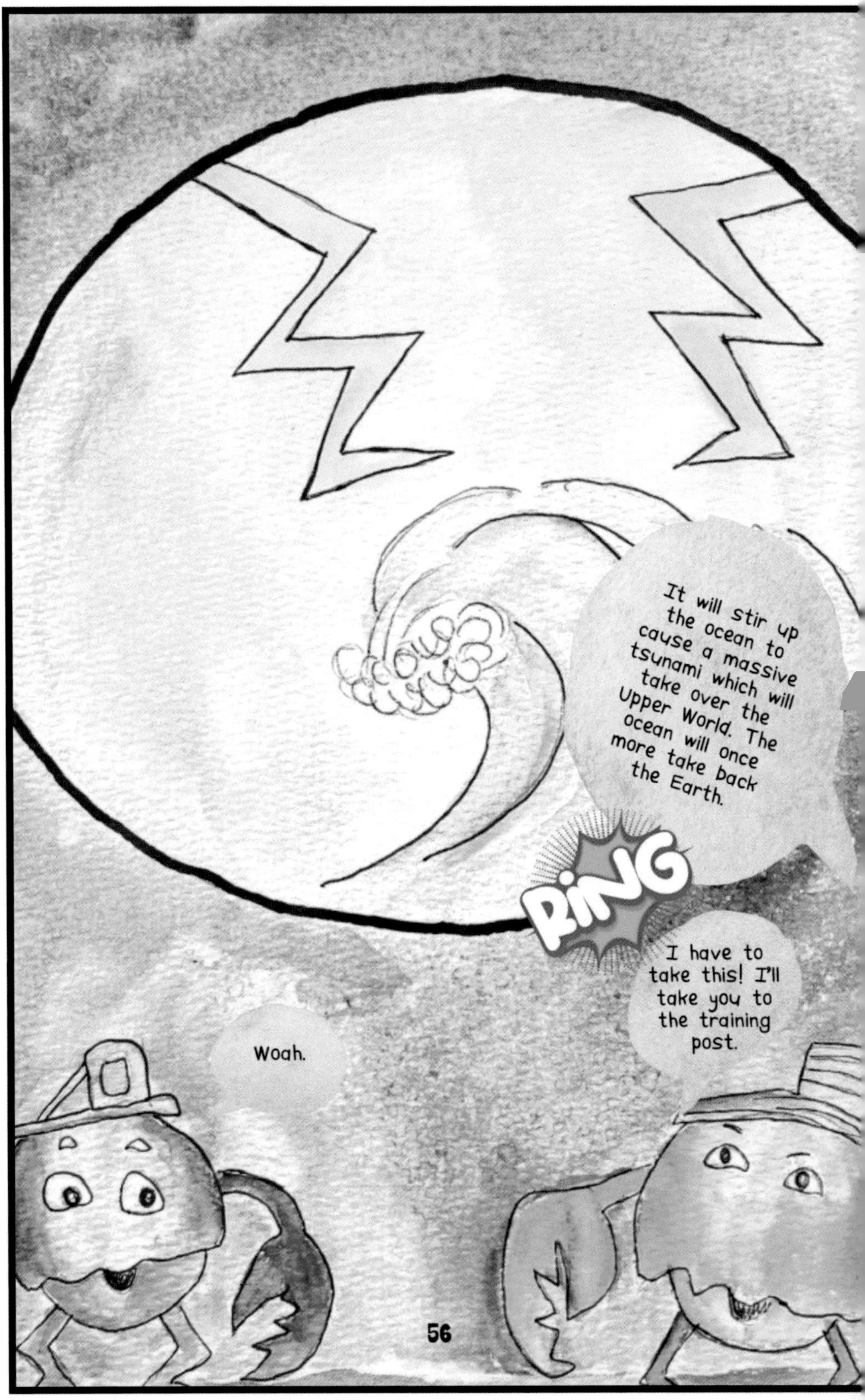
It will stir up the ocean to cause a massive tsunami which will take over the Upper World. The ocean will once more take back the Earth.
RING
I have to take this! I'll take you to the training post.
Woah.

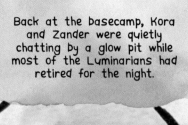

Back at the basecamp, Kora and Zander were quietly chatting by a glow pit while most of the Luminarians had retired for the night.

I'm sorry to hear about your mom. That must have been so hard.

Thank you, I don't talk too much about it.

Tomorrow we'll finally make it to the Transporter Station!

Yes, we better get some rest!

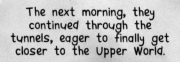

The next morning, they continued through the tunnels, eager to finally get closer to the Upper World.

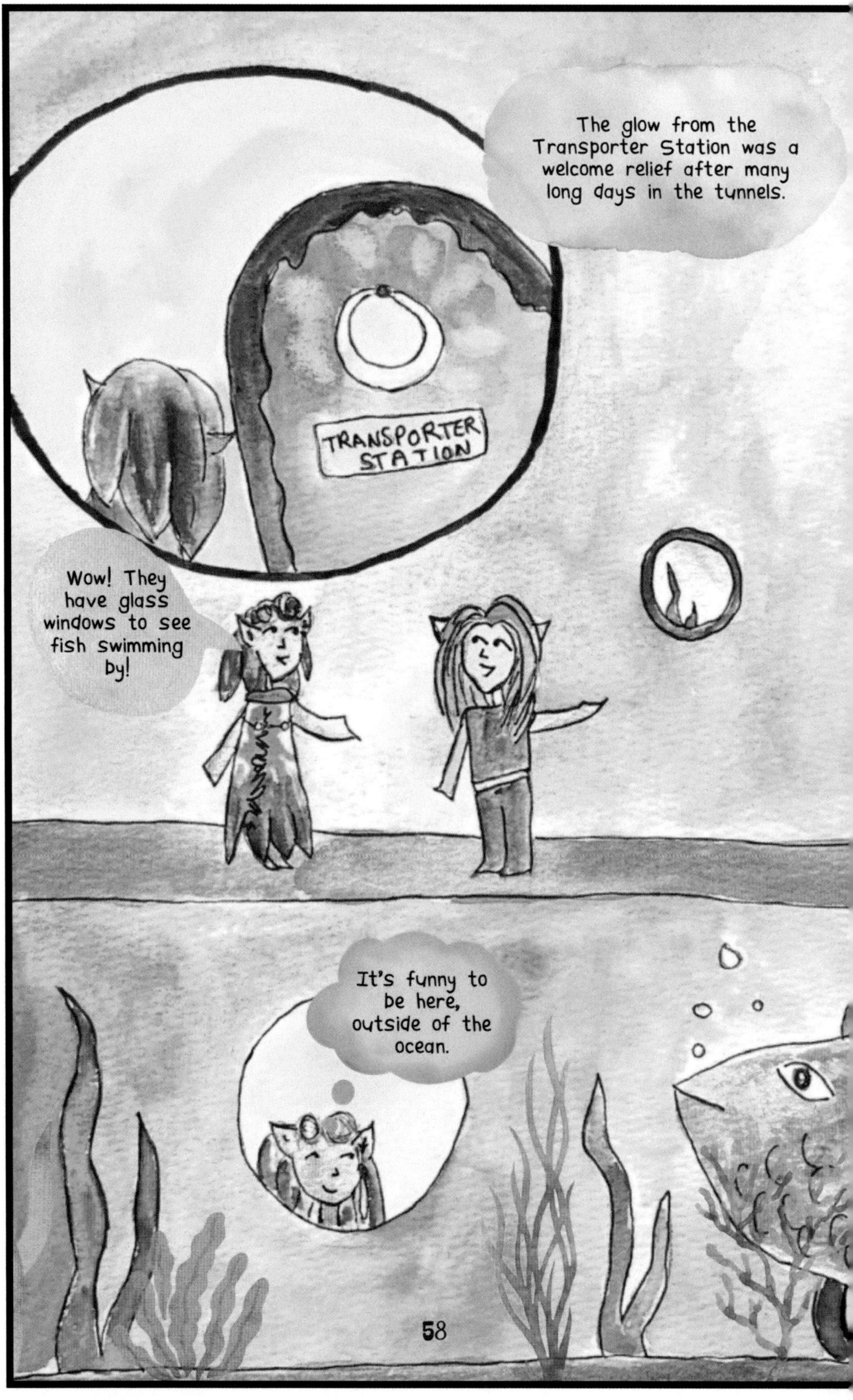
The glow from the Transporter Station was a welcome relief after many long days in the tunnels.
TRANSPORTER STATION
Wow! They have glass windows to see fish swimming by!
It's funny to be here, outside of the ocean.

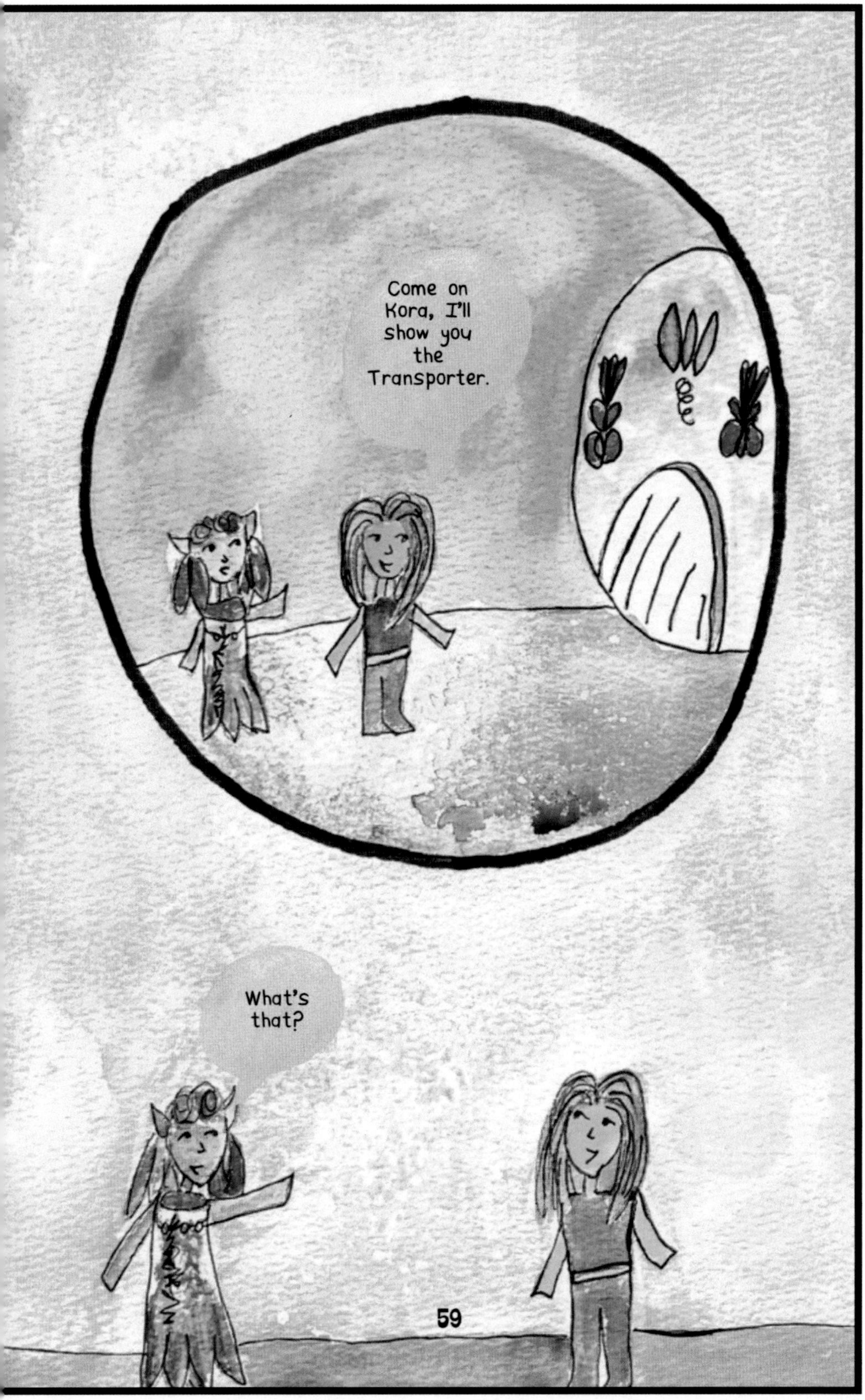
Come on Kora, I'll show you the Transporter.
What's that?

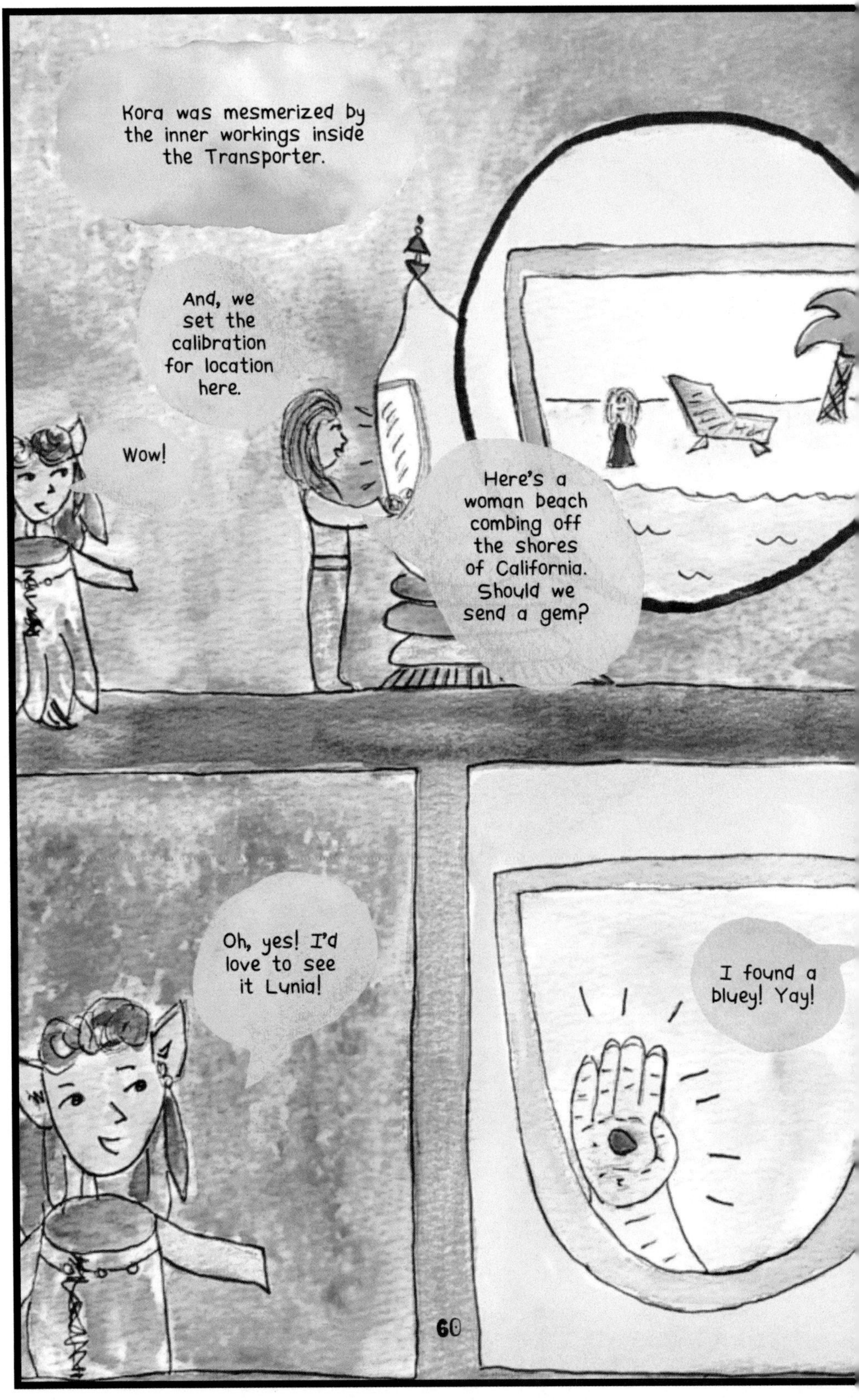
Kora was mesmerized by the inner workings inside the Transporter.
And, we set the calibration for location here.
Wow!
Here's a woman beach combing off the shores of California. Should we send a gem?
Oh, yes! I'd love to see it Lunia!
I found a bluey! Yay!

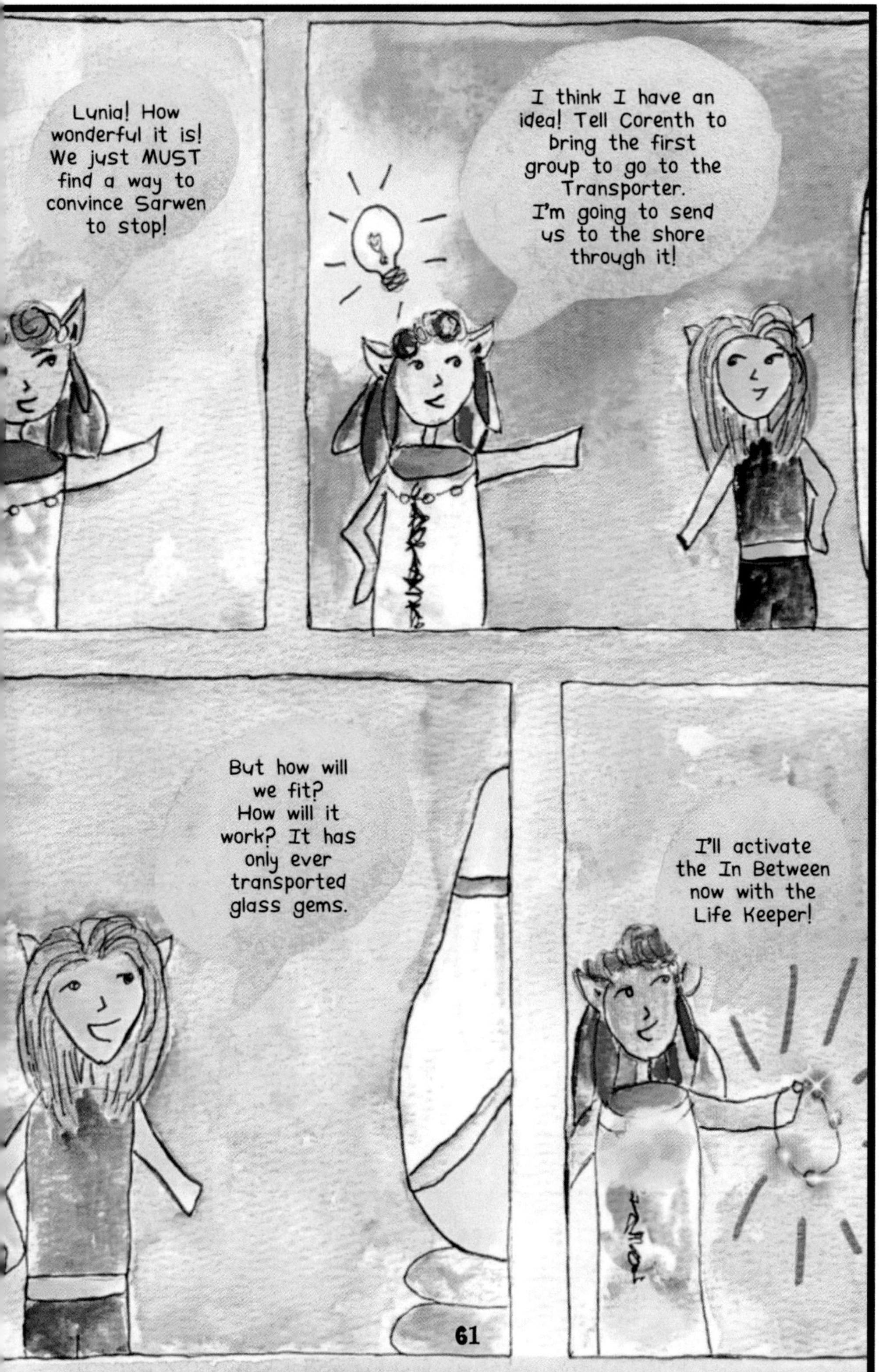
Lunia! How wonderful it is! We just MUST find a way to convince Sarwen to stop!
I think I have an idea! Tell Corenth to bring the first group to go to the Transporter. I'm going to send us to the shore through it!
But how will we fit? How will it work? It has only ever transported glass gems.
I'll activate the In Between now with the Life Keeper!

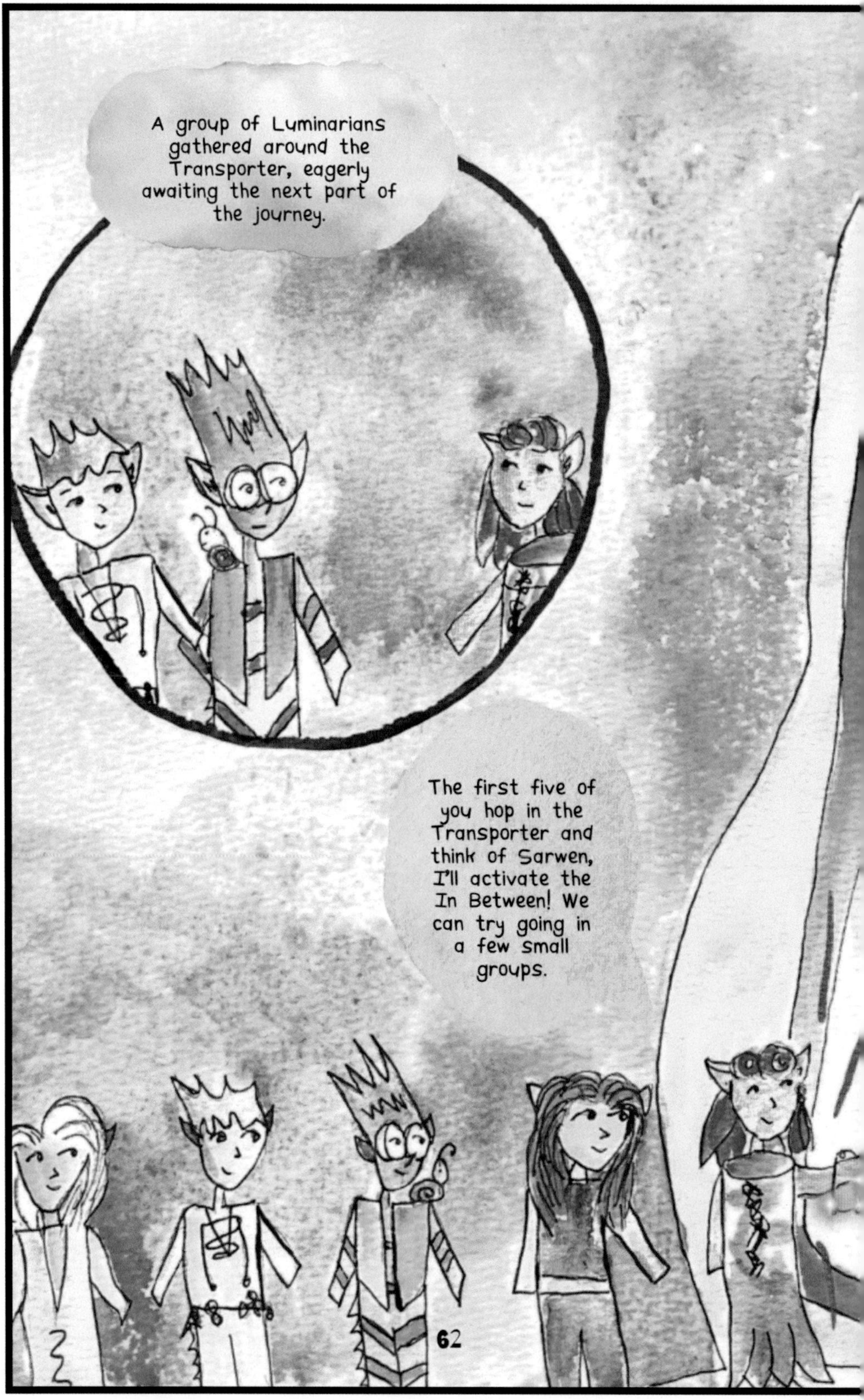
A group of Luminarians gathered around the Transporter, eagerly awaiting the next part of the journey.
The first five of you hop in the Transporter and think of Sarwen, I'll activate the In Between! We can try going in a few small groups.

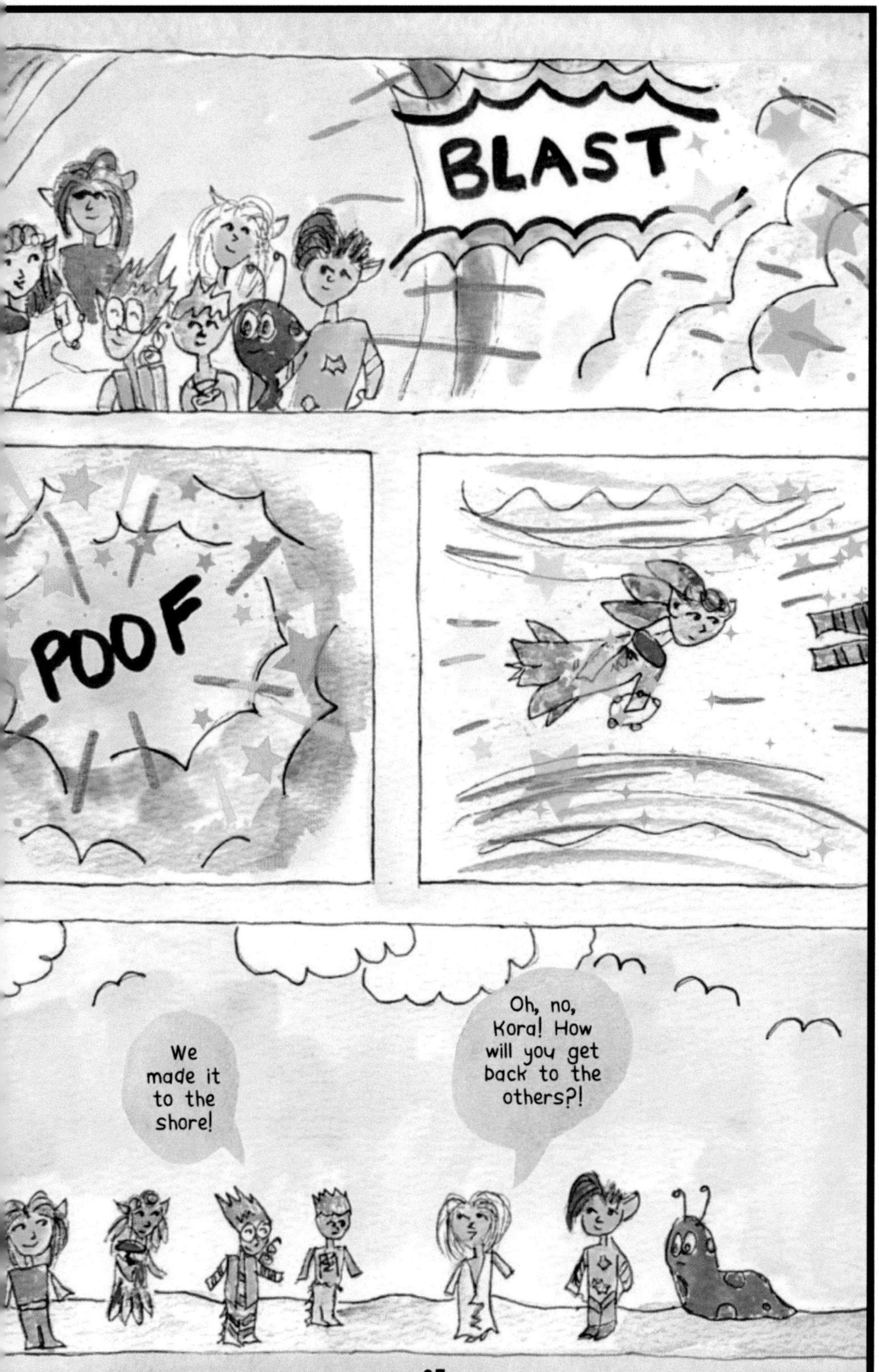

BLAST
POOF
We made it to the shore!
Oh, no, Kora! How will you get back to the others?!

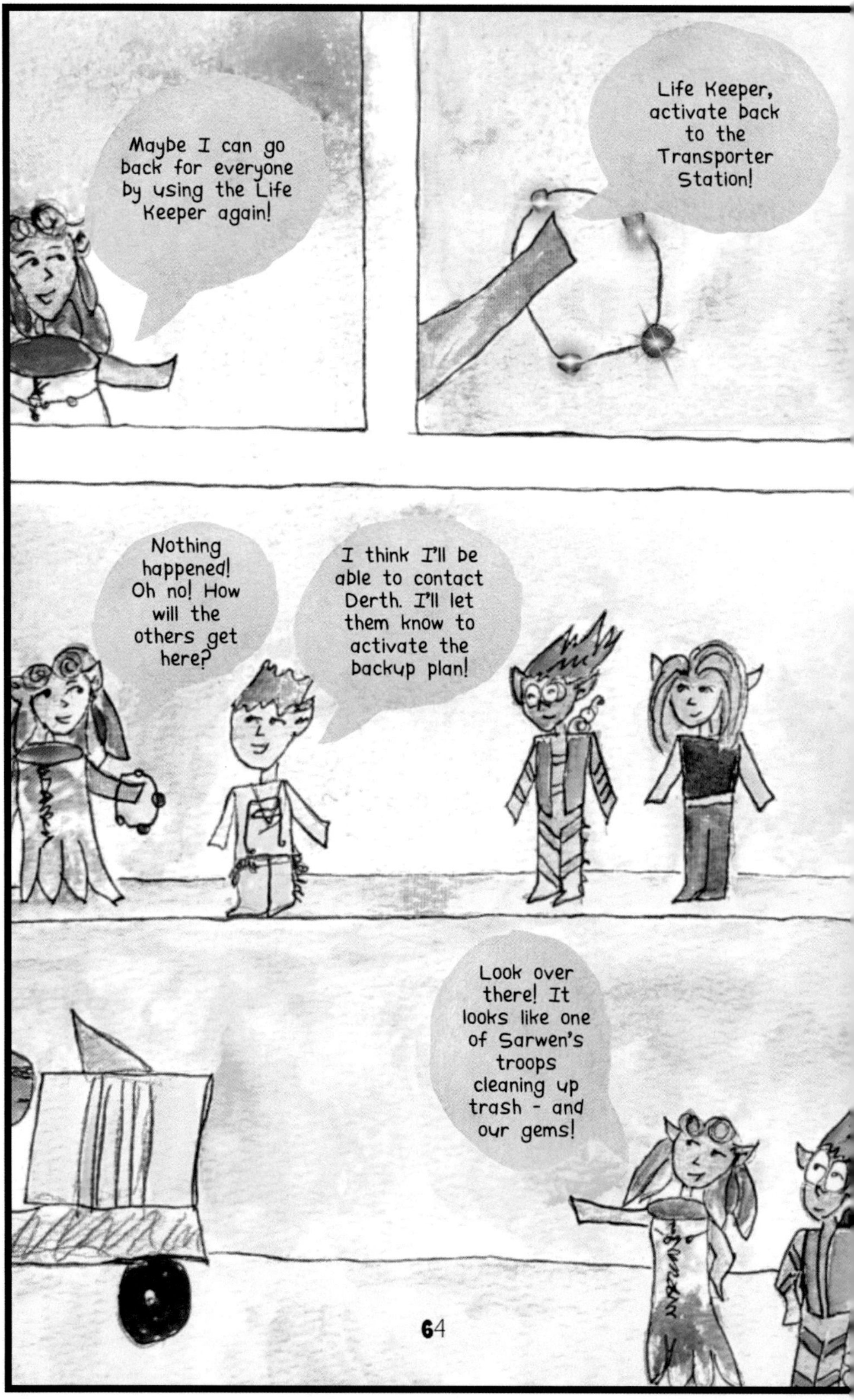
Maybe I can go back for everyone by using the Life Keeper again!
Life Keeper, activate back to the Transporter Station!
Nothing happened! Oh no! How will the others get here?
I think I'll be able to contact Derth. I'll let them know to activate the backup plan!
Look over there! It looks like one of Sarwen's troops cleaning up trash - and our gems!

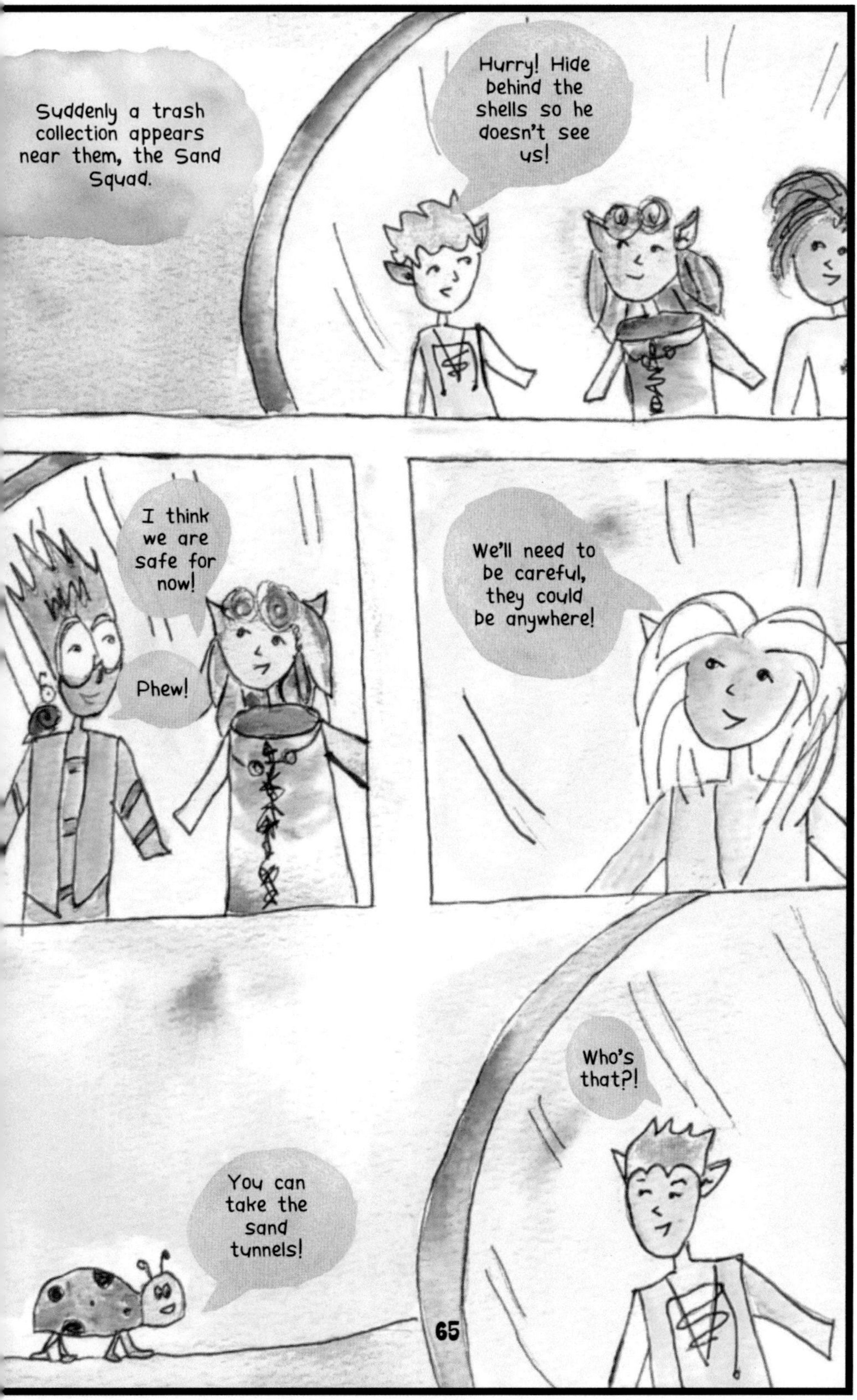
Suddenly a trash collection appears near them, the Sand Squad.
Hurry! Hide behind the shells so he doesn't see us!
I think we are safe for now!
Phew!
We'll need to be careful, they could be anywhere!
Who's that?!
You can take the sand tunnels!

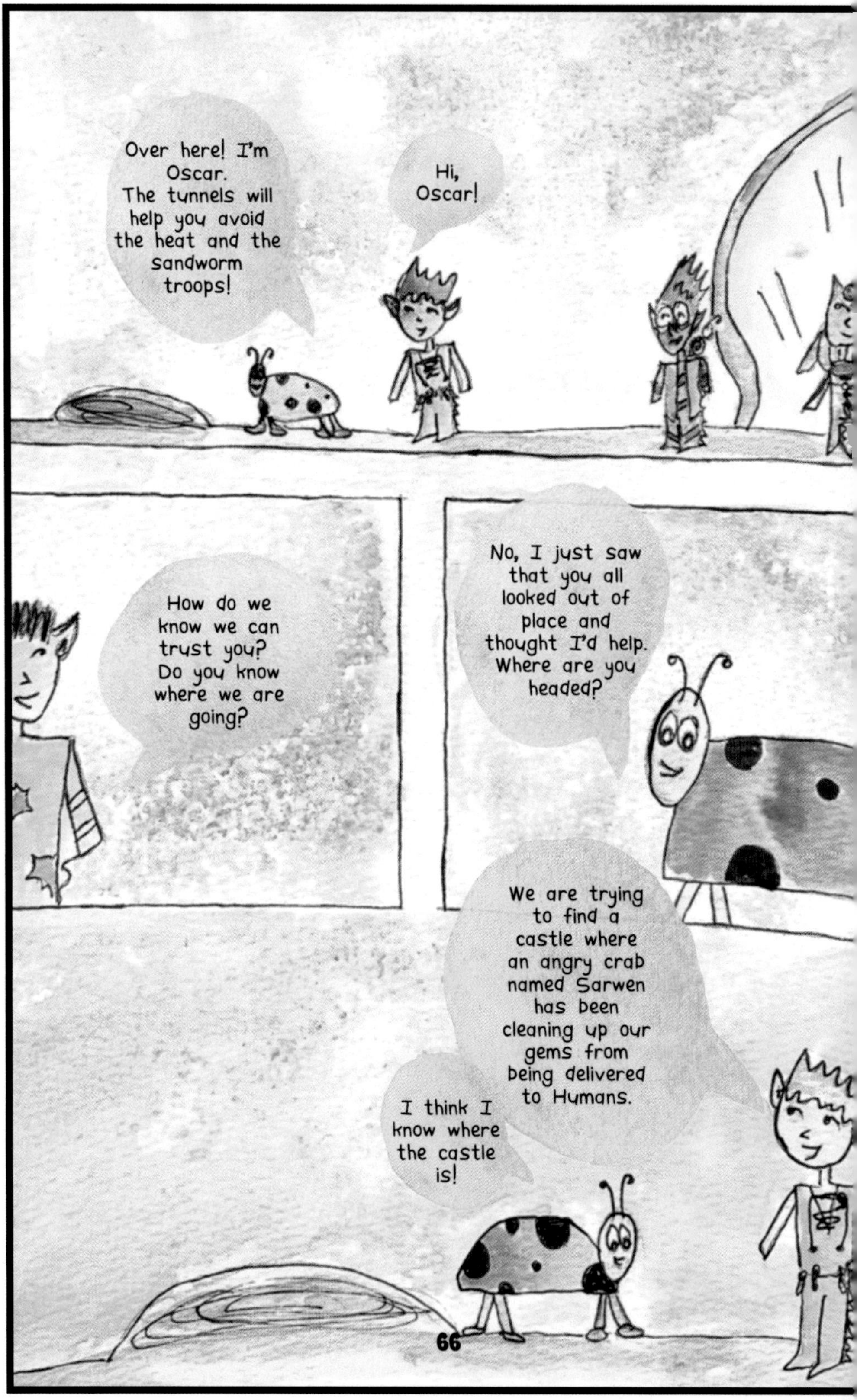

Over here! I'm Oscar. The tunnels will help you avoid the heat and the sandworm troops!
Hi, Oscar!
How do we know we can trust you? Do you know where we are going?
No, I just saw that you all looked out of place and thought I'd help. Where are you headed?
We are trying to find a castle where an angry crab named Sarwen has been cleaning up our gems from being delivered to Humans.
I think I know where the castle is!

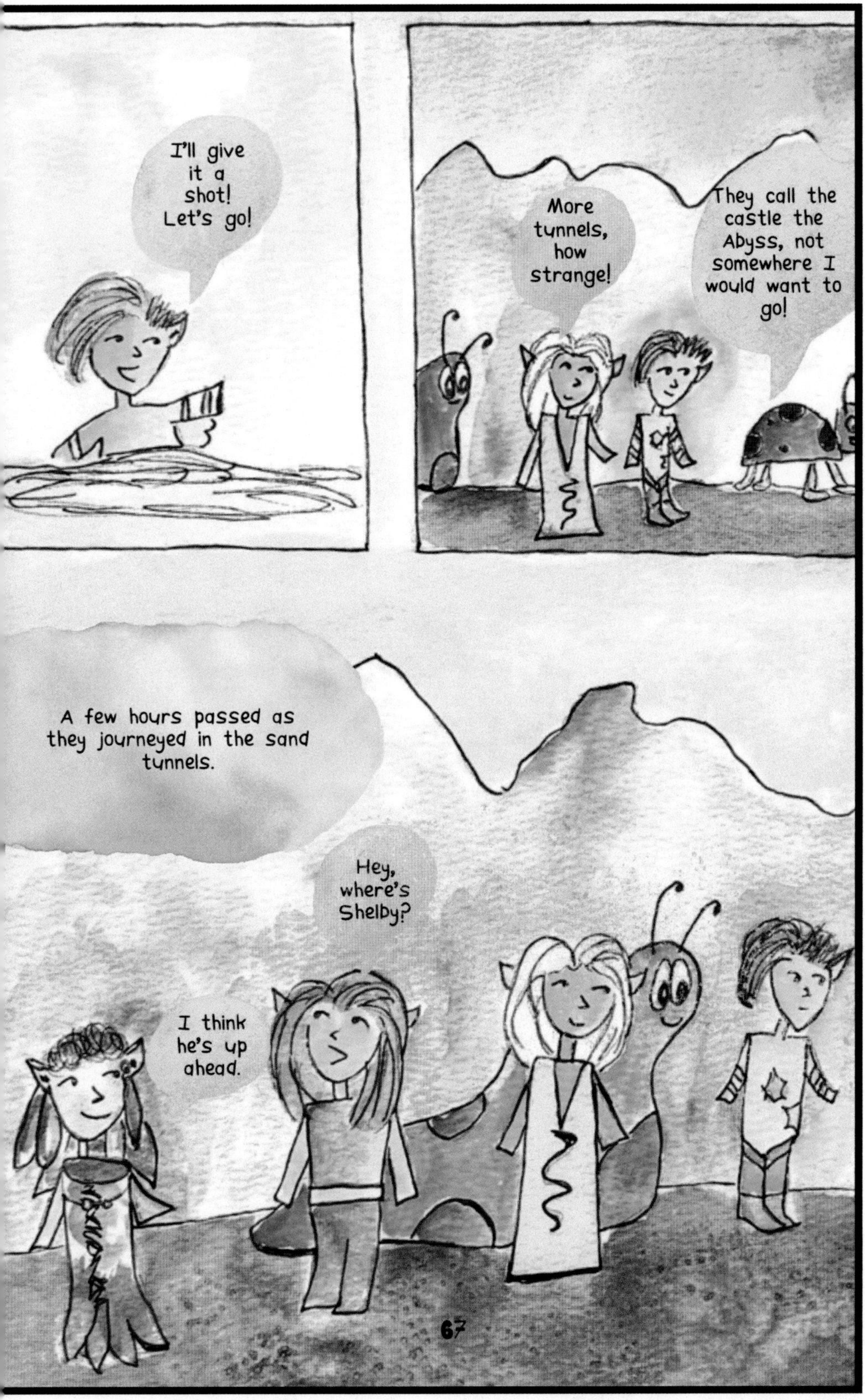
I'll give it a shot! Let's go!
More tunnels, how strange!
They call the castle the Abyss, not somewhere I would want to go!
A few hours passed as they journeyed in the sand tunnels.
Hey, where's Shelby?
I think he's up ahead.

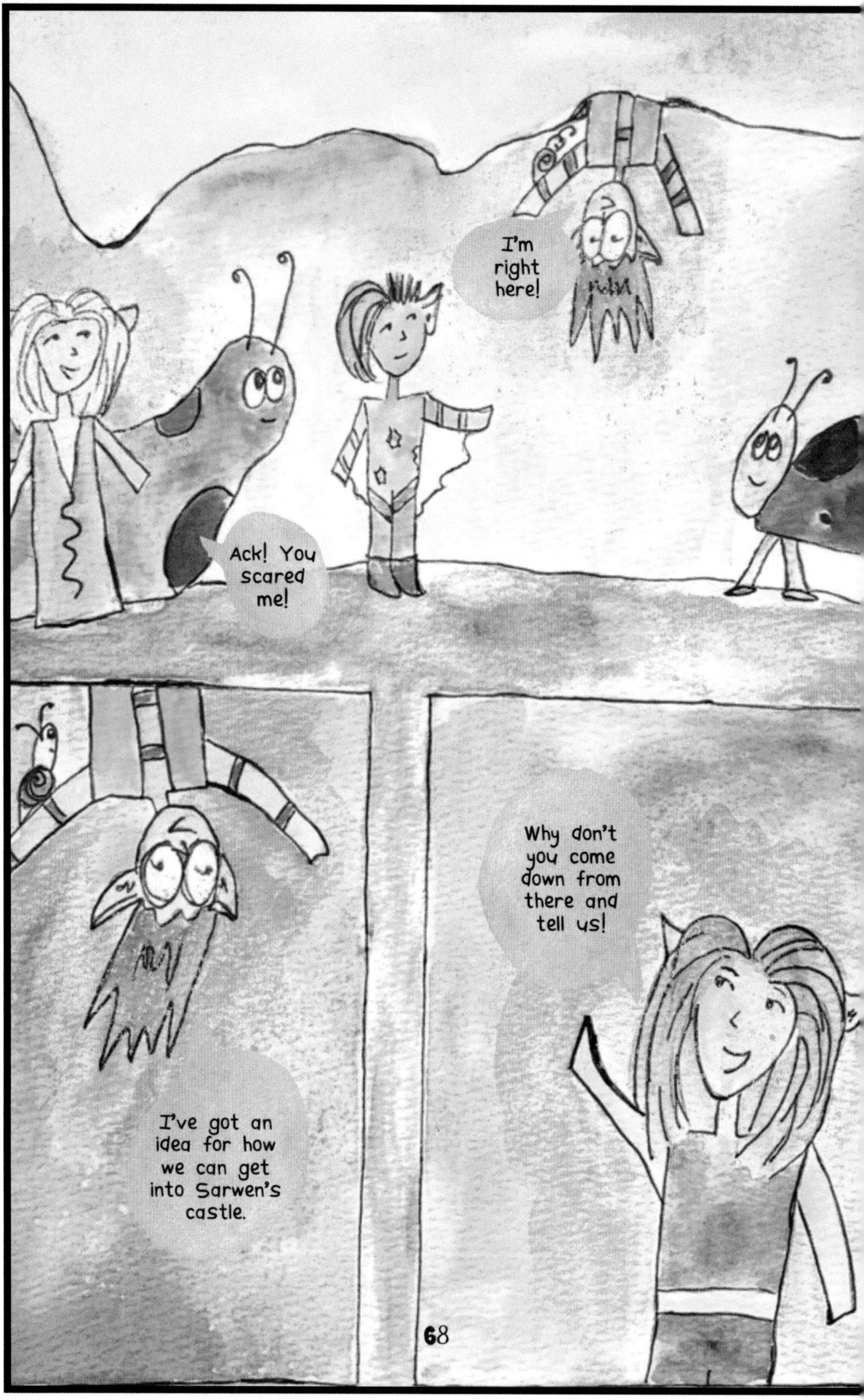
I'm right here!
Ack! You scared me!
I've got an idea for how we can get into Sarwen's castle.
Why don't you come down from there and tell us!

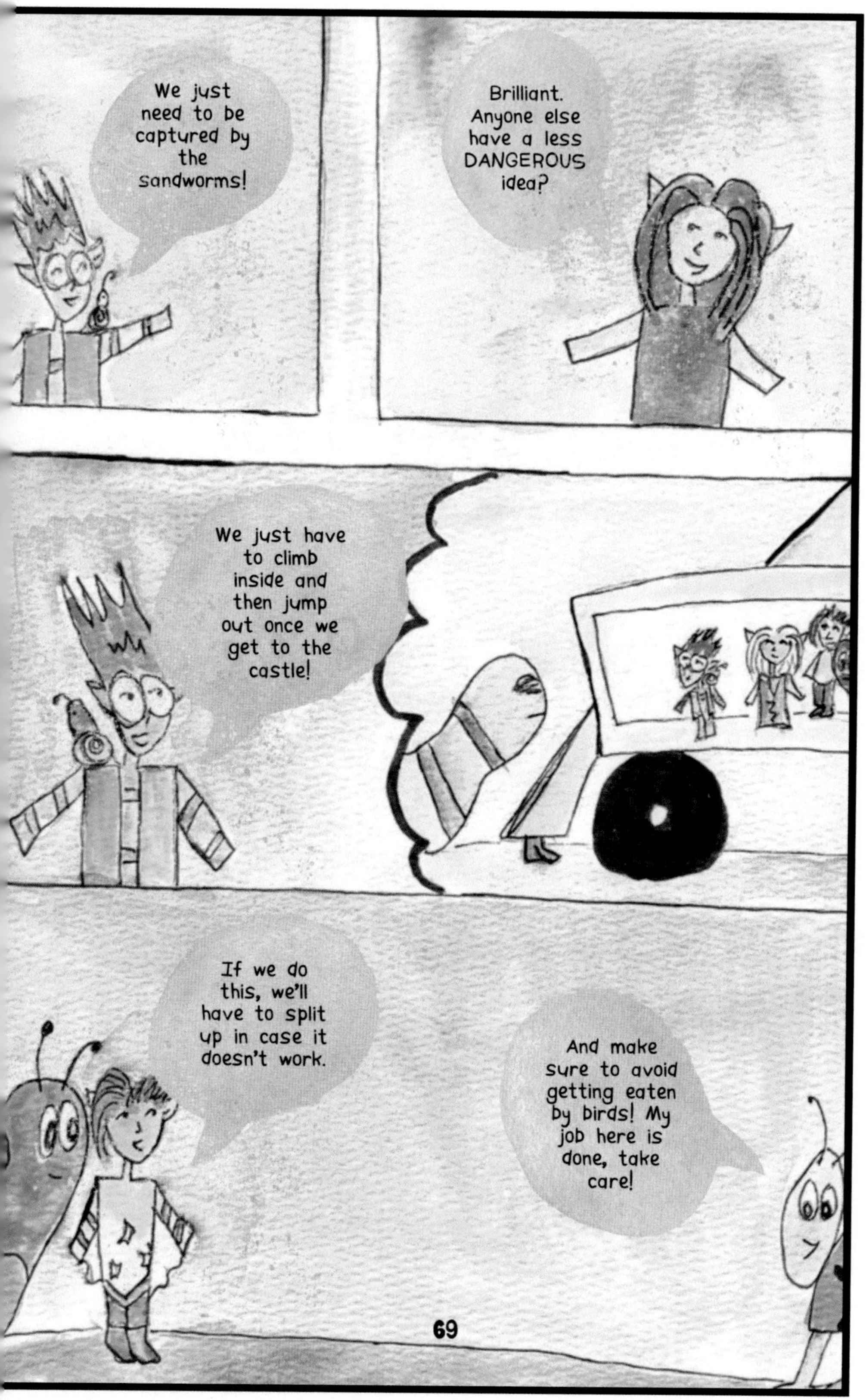
We just need to be captured by the sandworms!
Brilliant. Anyone else have a less DANGEROUS idea?
We just have to climb inside and then jump out once we get to the castle!
If we do this, we'll have to split up in case it doesn't work.
And make sure to avoid getting eaten by birds! My job here is done, take care!

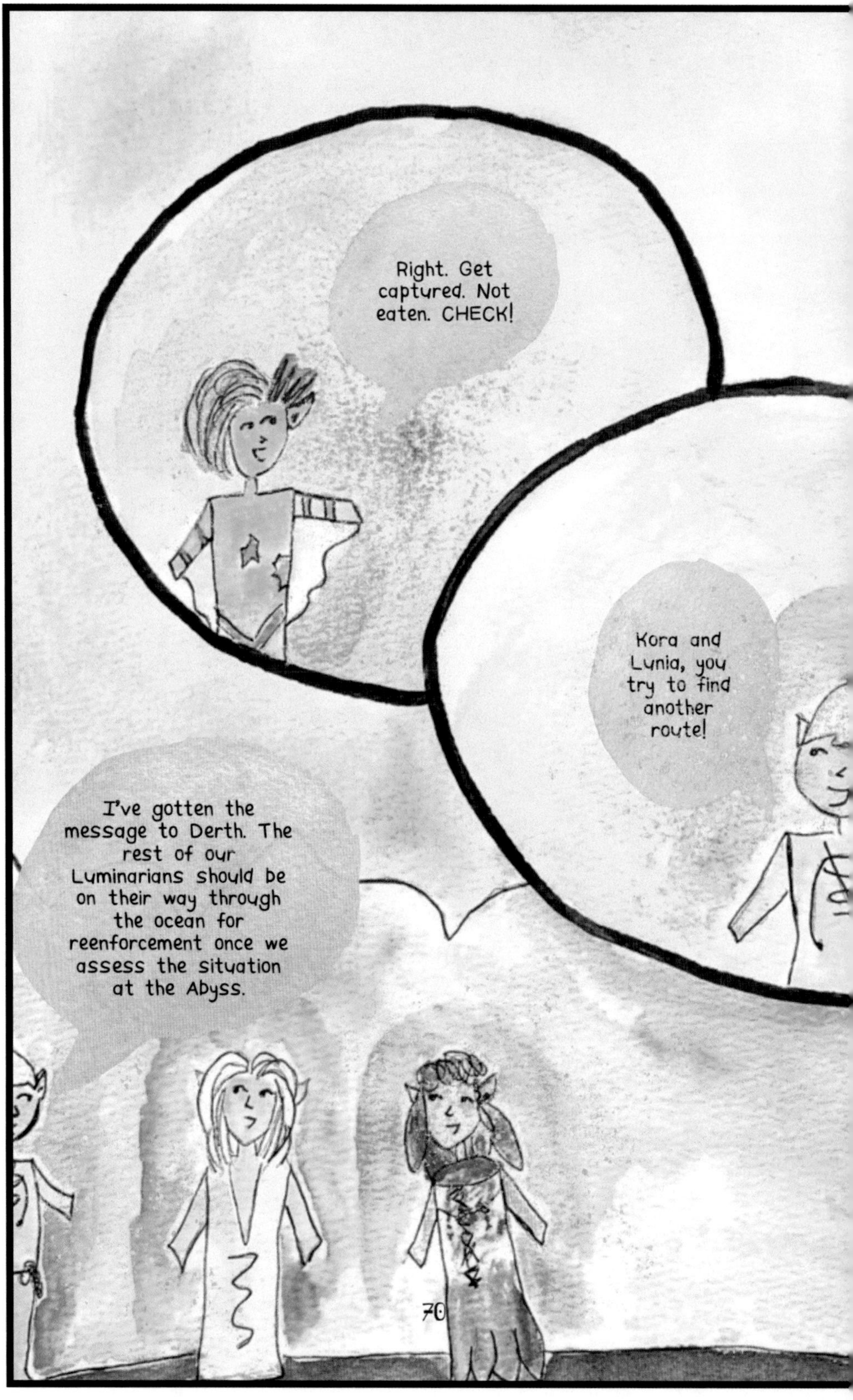
Right. Get captured. Not eaten. CHECK!
Kora and Lunia, you try to find another route!
I've gotten the message to Derth. The rest of our Luminarians should be on their way through the ocean for reenforcement once we assess the situation at the Abyss.

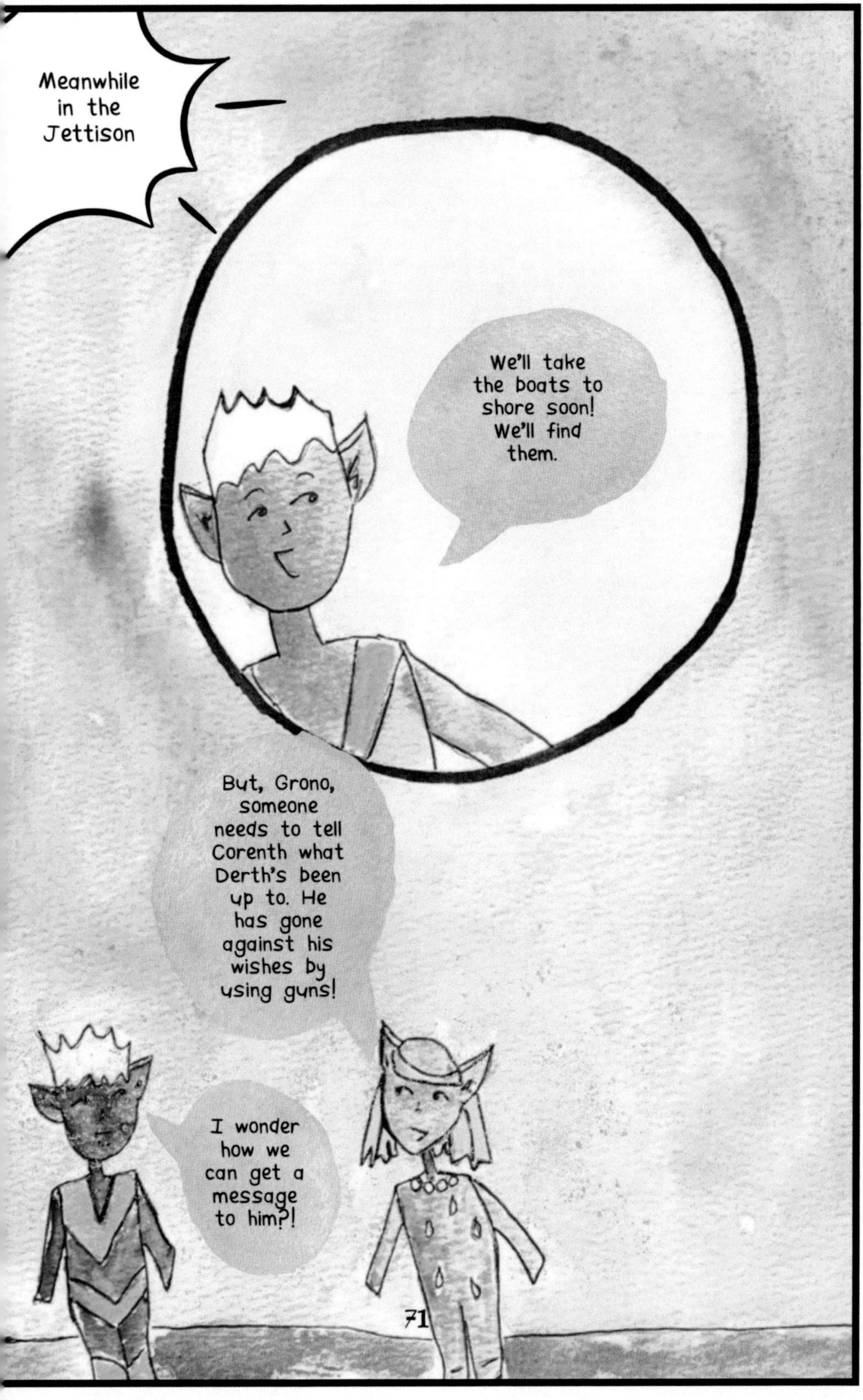
Meanwhile in the Jettison
We'll take the boats to shore soon! We'll find them.
But, Grono, someone needs to tell Corenth what Derth's been up to. He has gone against his wishes by using guns!
I wonder how we can get a message to him?!

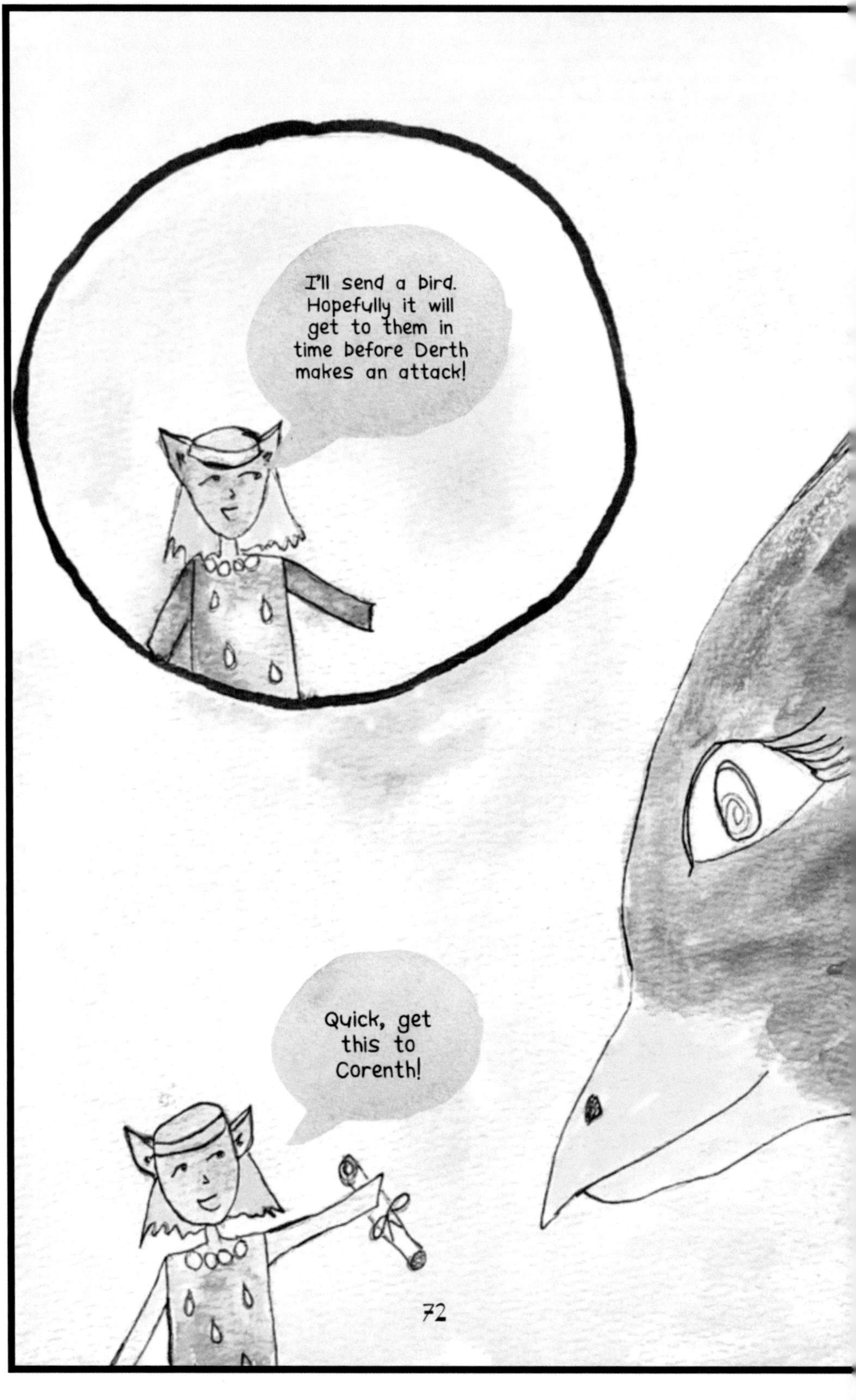
I'll send a bird. Hopefully it will get to them in time before Derth makes an attack!
Quick, get this to Corenth!

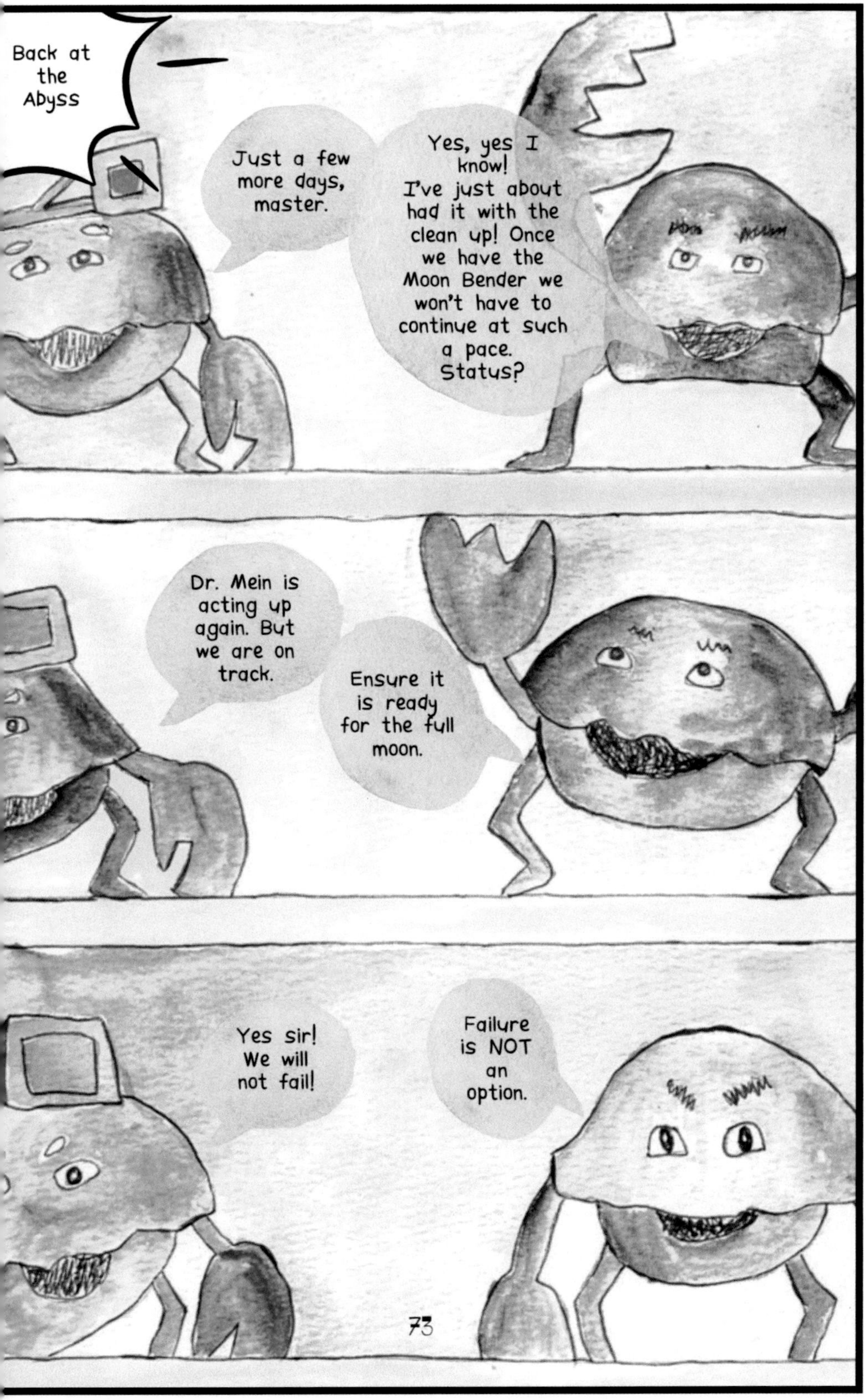
Back at the Abyss
Just a few more days, master.
Yes, yes I know! I've just about had it with the clean up! Once we have the Moon Bender we won't have to continue at such a pace. Status?
Dr. Mein is acting up again. But we are on track.
Ensure it is ready for the full moon.
Yes sir! We will not fail!
Failure is NOT an option.

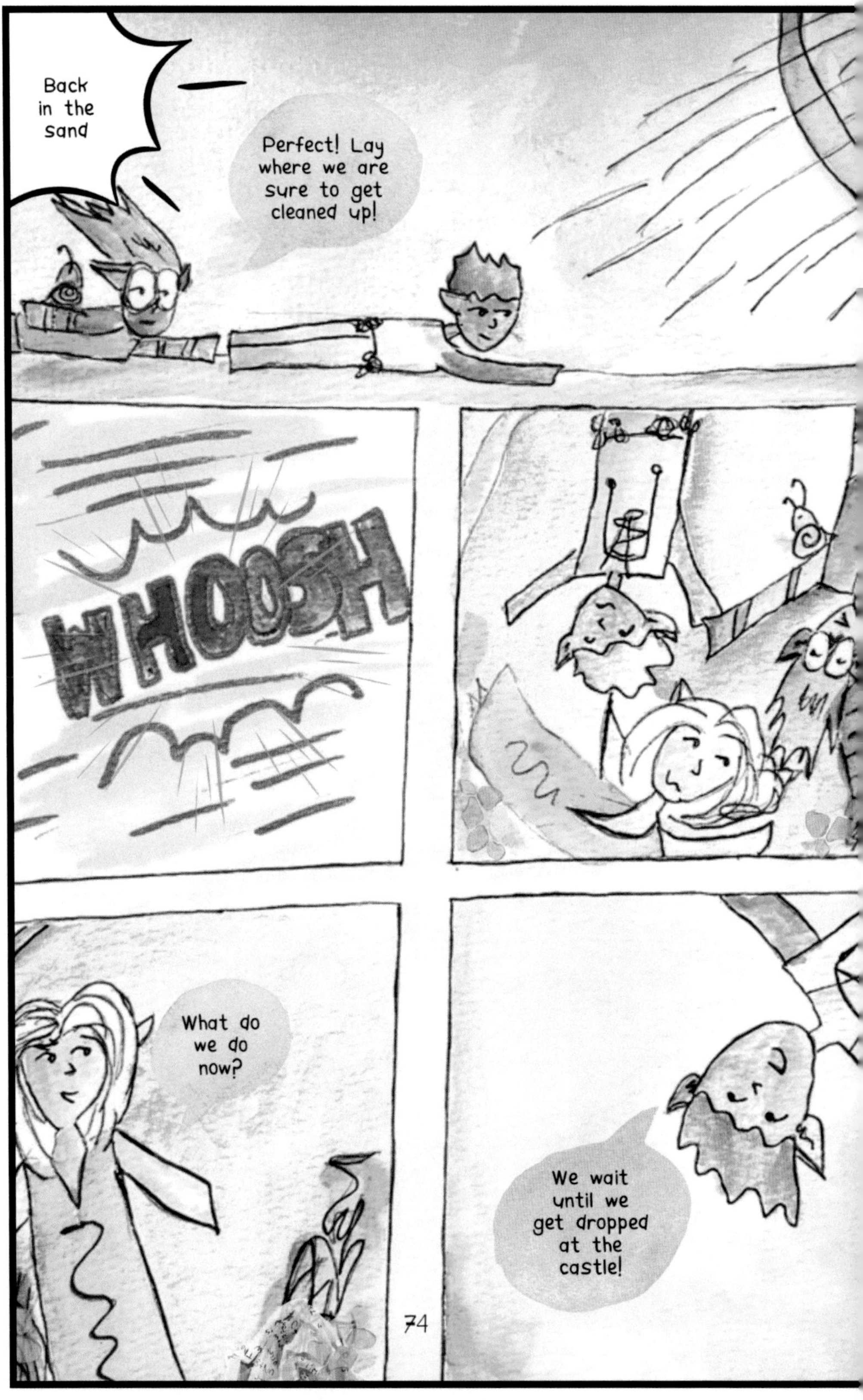
Back in the sand
Perfect! Lay where we are sure to get cleaned up!
WHOOSH
What do we do now?
We wait until we get dropped at the castle!

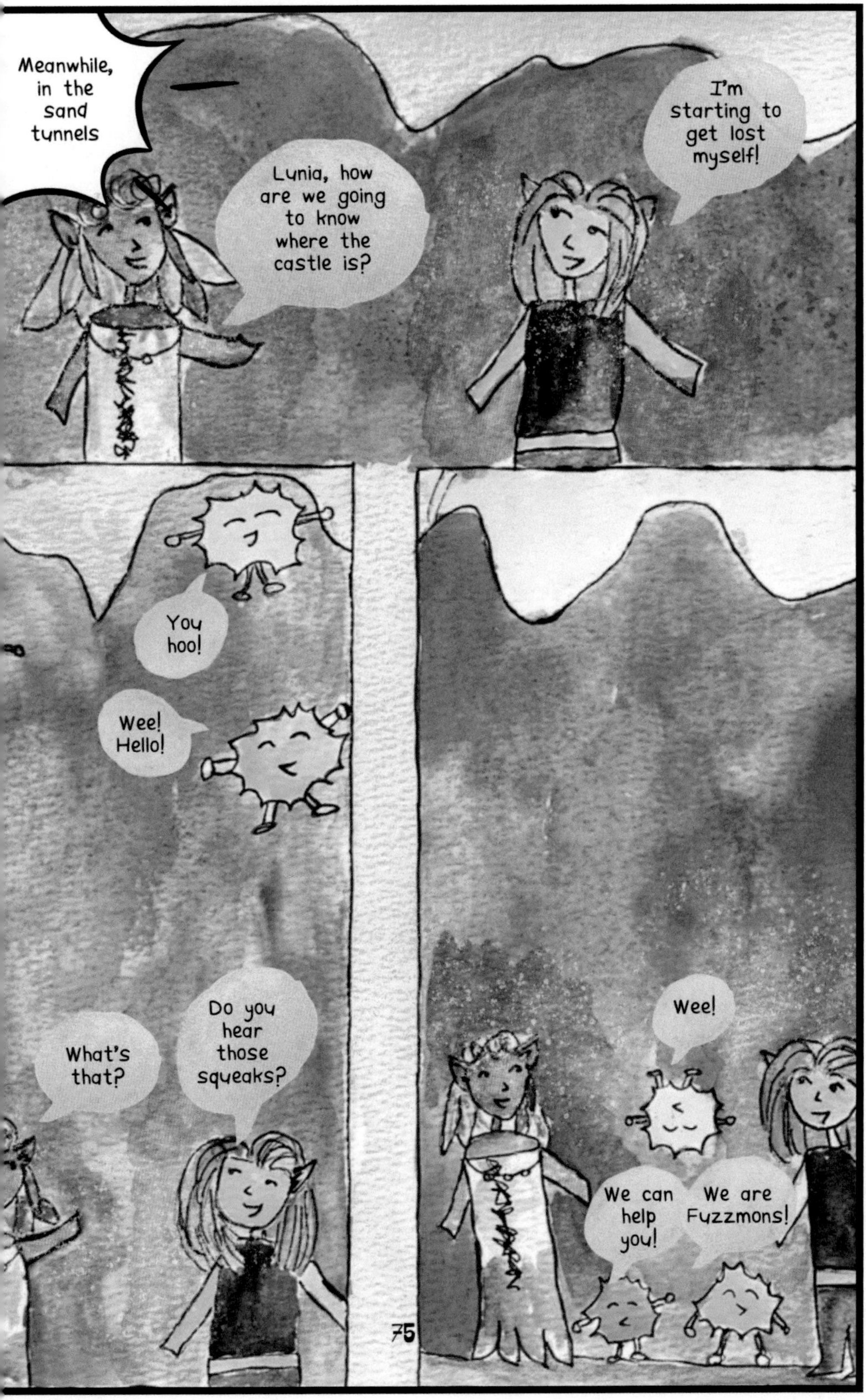
Meanwhile, in the sand tunnels
Lunia, how are we going to know where the castle is?
I'm starting to get lost myself!
You hoo!
Wee! Hello!
What's that?
Do you hear those squeaks?
Wee!
We can help you!
We are Fuzzmons!

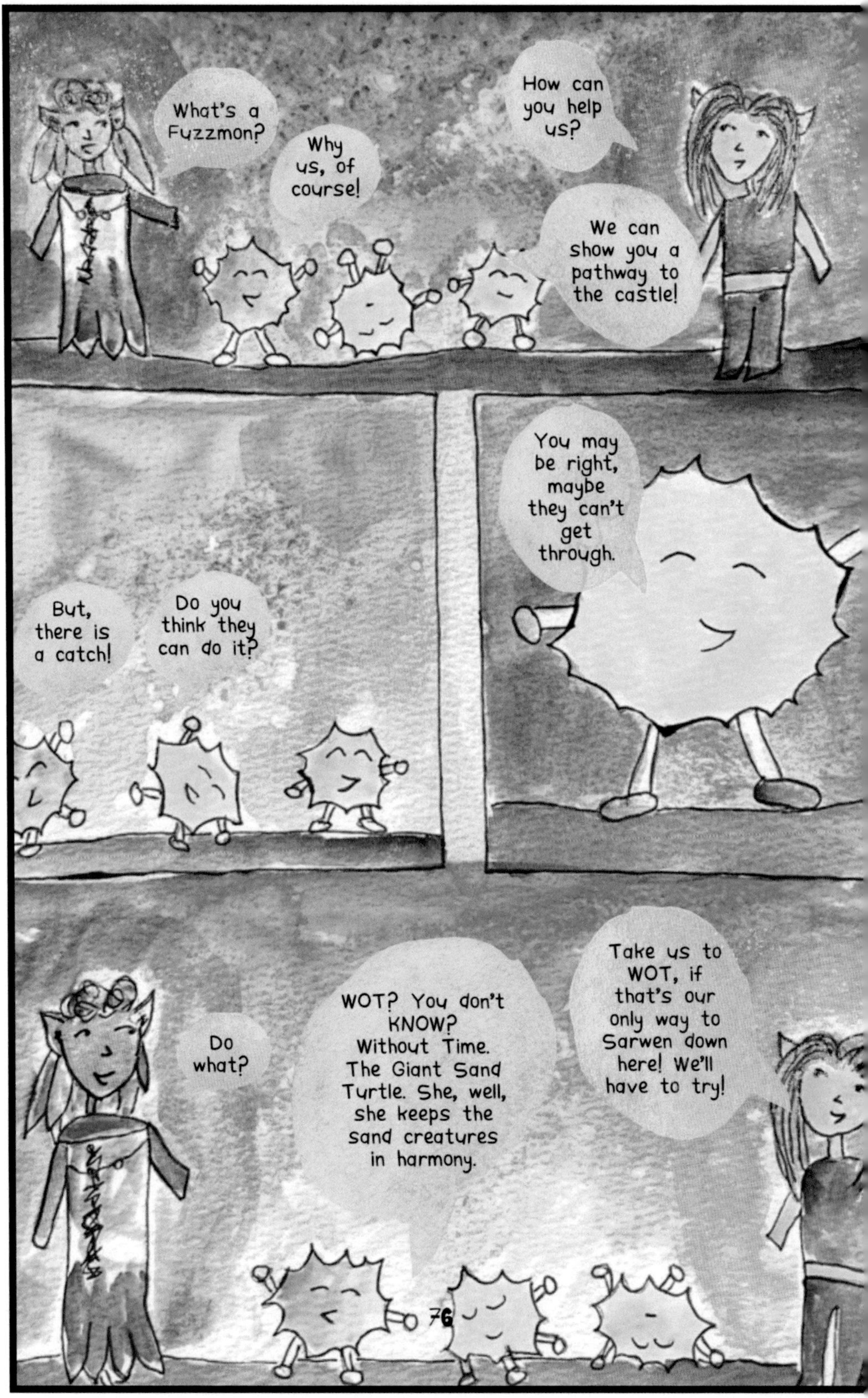
What's a Fuzzmon?
Why us, of course!
How can you help us?
We can show you a pathway to the castle!
But, there is a catch!
Do you think they can do it?
You may be right, maybe they can't get through.
Do what?
WOT? You don't KNOW? Without Time. The Giant Sand Turtle. She, well, she keeps the sand creatures in harmony.
Take us to WOT, if that's our only way to Sarwen down here! We'll have to try!

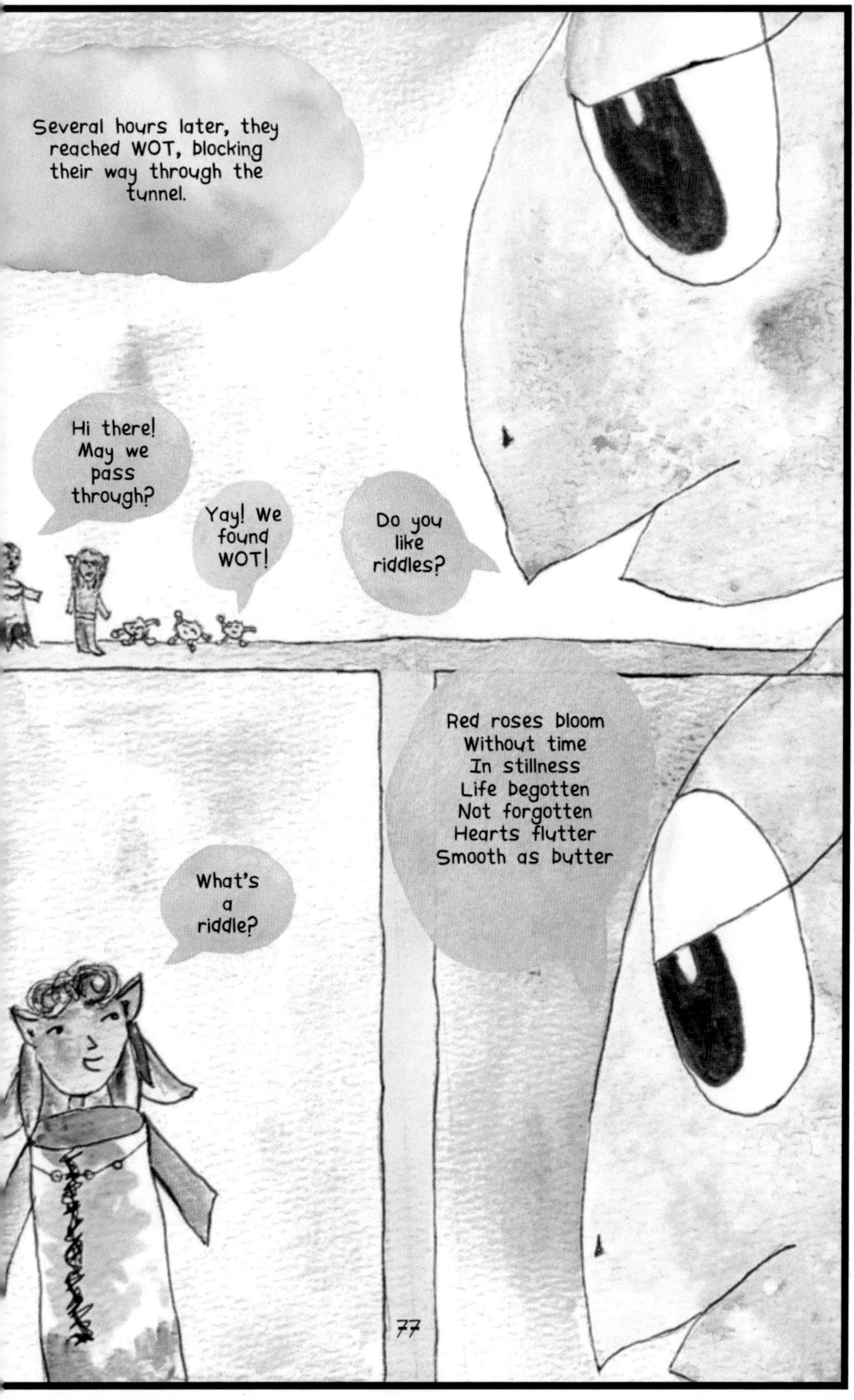

Several hours later, they reached WOT, blocking their way through the tunnel.
Hi there! May we pass through?
Yay! We found WOT!
Do you like riddles?
What's a riddle?
Red roses bloom
Without time
In stillness
Life begotten
Not forgotten
Hearts flutter
Smooth as butter

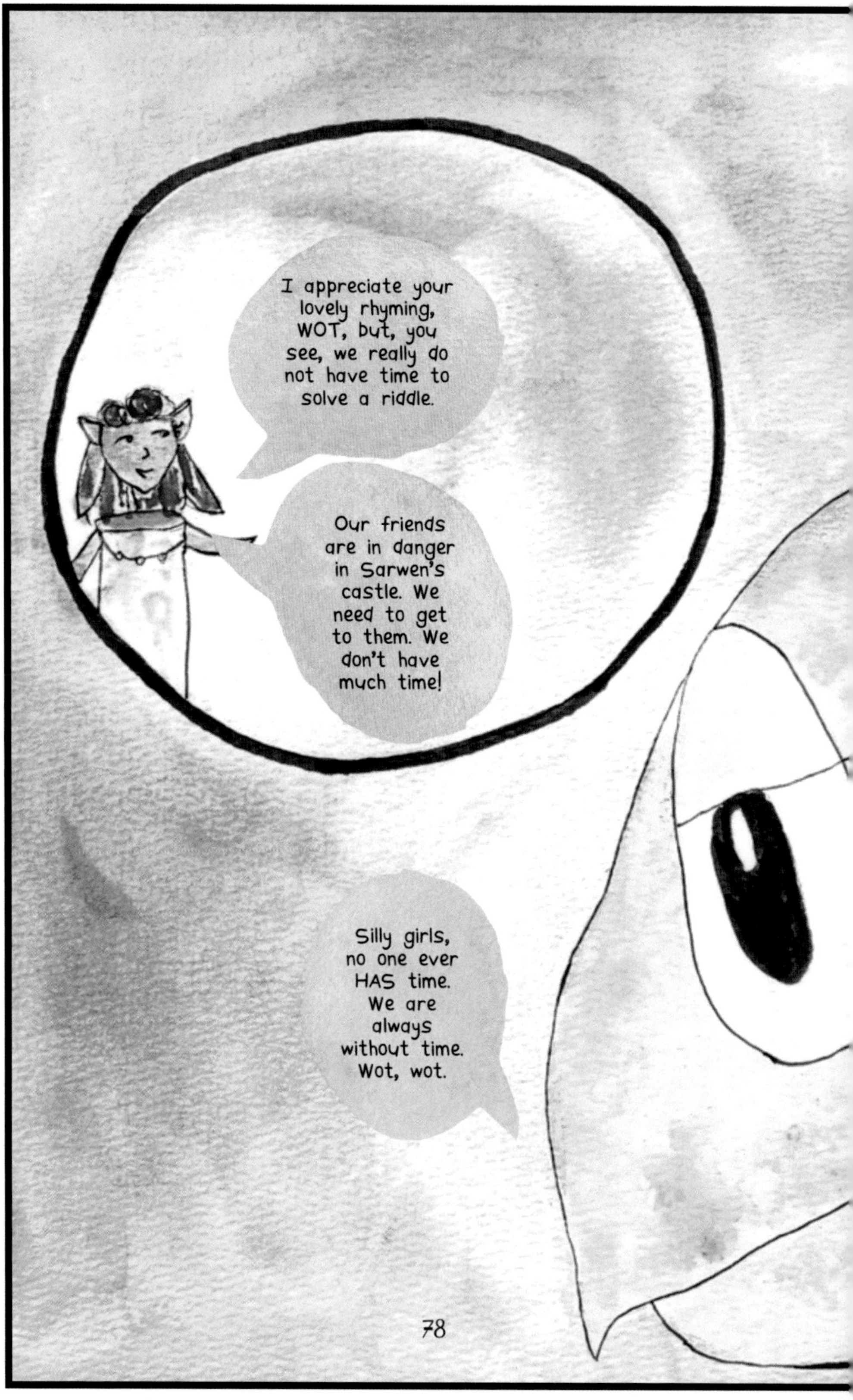
I appreciate your lovely rhyming, WOT, but, you see, we really do not have time to solve a riddle.
Our friends are in danger in Sarwen's castle. We need to get to them. We don't have much time!
Silly girls, no one ever HAS time. We are always without time. Wot, wot.

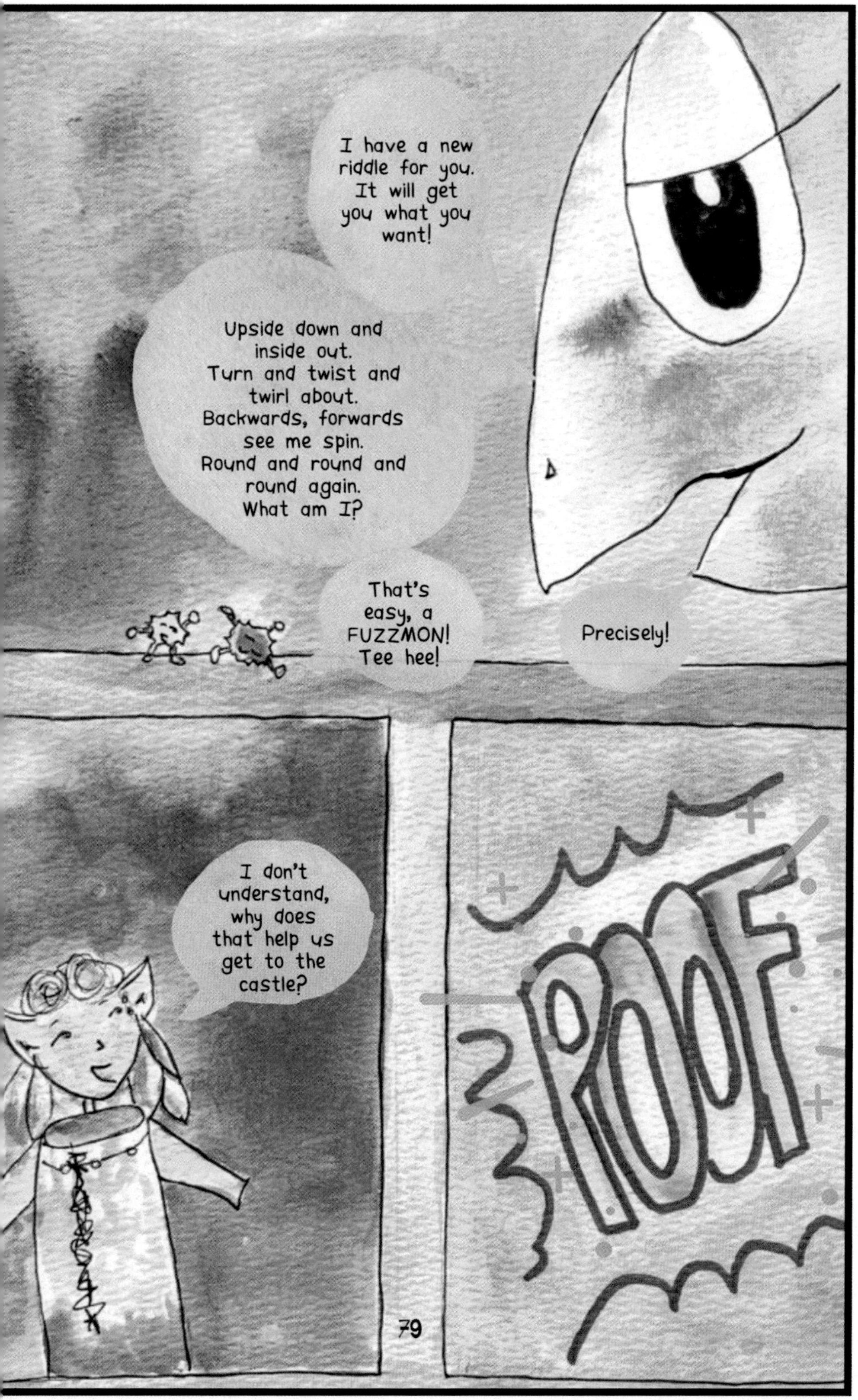
I have a new riddle for you. It will get you what you want!
Upside down and inside out. Turn and twist and twirl about. Backwards, forwards see me spin. Round and round and round again. What am I?
That's easy, a FUZZMON! Tee hee!
Precisely!
I don't understand, why does that help us get to the castle?
POOF

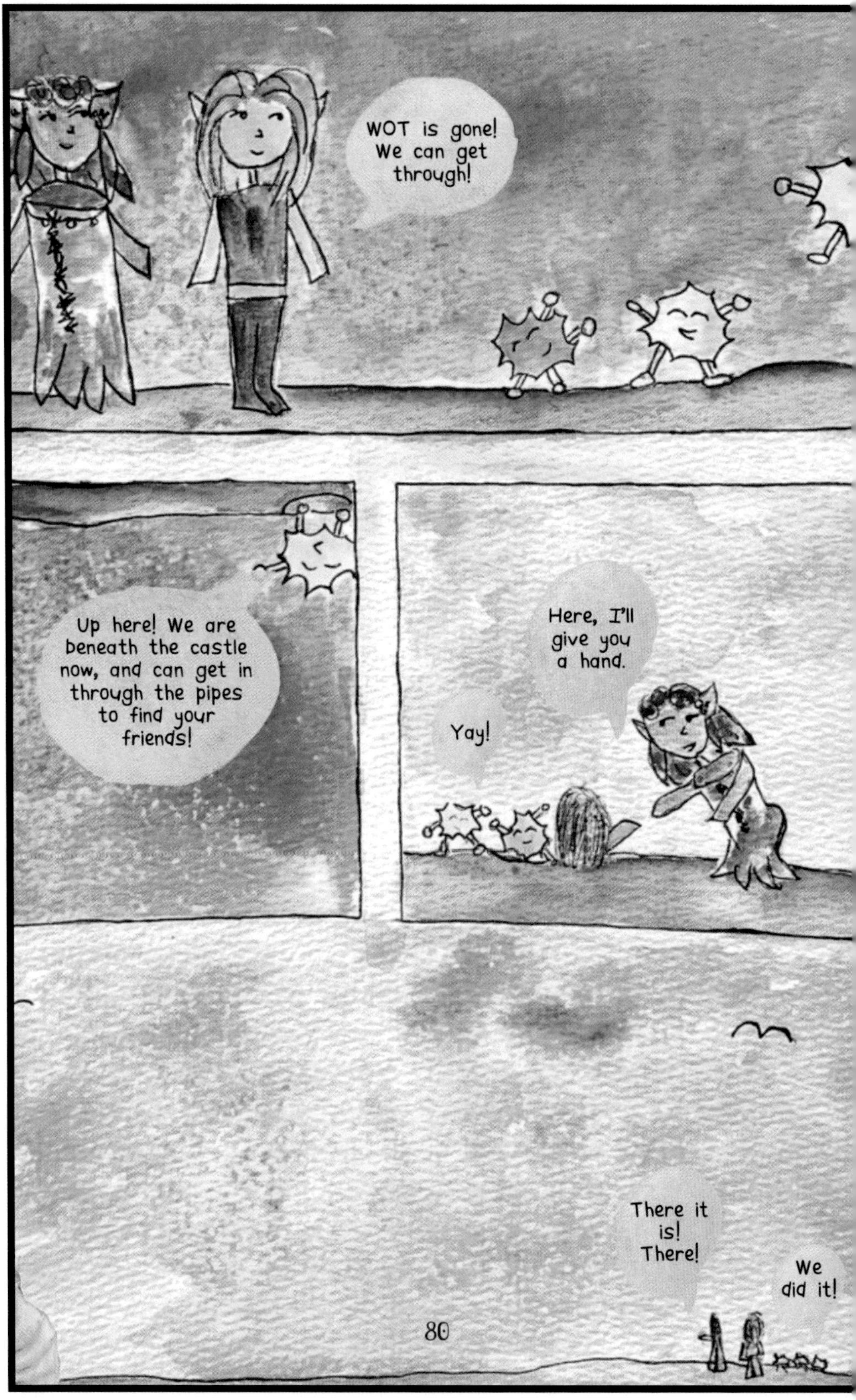
WOT is gone! We can get through!
Up here! We are beneath the castle now, and can get in through the pipes to find your friends!
Here, I'll give you a hand.
Yay!
There it is! There!
We did it!

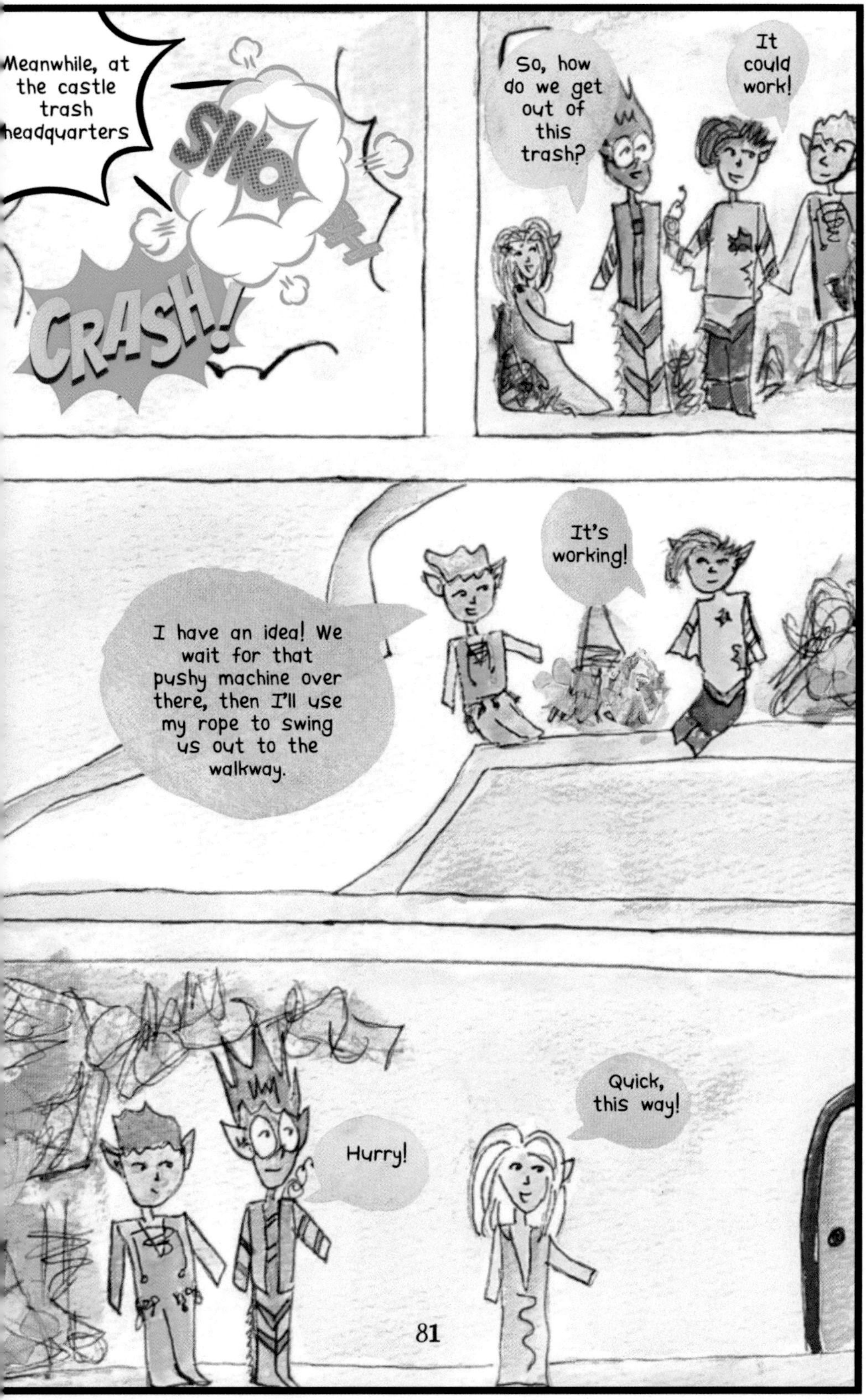
Meanwhile, at the castle trash headquarters
SWOOSH
CRASH!
So, how do we get out of this trash?
It could work!
I have an idea! We wait for that pushy machine over there, then I'll use my rope to swing us out to the walkway.
It's working!
Hurry!
Quick, this way!

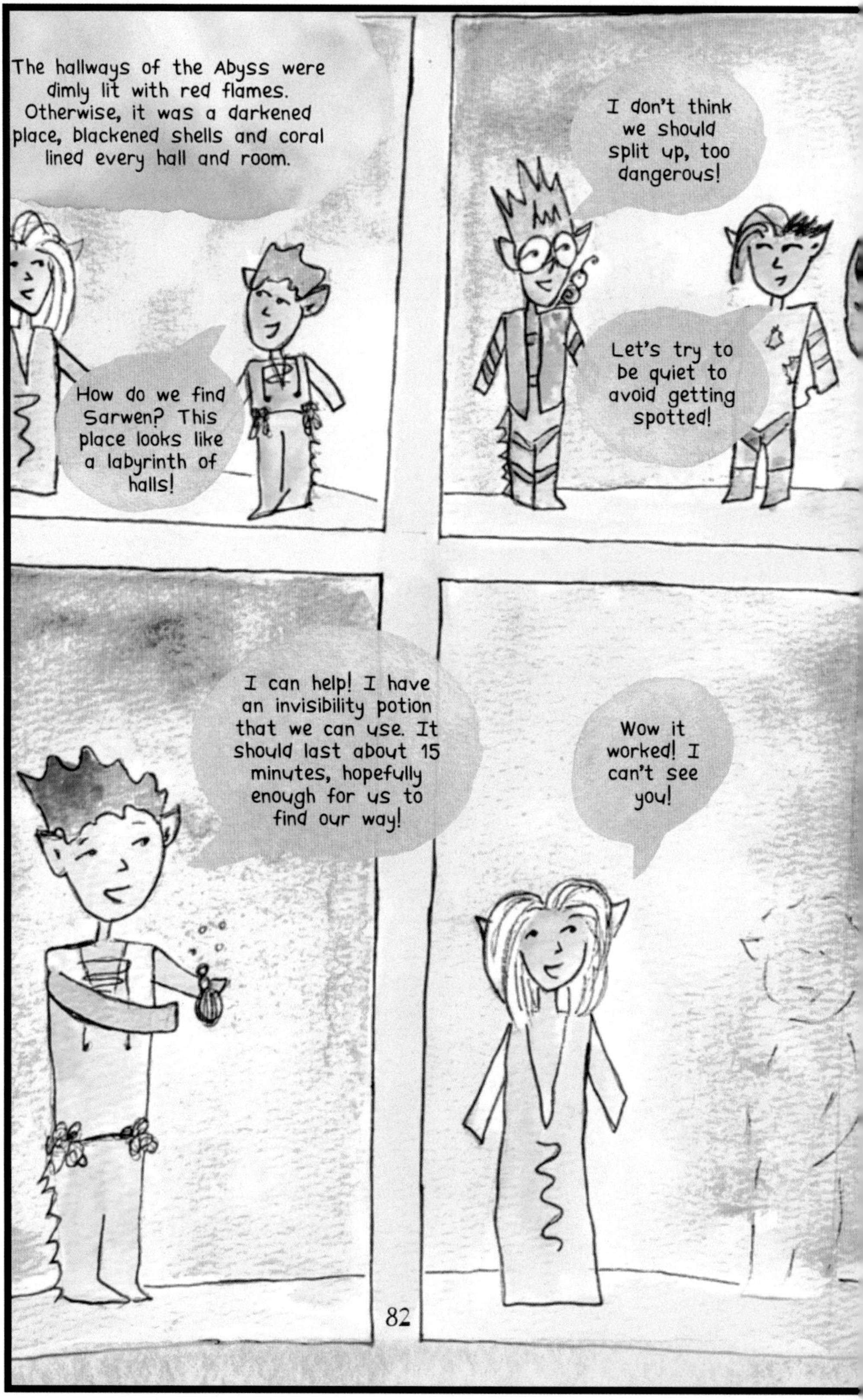
The hallways of the Abyss were dimly lit with red flames. Otherwise, it was a darkened place, blackened shells and coral lined every hall and room.
How do we find Sarwen? This place looks like a labyrinth of halls!
I don't think we should split up, too dangerous!
Let's try to be quiet to avoid getting spotted!
I can help! I have an invisibility potion that we can use. It should last about 15 minutes, hopefully enough for us to find our way!
Wow it worked! I can't see you!

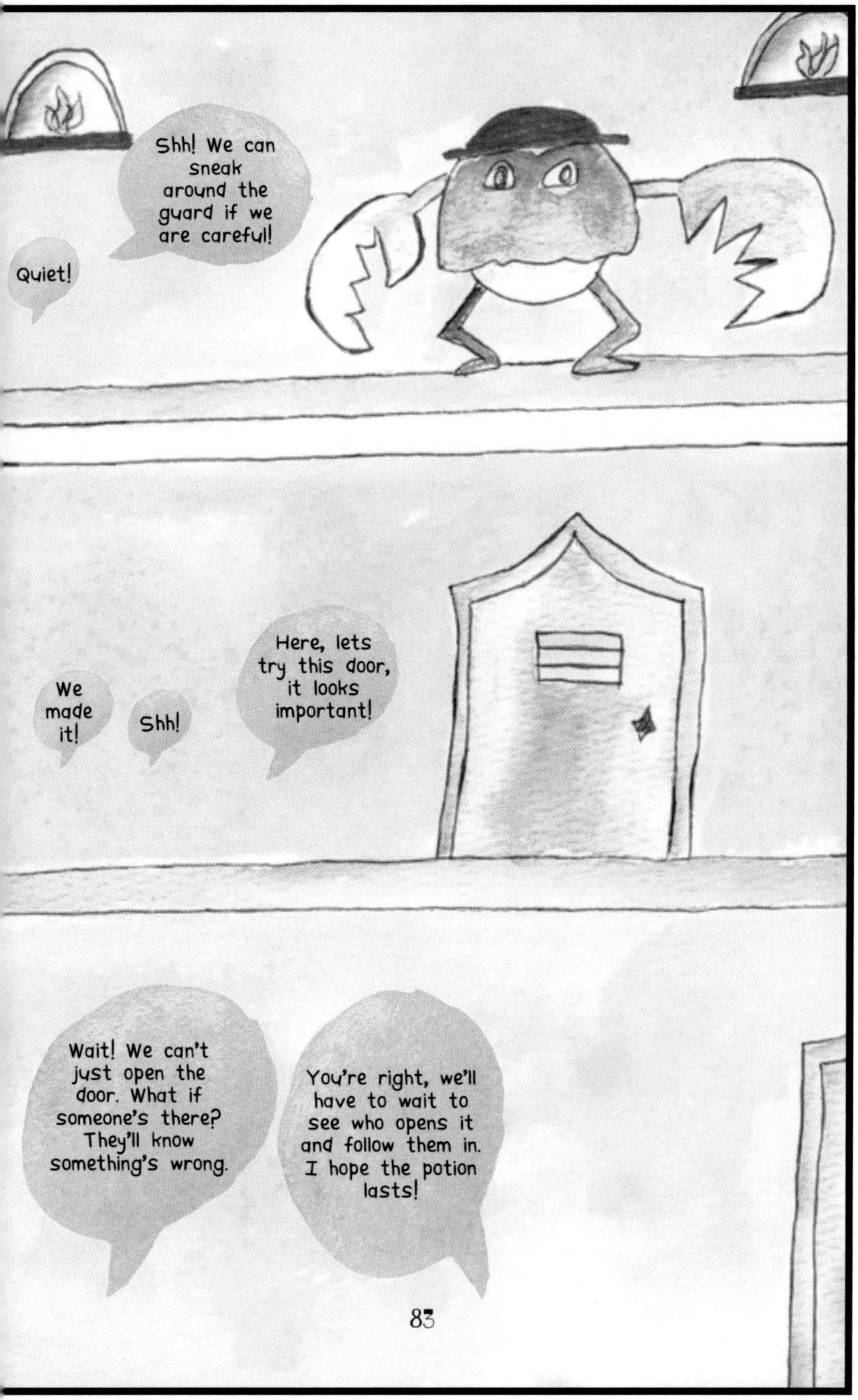
Quiet!
Shh! We can sneak around the guard if we are careful!
We made it!
Shh!
Here, lets try this door, it looks important!
Wait! We can't just open the door. What if someone's there? They'll know something's wrong.
You're right, we'll have to wait to see who opens it and follow them in. I hope the potion lasts!

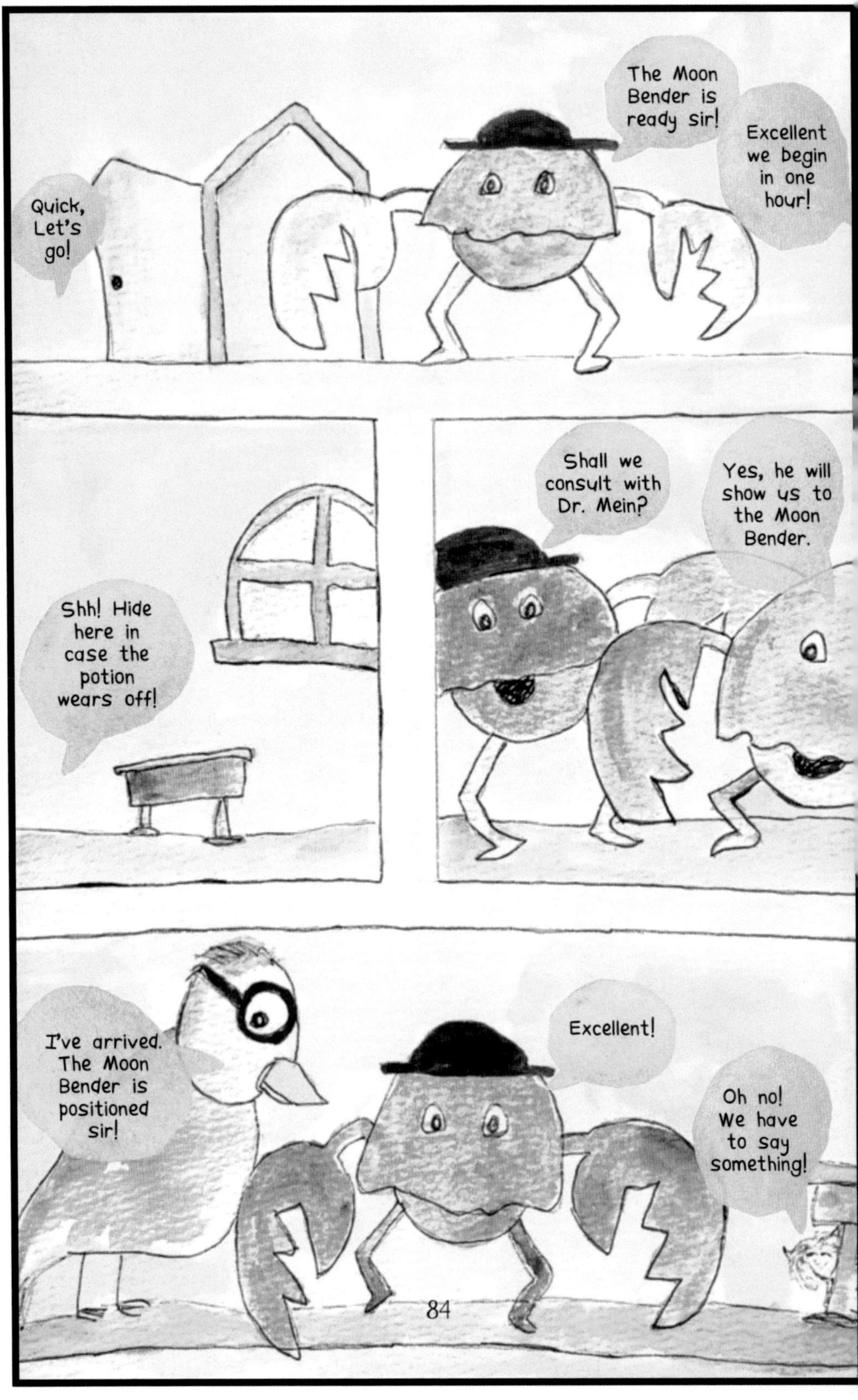
Quick, Let's go!
The Moon Bender is ready sir!
Excellent we begin in one hour!
Shh! Hide here in case the potion wears off!
Shall we consult with Dr. Mein?
Yes, he will show us to the Moon Bender.
I've arrived. The Moon Bender is positioned sir!
Excellent!
Oh no! We have to say something!

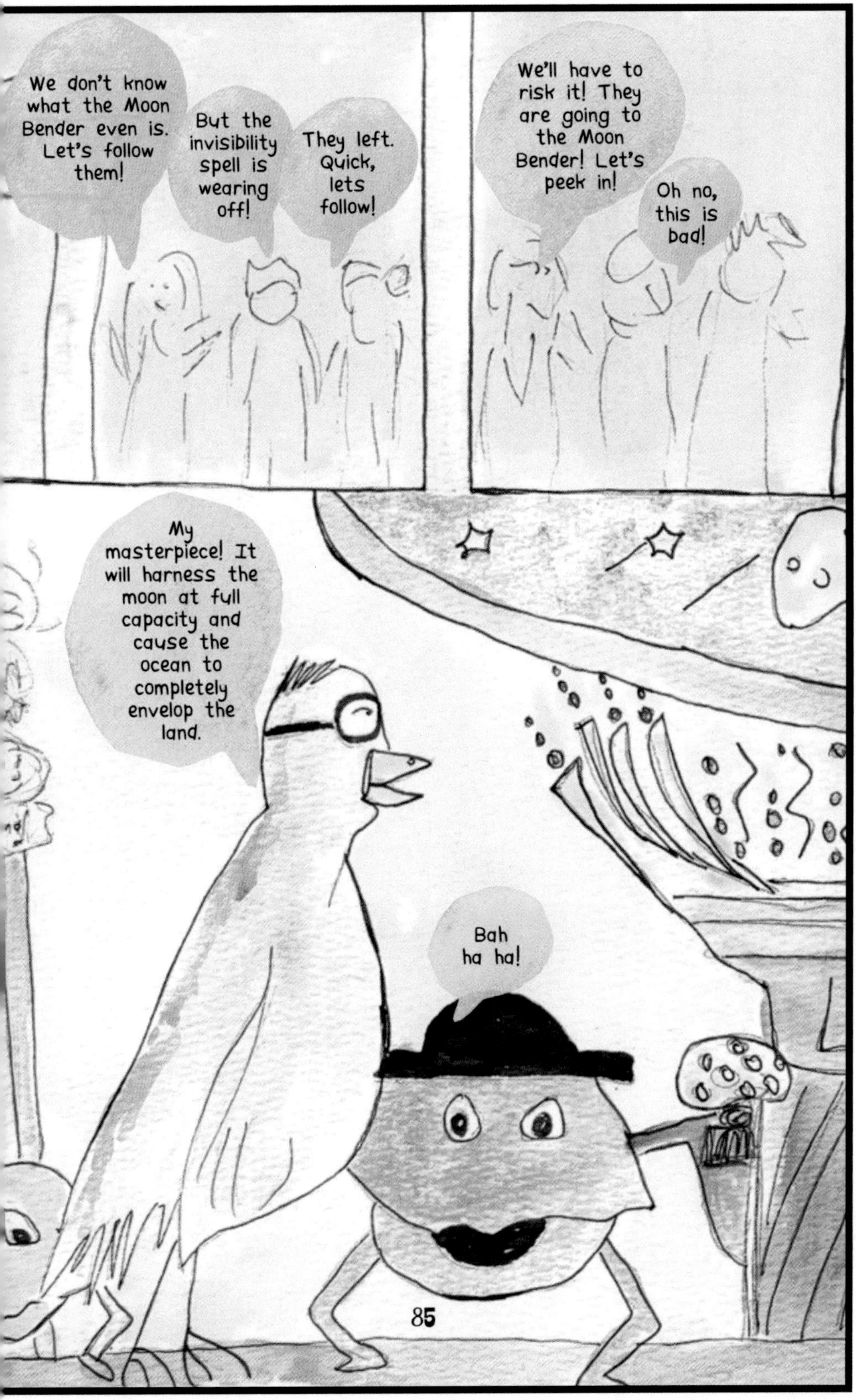

We don't know what the Moon Bender even is. Let's follow them!
But the invisibility spell is wearing off!
They left. Quick, lets follow!
We'll have to risk it! They are going to the Moon Bender! Let's peek in!
Oh no, this is bad!
My masterpiece! It will harness the moon at full capacity and cause the ocean to completely envelop the land.
Bah ha ha!

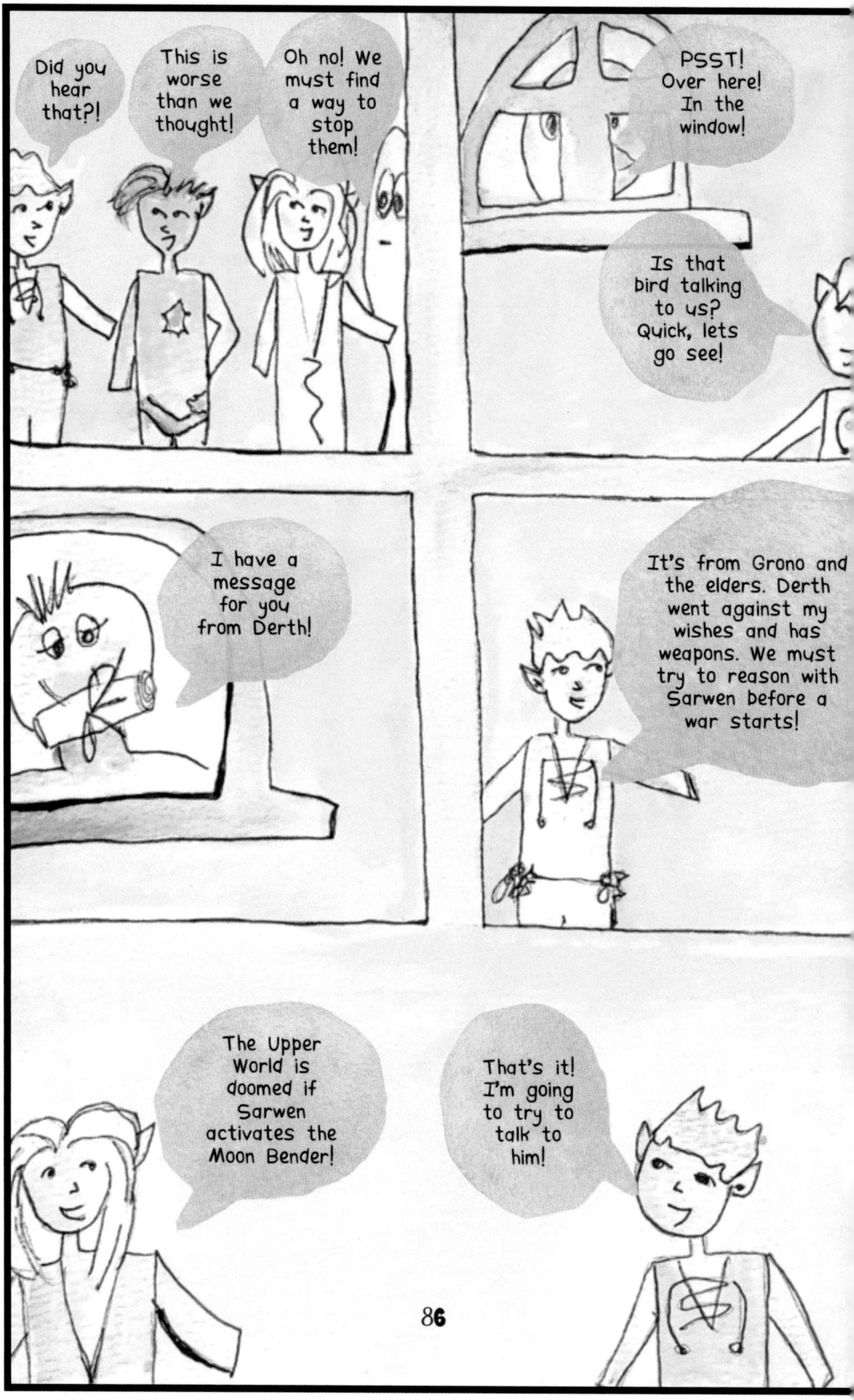
Did you hear that?!
This is worse than we thought!
Oh no! We must find a way to stop them!
PSST! Over here! In the window!
Is that bird talking to us? Quick, lets go see!
I have a message for you from Derth!
It's from Grono and the elders. Derth went against my wishes and has weapons. We must try to reason with Sarwen before a war starts!
The Upper World is doomed if Sarwen activates the Moon Bender!
That's it! I'm going to try to talk to him!

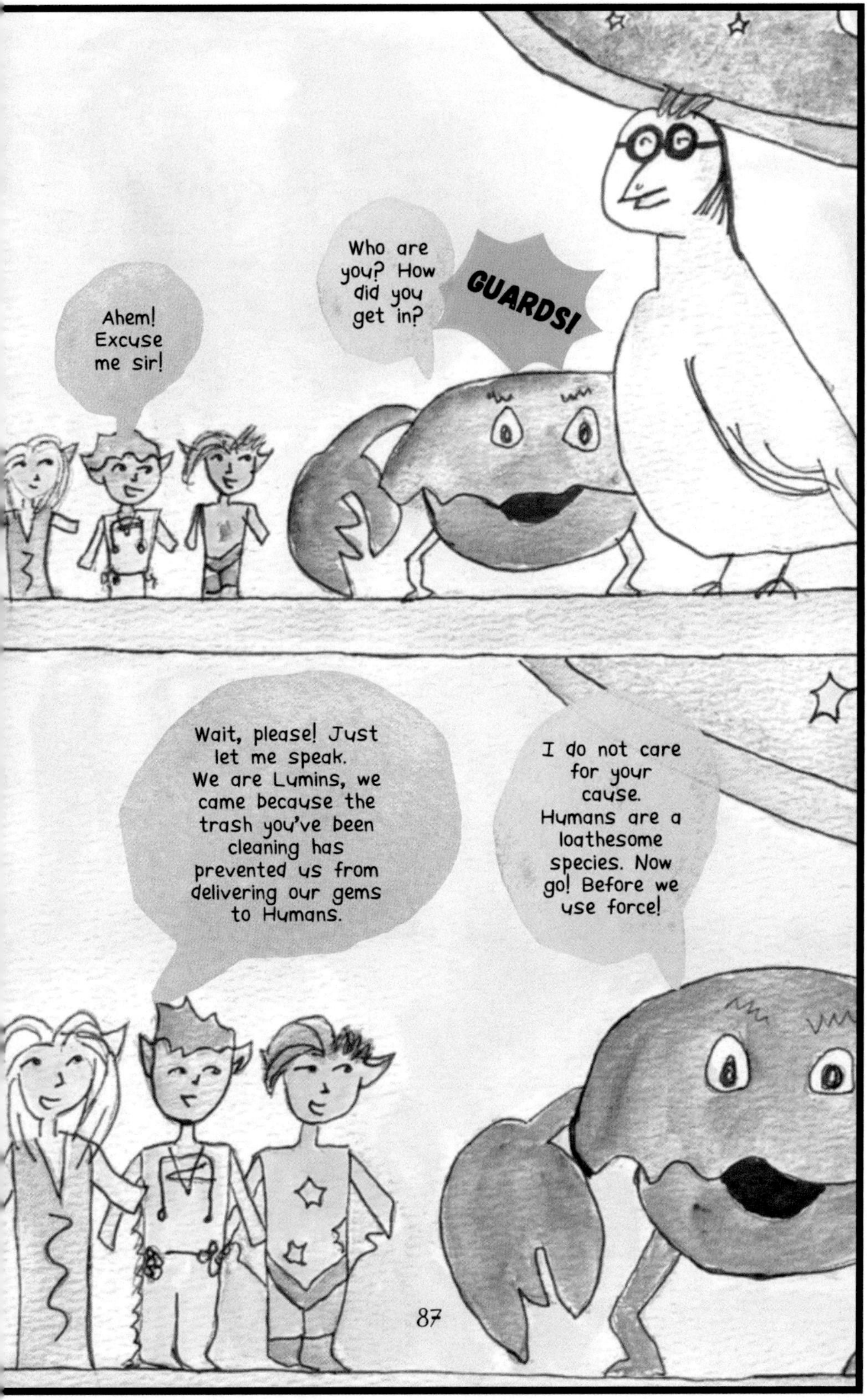
Ahem! Excuse me sir!
Who are you? How did you get in?
GUARDS!
Wait, please! Just let me speak. We are Lumins, we came because the trash you've been cleaning has prevented us from delivering our gems to Humans.
I do not care for your cause. Humans are a loathesome species. Now go! Before we use force!

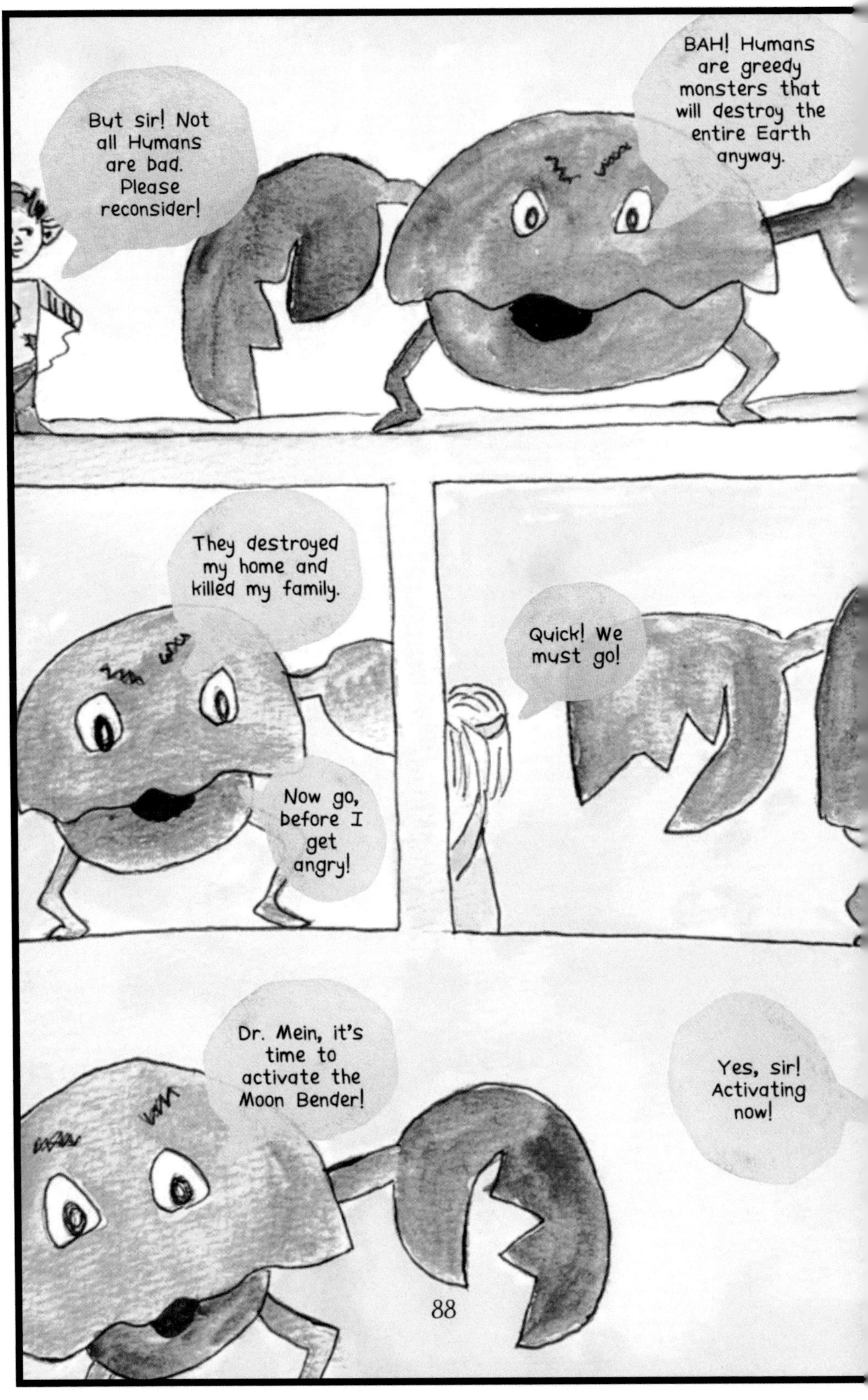
But sir! Not all Humans are bad. Please reconsider!
BAH! Humans are greedy monsters that will destroy the entire Earth anyway.
They destroyed my home and killed my family.
Now go, before I get angry!
Quick! We must go!
Dr. Mein, it's time to activate the Moon Bender!
Yes, sir! Activating now!

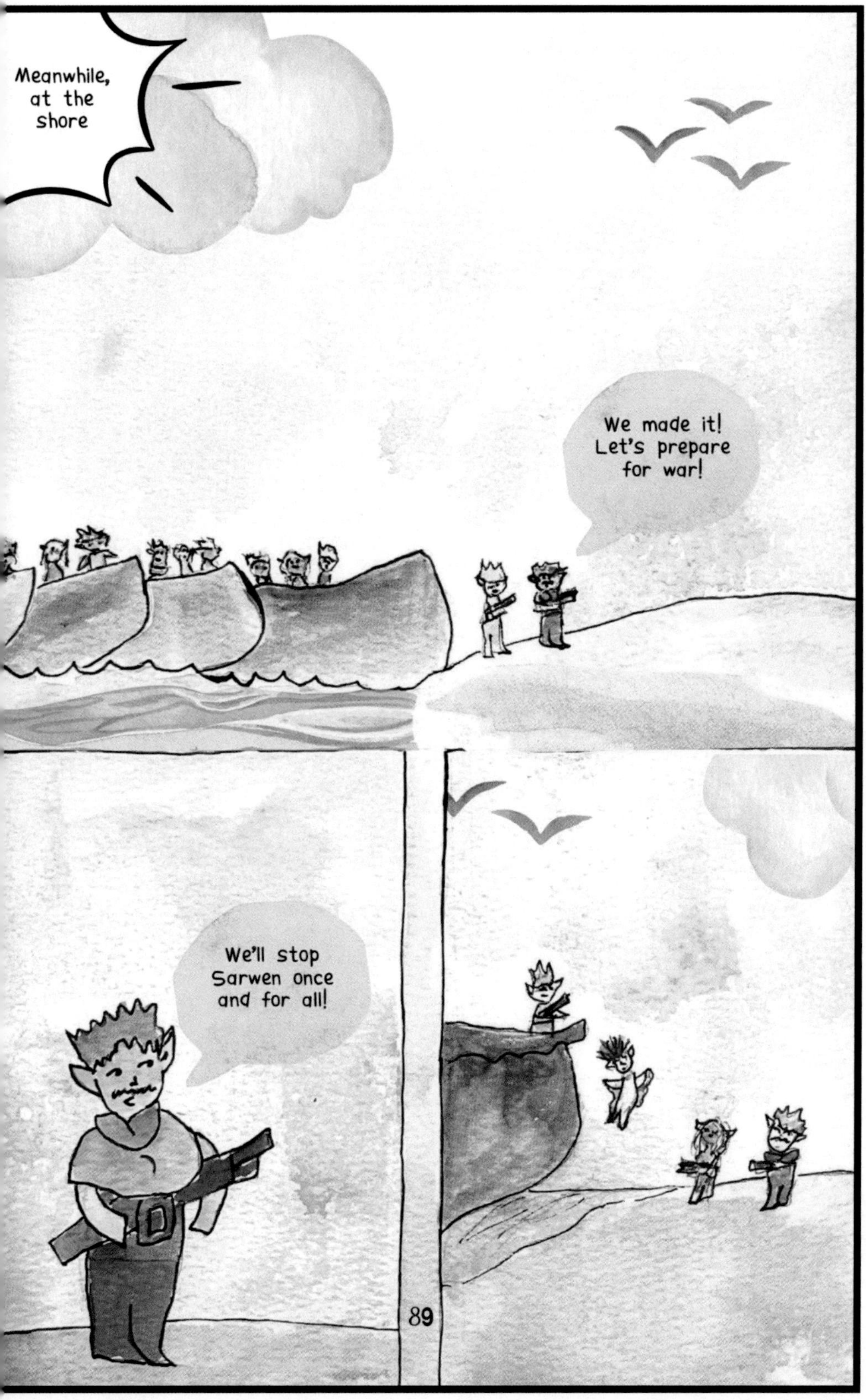
Meanwhile, at the shore
We made it! Let's prepare for war!
We'll stop Sarwen once and for all!

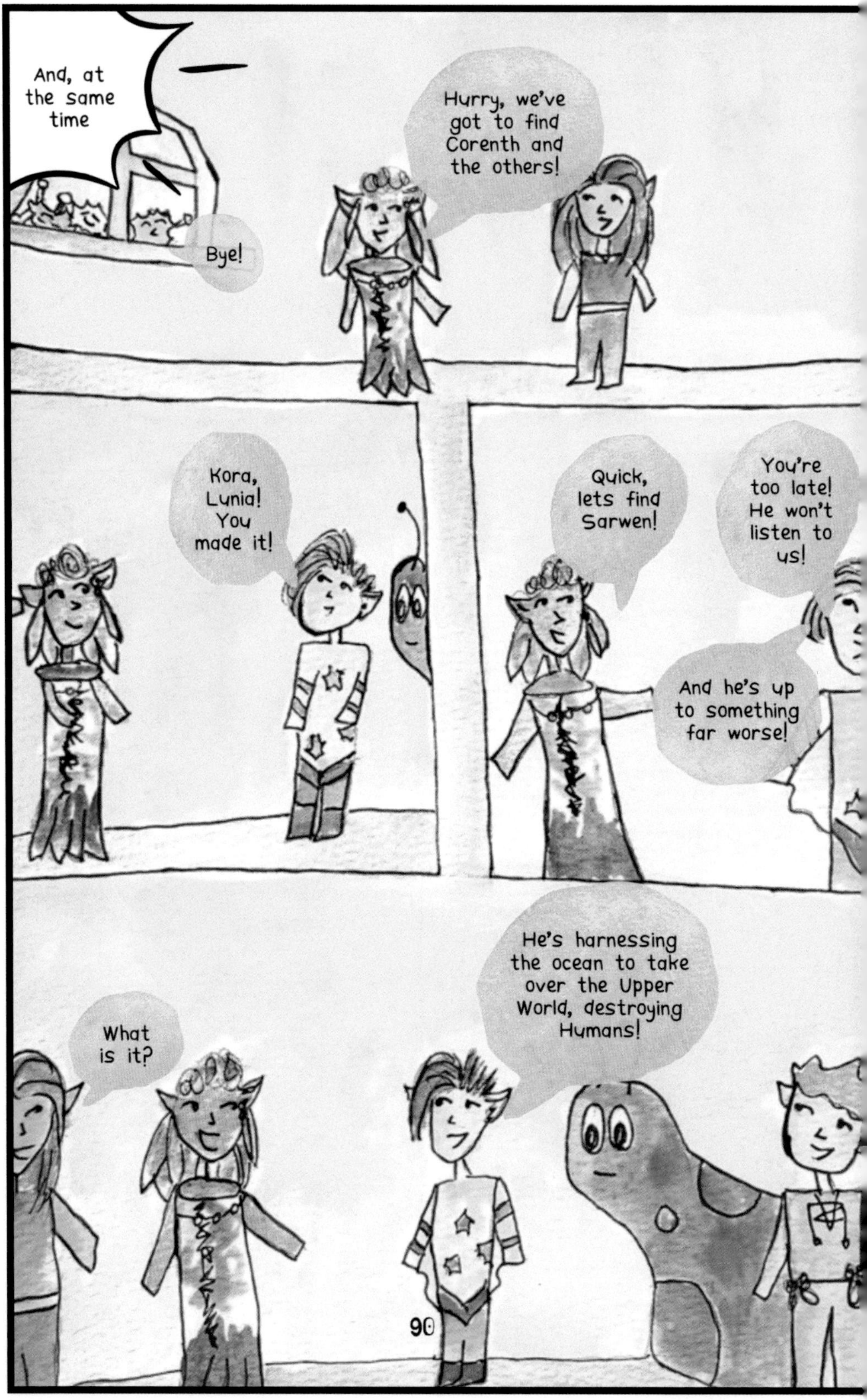
And, at the same time
Hurry, we've got to find Corenth and the others!
Bye!
Kora, Lunia! You made it!
Quick, lets find Sarwen!
You're too late! He won't listen to us!
And he's up to something far worse!
What is it?
He's harnessing the ocean to take over the Upper World, destroying Humans!

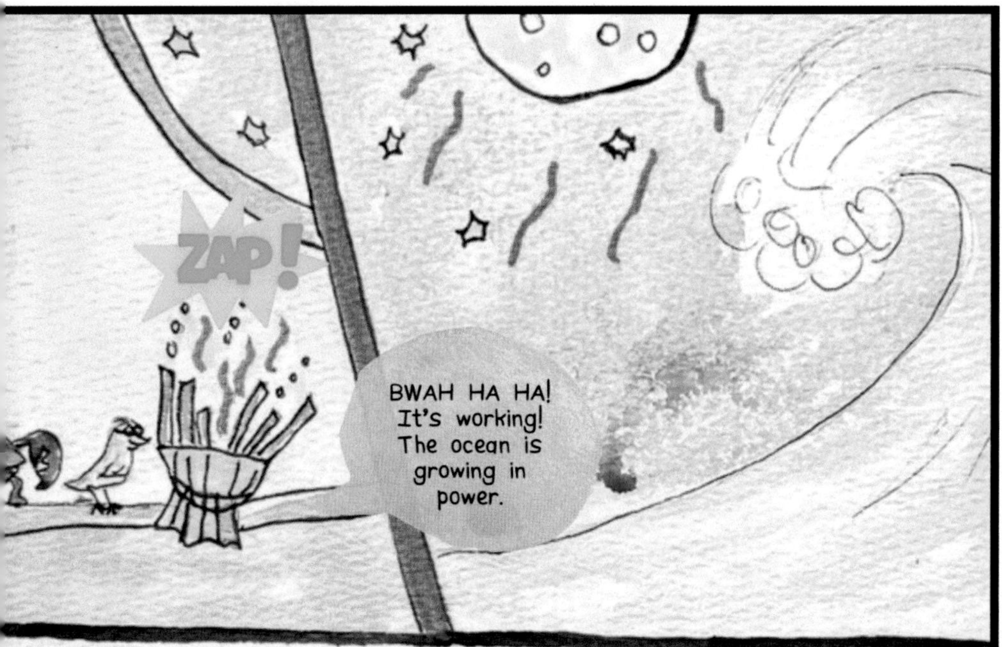
ZAP!
BWAH HA HA! It's working! The ocean is growing in power.

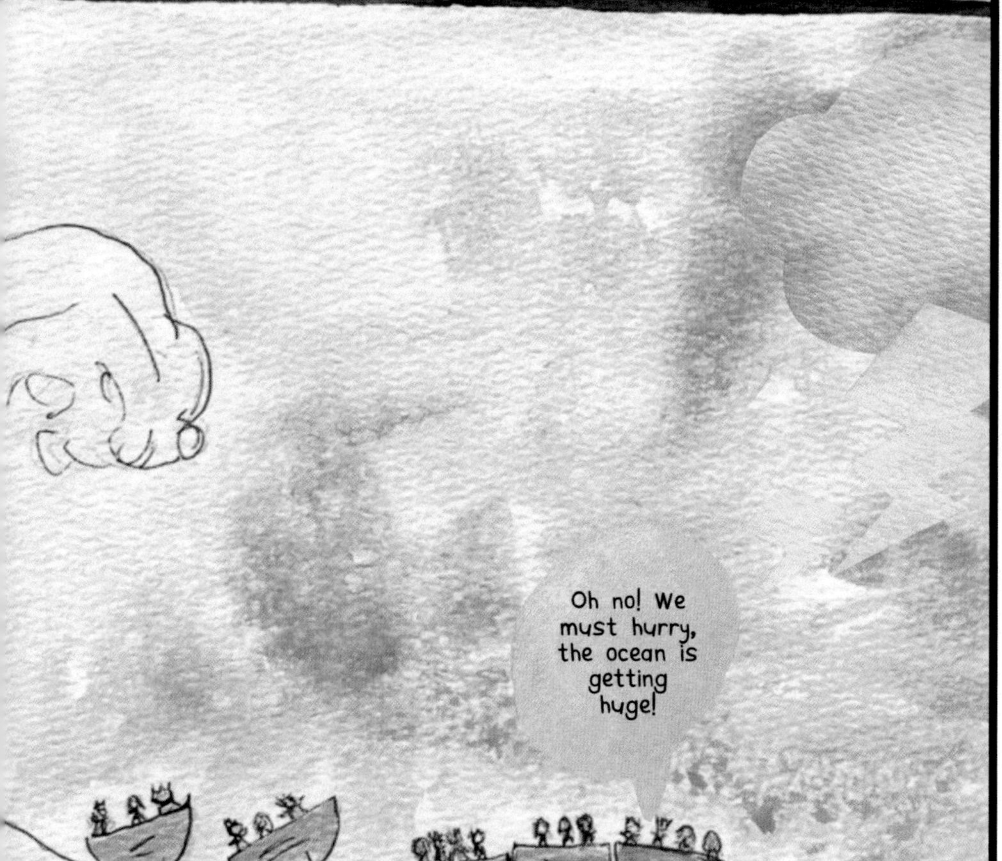
Oh no! We must hurry, the ocean is getting huge!

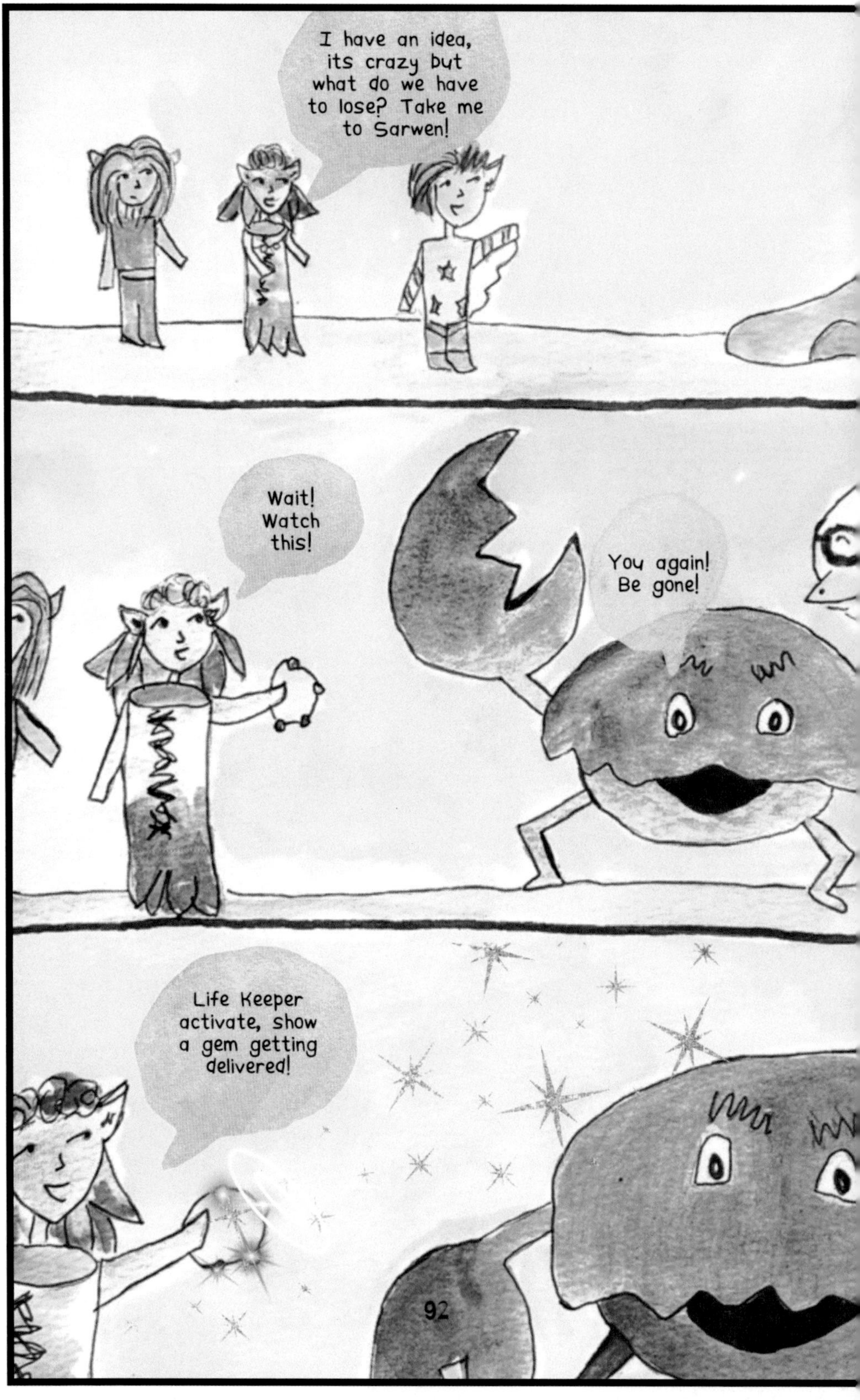
I have an idea, its crazy but what do we have to lose? Take me to Sarwen!
Wait! Watch this!
You again! Be gone!
Life Keeper activate, show a gem getting delivered!

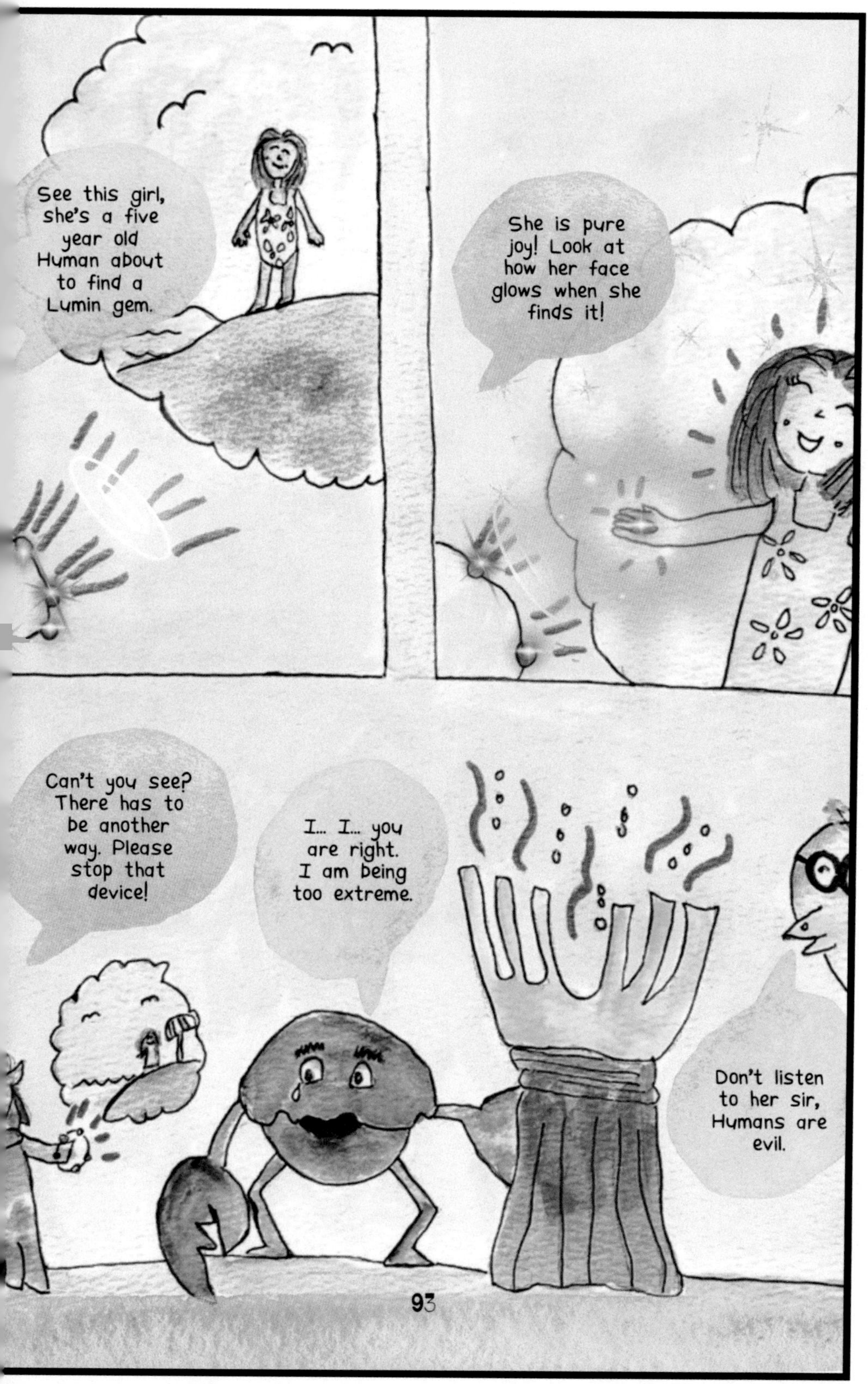
See this girl, she's a five year old Human about to find a Lumin gem.
She is pure joy! Look at how her face glows when she finds it!
Can't you see? There has to be another way. Please stop that device!
I... I... you are right. I am being too extreme.
Don't listen to her sir, Humans are evil.

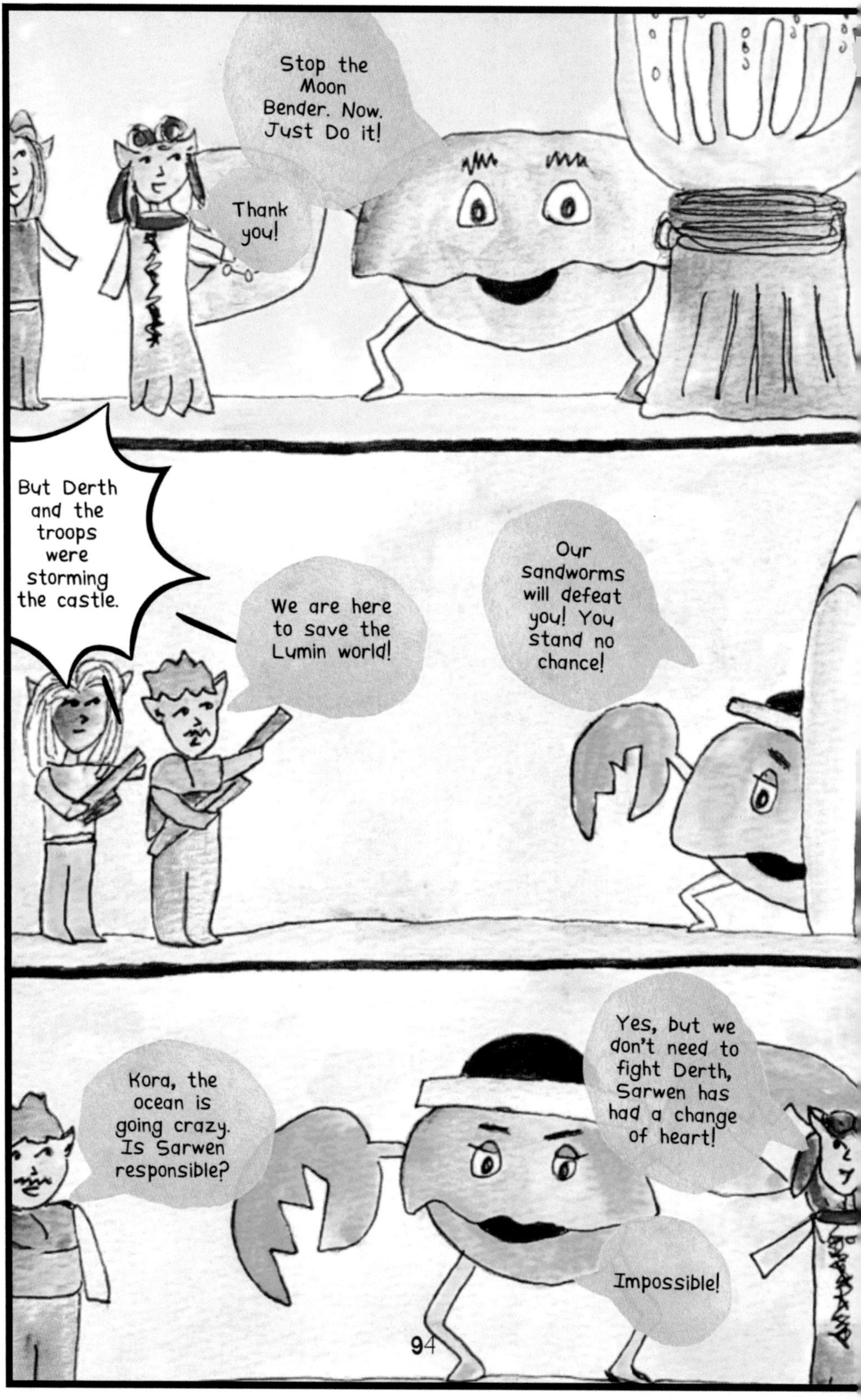

Stop the Moon Bender. Now. Just Do it!
Thank you!
But Derth and the troops were storming the castle.
We are here to save the Lumin world!
Our sandworms will defeat you! You stand no chance!
Kora, the ocean is going crazy. Is Sarwen responsible?
Yes, but we don't need to fight Derth, Sarwen has had a change of heart!
Impossible!

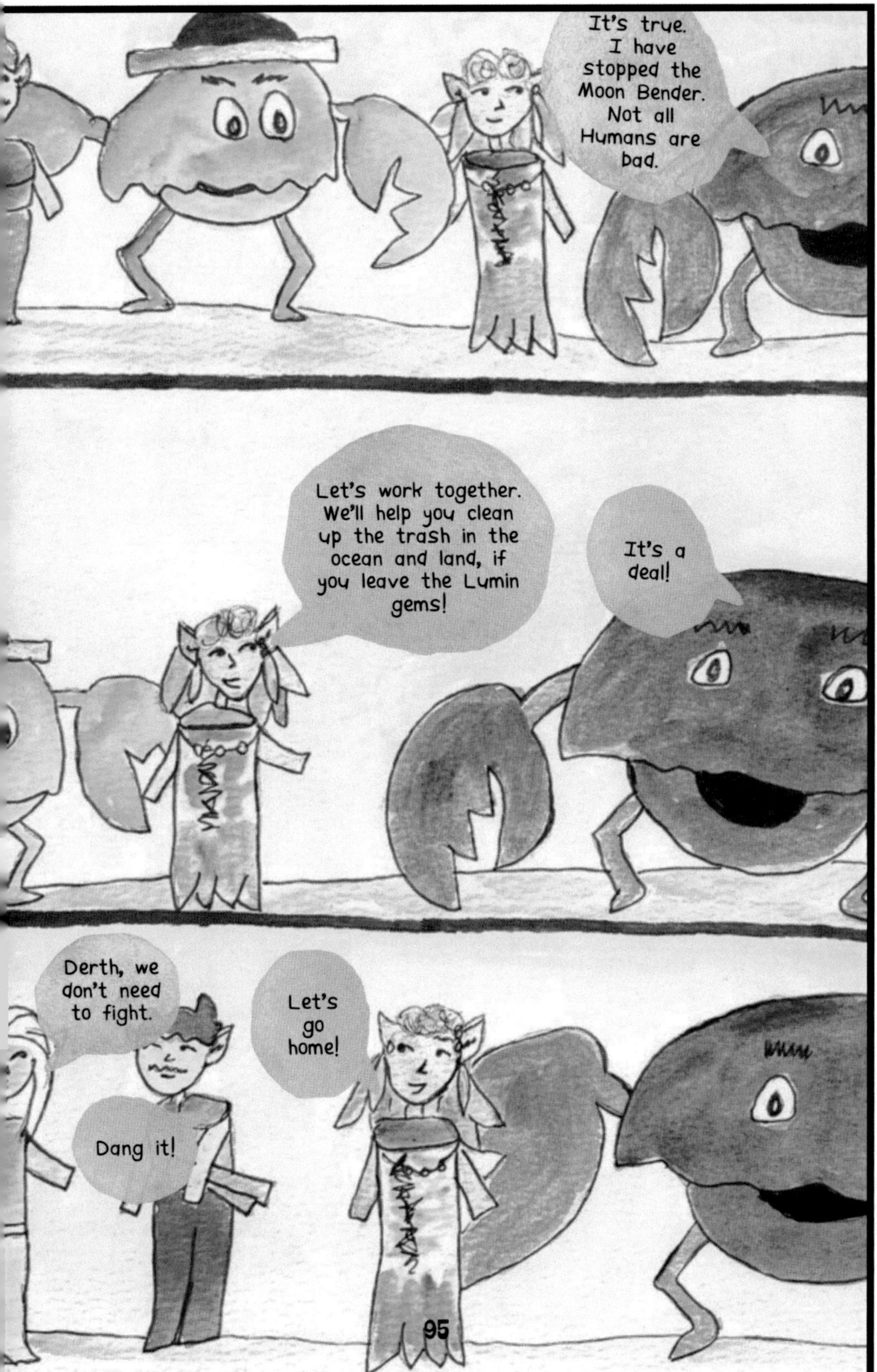
It's true. I have stopped the Moon Bender. Not all Humans are bad.
Let's work together. We'll help you clean up the trash in the ocean and land, if you leave the Lumin gems!
It's a deal!
Derth, we don't need to fight.
Dang it!
Let's go home!

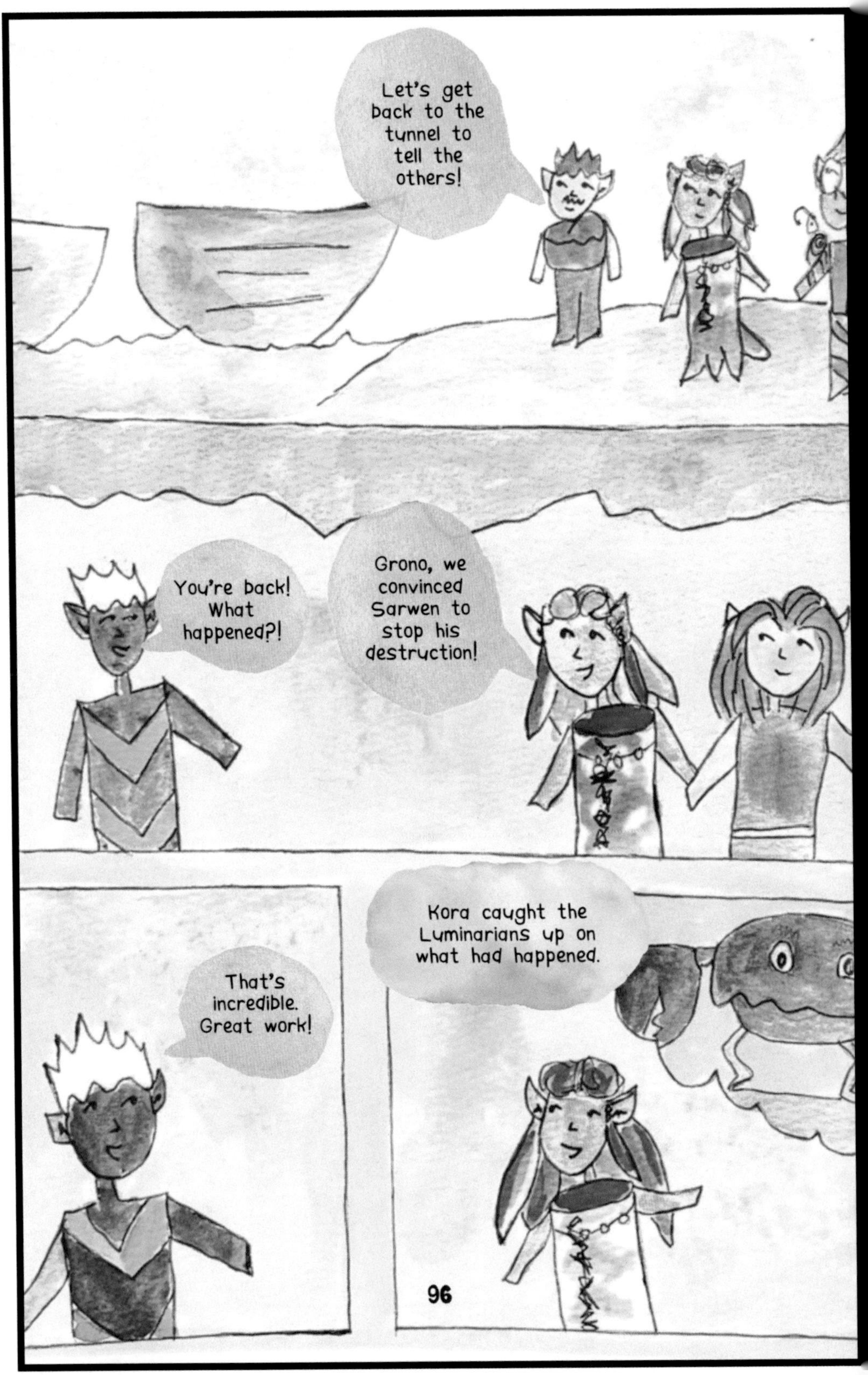
Let's get back to the tunnel to tell the others!
You're back! What happened?!
Grono, we convinced Sarwen to stop his destruction!
That's incredible. Great work!
Kora caught the Luminarians up on what had happened.

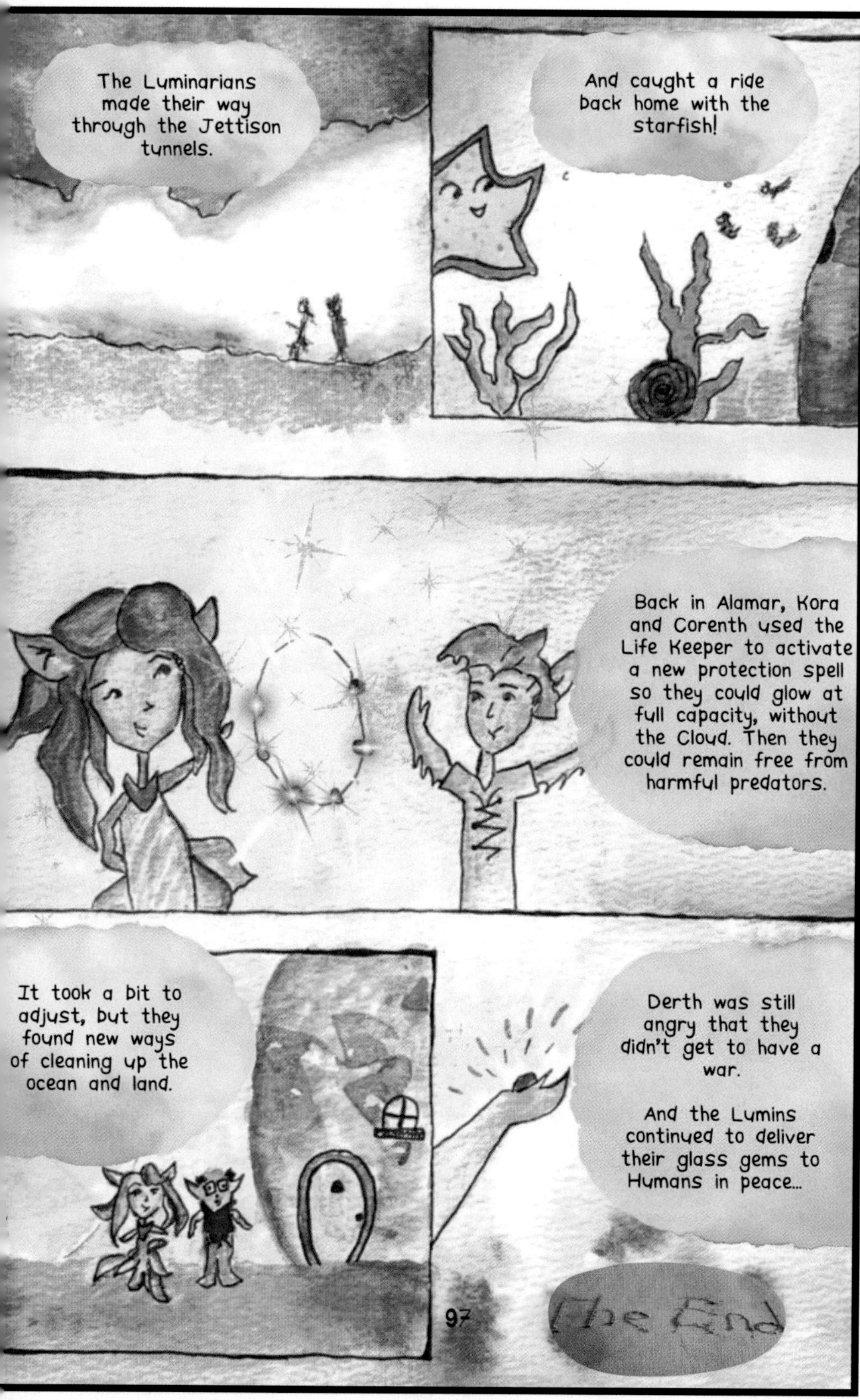
The Luminarians made their way through the Jettison tunnels.
And caught a ride back home with the starfish!
Back in Alamar, Kora and Corenth used the Life Keeper to activate a new protection spell so they could glow at full capacity, without the Cloud. Then they could remain free from harmful predators.
It took a bit to adjust, but they found new ways of cleaning up the ocean and land.
Derth was still angry that they didn't get to have a war.
And the Lumins continued to deliver their glass gems to Humans in peace...
The End

But wait, there's more...

Just when peace settles over the ocean and its magical shores, a new storm is brewing beneath the waves! In Kora Kelly and the Dark Star, book 2 of the Glimmer Series, our favorite Lumin faces a cosmic challenge. Derth, the once-powerful Cloud Collector, is fuming. His dreams of battle shattered, his thirst for chaos reignites a simmering feud with Sarwen the crab. This time, his scheme threatens not just the ocean, but the entire universe!
Kora and her brave band of ocean friends are catapulted into an adventure beyond their wildest imaginations. Through a mysterious portal, they find themselves among the stars, guided by celestial beings who shine with ancient wisdom. Can Kora and her friends navigate this dazzling yet dangerous realm, where the stars hold secrets and perils unknown?

Packed with starry-eyed wonder, heroic feats, and heart-pounding moments, Kora Kelly and the Dark Star will transport you to a galaxy where friendship and courage sparkle brighter than the stars themselves.

Are you ready to reach for the stars with Kora?

Support the Lumin world creator by buying copies, leaving reviews, sharing, reading at schools and engage with us at:

@CreativelyFreeStudios
CreativelyFreeStudios.com